COMMUNICATION:

Strategic Action
in Context

COMMUNICATION

A series of volumes edited by:
Dolf Zillmann and Jennings Bryant

ZILLMANN and BRYANT • *Selective Exposure to Communication*

BEVILLE • *Audience Ratings: Radio, Television, and Cable*

BRYANT and ZILLMANN • *Perspectives on Media Effects*

GOLDSTEIN • *Reporting Science: The Case of Aggression*

ELLIS and DONOHUE • *Contemporary Issues in Language and Discourse Processes*

WINETT • *Information and Behavior: Systems of Influence*

HUESMANN and ERON • *Television and the Aggressive Child: A Cross-National Comparison*

GUNTER • *Poor Reception: Miscomprehension and Forgetting of Broadcast News*

RODDA and GROVE • *Language, Cognition, and Deafness*

HASLETT • *Communication: Strategic Action in Context*

DONOHEW, SYPHER, and HIGGINS • *Communication, Social Cognition, and Affect*

Olasky • *Corporate Public Relations and Private Enterprise: A New Historical Perspective*

Beth Haslett

University of Delaware

COMMUNICATION:

Strategic Action
in Context

LAWRENCE ERLBAUM ASSOCIATES, PUBLISHERS
1987   Hillsdale, New Jersey   London

Lawrence Erlbaum Associates, Inc., Publishers
365 Broadway
Hillsdale, New Jersey 07642

Library of Congress Cataloging in Publication Data

Haslett, Beth.
  Communication, strategic action in context.

  (Communication)
  Bibliography: p.
  Includes indexes.
  1. Communication. 2. Pragmatics. I. Title.
II. Series: Communication (Hillsdale, N.J.)
P91.H375 1987   401'.9   86-32806
ISBN 0-89859-871-0

Printed in the United States of America
10 9 8 7 6 5 4 3 2 1

To My Parents,
Clifford W. *Bonniwell* and *Edna Stoeckmann Bonniwell*
and My Family,
David, Heidi and *Erik*

Contents

Preface

This book attempts to outline a descriptively adequate basis for the study of human communication. It does so by advocating a pragmatic approach to communication, an approach based on the study of language use in context. This approach provides a basis for integrating the study of verbal communication across diverse settings, tasks, and participants. In addition, this approach may provide a basis for studying nonverbal communication as well because many scholars suggest that nonverbal communication is organized like verbal communication and that both communicative systems complement one another. A pragmatic approach thus offers a perspective through which an integrated study of human communication processes is possible. However, pragmatics, as an approach to the study of human communication, is distinct from pragmatics as a sub-area of linguistics.

As such, this book is broad in its scope and goals. It covers work on verbal communication in many disciplines, and represents a variety of underlying assumptions and methods of analysis. However, as I argue in chapter 1, important common assumptions underlie research on pragmatics and it is this convergence, I believe, that offers the promise for an integrated study of human communication.

A promising convergence is also occurring within the social sciences. The convergence of concepts, assumptions, and methods from multiple disciplines is an exciting intellectual phenomenon. Some of this convergence is due to a sense of crisis in the social sciences; increasing attention is being given to basic reformulations concerning the nature of knowledge itself and concerning the conduct of social science research (Foucault, 1972; Giddens, 1976, 1979, 1982; Kuhn, 1970). Increasingly, scholars are calling for integration of research findings in communication (M. Atkinson, 1981; Duck, 1980; Hinde, 1981) and for the use of multiple methods of analysis.

The possibility of an integrated pragmatic approach to analyze communication, supported by models of social science research emphasizing such integrated approaches, provides strong intellectual support for the synthesis attempted here. The very structure of the book itself is an argument about *how* communication should be studied: the topics included, and their organization and integration in this book, are meant as a statement about how communicative processes take place.

I have, in some cases, reframed and extended other's research to show how their work fits into the analysis of human communication. In all instances, I have tried to remain faithful to the original formulations intended by these scholars. However, I may *use* their research in ways unintended by them, yet compatible with their original formulations. For example, the work on speech markers has been done primarily in the context of intergroup communication. I have, however, viewed speech markers here as accountability practices—a view, insofar as I can determine, not intended by any of the scholars researching speech markers, but certainly compatible with their views on intergroup communication processes. In addition, this book blends both European and North American scholarship. As such, I hope it will direct readers to additional sources of information, and contribute to the cross-disciplinary sharing of ideas.

The book is divided into three sections. The first section outlines the major approaches to pragmatics—the structural, functional, and contextual approaches. The next section synthesizes these approaches into an integrated, descriptively adequate basis for the study of human communication. Finally, the third section deals with pragmatic research in the major contexts in which communicative skills are acquired—the developmental environment during the first 5 years; the context of interpersonal relationships, and educational settings. Each chapter in this section represents a coherent view of communication research in those areas, although obviously not an exhaustive view.

Each chapter can be read independently and thus stands alone. However, I believe readers will benefit from reading the chapters in the order they are presented. Each chapter leads logically into subsequent chapters and thus contributes to an overall sense of how communication should be analyzed.

Through this book, I wish to present a general view of how verbal communication works and to describe significant influences on communicative processes. At this level of analysis, for example, I want to demonstrate the richness and complexity of contextual influences on communication rather than articulate a fully worked-out model of how a particular aspect of context influences communication. In so doing, and in view of the book's scope, comprehensive discussion of every approach has not been possible. Important distinctions among the various approaches that are not critical to the level of analysis undertaken here are not discussed. Briefly put, I am focusing on the underlying themes that permit an overall, integrated pragmatic approach to emerge—not on important (yet, from my view, not critical) distinctions among approaches.

Both broadly focused and narrowly focused analyses of communication are needed: I have chosen to do the former, while many scholars choose to do the latter. I believe there is an imbalance between these two alternatives; too much attention has been directed at fully developing views on a particular aspect of communication, and not enough attention paid to how various aspects of communication fit together in the process of humans communicating. I am certainly not suggesting here that we abandon more detailed analyses of specific features of communication, but merely that we place those efforts in the context of a more comprehensive view of communication. Most especially, as I argue in Chapter 6, we need to examine relevant, previously unexplored interrelationships among communicative features.

Acknowledgments

I wish to thank many colleagues who, through discussions of their own work and/or their thoughtful responses to my work, have contributed to my views: George Borden, David Clarke, Don Cushman, Robert DiPietro, John Dore, Steve Duck, William Frawley, Adrian Furnham, Howard Giles, Edmund Glenn, Stephen Levinson, John Shotter, and Joan Tough.

Special thanks are due to Charles Berger and Robert Hopper who, through extensive discussions with me and through their own insightful contributions to the study of communication, have stimulated my own thinking in many ways. To Paul Drew, John Heritage, and Tony Wootton, goes my appreciation for clarifying conversational analysis and for their excellence as practitioners of the art of conversational analysis. I also wish to thank Deidre Wilson for her helpful comments on my work, and for sharing a pre-publication copy of the Sperber and Wilson book with me. And to Teun van Dijk, my thanks for his helpful discussions of his work and for his insightful comments on my own.

I am very grateful to all of these colleagues, for their thinking and insights, which have been instrumental in developing my own views. I, of course, accept full responsibility for any errors in the interpretation of their views, and hope that they are few in number!

Two mentors deserve special mention. To Fred Williams, my thanks for introducing me to linguistics and its importance in analyzing communication. And to Jim Jenkins, my deepest appreciation for enhancing my understanding of language and communication; for modeling, through his own research and teaching, intellectual excellence; and for being, in the finest sense of these words, "a true scholar and gentleman."

I also wish to thank the University of Delaware for providing a research sabbatical in England, during which time I completed this book. My thanks also to friends and colleagues at the University of Hull, Kingston-Upon-Hull, England, who made my stay in England such a rewarding experience. My heartfelt appreciation also to the Electronics Laboratory at the University of Hull who performed the necessary "magic" to make a U.S. computer compatible with British electrical current. My thanks also to Myrna Hoffman who typed portions of the manuscript and the bibliography.

I wish to thank the editors and publisher of *Communication Yearbook, Volume 9,* for permission to use materials from my article on communicative development. I also wish to thank Edward Arnold, publishers of *Intergroup Communication* (edited by W. Gudykunst), part of their series on the social psychology of language, for their permission to use materials and reprint a table from my article, "The influence of age, sex and social class on intergroup communication."

Finally, I convey my deepest appreciation to the individuals who made it all possible with their love and support: Eor, Horse-Climber, and Sheep-Stalker.

Beth Haslett

CONCEPTUAL APPROACHES TO PRAGMATICS

1 Conceptual Foundations of the Pragmatic Perspective

Questions concerning the appropriate definition of a field, its central issues and boundaries confront any new developing discipline. As Kuhn (1970) observes, such debate characterizes developing, pre-paradigmatic fields of study. Both communication and pragmatics, as fields of study, may be characterized as pre-paradigmatic.

Pragmatics—the use of language in context—has emerged as a serious research area in several disciplines. Linguists have concentrated primarily on syntax and semantics, and have only recently focused increasing attention on pragmatics. However, most linguists now acknowledge that an adequate understanding of language itself will rely heavily on pragmatics (see, for example, Chafe, 1976; Halliday, 1970; Leech, 1983; Levinson, 1983). Psycholinguists have focused on the role language plays in information processing, memory and learning. And sociologists now emphasize the role of verbal communication in social organization and social cooperation. A separate discipline, focusing primarily on verbal communication, has become an increasingly important area of study. Thus, from a wide variety of perspectives, the importance of studying language usage is now clearly recognized.

Since language is the predominate symbolic code used in communication, pragmatic approaches could be usefully applied to the study of communicative processes. Parret, Sbisa, and Verschuren (1981), for example, suggest that pragmatics be defined as the study of the underlying principles of meaningful language use—that is, as the study of verbal communication. The study of how individuals use language is one way to investigate how individuals communicate verbally. Thus, a pragmatic approach to analyzing human communication would enhance our understanding of verbal communication, and provide a basis for integrating the diverse aspects of communication. This integration would be instrumental in building a general model of human communicative processes.

Since I am advocating a pragmatic perspective on human communication, some clarification of both concepts is needed at the outset. In this chapter, I develop a set of assumptions underlying the concepts of communication and pragmatics utilized in this book, establish some boundary conditions for both concepts, and then look at the interrelationships between them. As we shall see, the issues involved are complex and not easily resolved.

The study of language use has been developed in a wide variety of disciplines, with each discipline focusing on different issues and selecting different methods of analysis. The first section of this book deals with the varied approaches taken toward pragmatics. The second section attempts a synthesis of these perspectives, and uses this synthesis to analyze human communication. The final section applies a pragmatic analysis to interpersonal communication, communicative development, and communication in educational settings. Each of these contexts provides a significant setting for acquiring and developing communication skills.

I. COMMUNICATION, LANGUAGE, AND THE EMERGENCE OF PRAGMATICS

Communication

Everyone communicates, everyday, in diverse ways and in varied settings. However commonplace the act of communication, it is, nonetheless, very difficult to analyze. And the more we learn about human communicative processes, the more complex and fascinating these processes appear to be.

Definitions are rarely satisfactory, but some are more useful than others. One very useful definition of communication is that proposed by Albert Scheflen, the noted psychiatrist and nonverbal communication scholar. Scheflen (1963) views communication as an organized, standardized, culturally patterned system of behavior that sustains, regulates, and makes possible human relationships.

Several important underlying assumptions are presupposed by this definition of communication. First, communication is a *shared* activity that enables human relationships to be established and maintained. As Duck (personal communication) notes, communication is shared because it involves shared time, space, interaction, and activities, as well as shared beliefs about the interactants' relationship and their purposes for interacting. Second, communication is multi-modal: communication occurs verbally and nonverbally. Kreckel (1981), for example, views communicative acts as socially meaningful units of *verbal/nonverbal* behavior that transmit a particular message. Third, communication is structured; it is not random or haphazard, but purposive and goal-directed. The most fundamental purpose of communication is, of course, to establish human relationships. Fourth, communication patterns vary from culture to culture. And finally, communication is basically a *conventional* (i.e., standardized) process. While there are many individual differences across communicative behaviors, communicative behaviors depend upon conventional, socially shared meanings.

Language, Communication, and Pragmatics

Despite these different perspectives on communication, underlying most, if not all, communication is language, the symbolic code used in verbal communication. Many scholars also suggest that verbal and nonverbal communicative behaviors are related, and that language may be regarded as a model for analyzing nonverbal communication (Birdwhistell, 1970; Hall, 1959). More recently, significant relationships have been demonstrated between verbal and nonverbal dimensions of communication during interaction (Duncan & Fiske, 1977; Goodwin, 1981).

The strong relationships between language and communication suggest that language can be useful as a tool for analyzing human communicative processes. Traditional models of language, however, have focused on grammatical issues and generally excluded other dimensions of analysis (Chomsky, 1965; Gumperz, 1981; Hymes, 1972). While Chomsky's distinction between linguistic competence (knowledge of language) and linguistic performance (production of language) has contributed significantly to the study of language as a system, pragmatic issues were relatively ignored in this view. There was little concern for issues like the speaker/listener's motivation, social status, culture, and so forth that influence language processing.

By the late 1970's, the inability of transformational grammars to deal adequately with the extra-linguistic context of utterances, anaphoric and definite reference, pronominalization, elliptical comments, and presuppositions became clear. These failures, as well as the need to deal with connected discourse, led to the development of new grammars—text grammars—which examine connected utterances rather than a single utterance (van Dijk, 1977a, 1980; Grimes, 1975; Levinson, 1983). In a parallel fashion, scholars also began to analyze the meanings of utterances, rather than just single words.

Text Grammars.   Reisser (1977) notes that two major concerns of text grammars were (1) the connections between sentences in discourse, and

(2) the difficulty of developing intersubjectively valid interpretations of texts. According to Reisser, these early grammars failed to make an explicit distinction between syntax and semantics, and ignored the constraints of processing texts in real time.

Other scholars raised important objections as well. Van Dijk (1981) points out that text grammars treated the text as a single complex utterance. Frederiksen, Harris, and Duran (1975) argue that a discourse grammar ought to include three levels of context: conceptual context (presuppositions and intentions), extra-linguistic context (time, place, identity and location of the interactants) and linguistic context (the context created by the preceding discourse). Thus, within linguistics itself, objections to early text grammars led to the inclusion of more communicative features, such as the extra-linguistic context, in these grammars. However, even with these extensions, Gumperz (1982) observes that such language constructs cannot adequately account for situated interpretations, and include only a small part of the information interactants use in interpreting utterances.

Thus, critical issues within the linguistics discipline itself, as well as interest from other disciplines, focused increasing attention on pragmatics (Levinson, 1983). With its emphasis on language use in context, pragmatic approaches can readily incorporate contextual and communicative features in their analyses. Although considerable debate still focuses on the nature of pragmatics, nevertheless it can be characterized in terms of a set of underlying conceptual assumptions. In what follows, I hope to clarify the conceptual foundations that characterize pragmatic perspectives and to begin to integrate these diverse approaches. Throughout this book, I emphasize the implications of a pragmatic perspective for the study of human verbal communication, rather than its implications for the study of language itself.

II. THE SCOPE OF PRAGMATIC INQUIRY

There are a number of distinct approaches to pragmatics. These alternative views are now discussed in terms of their strengths, their weaknesses and their implications for analyzing communication. What I suggest is that an integrated pragmatic perspective, building upon a set of common underlying assumptions shared the alternative approaches discussed, is the most adequate approach for analyzing human communication. In what follows, I discuss these alternative approaches. Finally, in section III of this chapter, the shared underlying assumptions of an integrated pragmatic perspective are discussed.

Cicourel's Overview of Pragmatic Approaches

Cicourel (1980) suggests that three general models of language use have emerged: the speech act model, the expansion model, and the information processing model. The *speech act* model deals with an utterance's propositional content (its assertions) and illocutionary force (its intended effect). This model presupposes Grice's cooperative principle, and assumes shared knowledge among participants. Cicourel argues that the speech act model does not allow for possible multiple meanings of an utterance, nor does it adequately specify the participants' contextual knowledge.

The *expansion* model broadens an utterance's meaning to include its meaning in context. Expansion models rely on the following assumptions: (1) the cultural basis of communication is explicitly recognized; (2) the participants' shared knowledge is recognized; (3) that an utterance can perform several speech acts in a particular context; and (4) an utterance's meaning may also be conveyed by nonverbal cues. This model, like the speech act model, faces the same problem of carefully specifying the relevant contextual cues and conventions operating in a given context.

Finally, the *information processing* model relies upon cognitive schemata to interpret texts. These schemata represent the meanings of concepts and the user's normal, conventional knowledge of typical interactional settings. Such a model, according to Cicourel, is expectation-driven as well as data-driven. That is, individuals anticipate what is to come, and respond to incoming information in view of those expectations (e.g., is this a usual or unusual happening, etc.).

Cicourel concludes by arguing that a synthesis of these models is necessary for an adequate theory of discourse. The expansion model is too general and inclusive, while the problem-solving model does not identify the properties of the text that develop during interaction. All language analyses must be carefully qualified since, as Cicourel notes, not everything that is said may be meaningful. Finally, he argues that a theory of verbal interaction should specify a participant's knowledge base, as well as the structural and organizational constraints on interaction.

Van Dijk's View of Pragmatics

Like Cicourel, van Dijk calls for "an integrated theory of the abstracted structures and functions of verbal utterances" and argues that pragmatics plays an essential role in developing this theory (van Dijk, 1981, p. 8). An integrated theory of verbal interaction must describe (1) the functions an utterance performs, (2) the contextual conditions necessary for that utterance to perform those functions, and (3) the appropriateness of the utterance. These conditions must apply to language as it is used in normal settings.

Special discourse constraints, such as those found in narration or argumentation, would not be included since not all utterances fall under these constraints.

Pragmatic theories are used to assess the appropriateness of an utterance in context. To judge an utterance's appropriateness, pragmatic theories must be able to specify the contextual features related to situational appropriateness, as well as specify the participants' relationship with one another. Van Dijk concludes that pragmatic theories need to be integrated with theories of cognition and social interaction in order to construct an overall theory of communication.

Levinson's View of Pragmatics

Another illuminating discussion of the scope of pragmatics, especially from the standpoint of integrating pragmatics into mainstream linguistic theory, is Stephen Levinson's discussion of alternative approaches to pragmatics (Levinson, 1983). His analysis surveys different approaches to pragmatics (e.g., pragmatics defined as communicative appropriateness, pragmatics defined as the functions of language, etc.), and points out strengths and weaknesses of each perspective. Keep in mind, however, that Levinson's analysis focuses on pragmatics as a subpart of linguistics. In contrast, according to the perspective being developed here, pragmatics is a way of conceptualizing verbal communication.

Levinson views these alternative approaches as *competing theories* of pragmatics. However, I view these approaches not as different theories, but as attempts to focus on different *aspects* of pragmatics. Furthermore, I believe these differing approaches can be synthesized into an analytic framework which examines verbal interaction. While Levinson and I thus disagree on how these diverse approaches are to be viewed, nevertheless, his discussion raises important issues that affect both pragmatic theories and communication theories.

Levinson suggests that pragmatics may be defined as the interpretation of language form in context; this includes both the linguistic form and communicative content of an utterance. The communicative content of utterances include truth-conditions (or entailment); conventional implicature; presuppositions; felicity conditions; conversational implicature; and inferences based on conversational structures (Levinson, 1983, p. 14). As such, pragmatics has both a universal level (those aspects of context that are marked in all languages) and language specific aspects (those contextual aspects marked in only one or several languages). In order to be considered pragmatic, a language form must be (1) intentionally used, (2) a conventional part of a contrastive set (i.e., the absence of this feature or selection of another feature marks something of different significance) and (3) subject to regular grammatical processes.

Levinson (1983) subsequently broadens his definition and suggests that "pragmatics is the study of the relations between language and context that are basic to an account of language understanding" (p. 21). Language understanding, according to Levinson, is what many define as communication: "communication is a complex kind of intention that is achieved or satisfied just by being recognized" (p. 16). That is, both the speaker and the listener mutually acknowledge a communicative intention. Achieving this mutual recognition of communicative intentionality requires rigorous, systematic inferences by both speakers and listeners. Levinson suggests that "for each systematic set of constraints on the use of language, there will be a corresponding set of inference-procedures that will be applied to language understanding" (p. 21).

Levinson argues, as do others, that this view of pragmatics is inherently problematic because specifying the interactants' commonsense knowledge that supports such inferences would be impossible. However, keep in mind that *only* commonsense knowledge *relevant* to language understanding in a given context needs to be specified. As Levinson himself points out, scholars (Argyle, 1973; Goffman, 1976; Lyons, 1977) are beginning to specify what constitutes this relevant knowledge base. This relevant knowledge includes the conventions of the language being used (Gumperz' contextualization cues), knowledge of the interactants' status and role, the level of formality, the appropriateness of the subject matter, goals of the interaction, and so forth.

In addition to developing his own view, Levinson also discusses two other well-known approaches to pragmatics: those emphasizing an utterance's appropriateness, and those emphasizing an utterance's functions. The appropriateness model is limited by its requirement of a culturally homogenous speech community, by its failure to account for inappropriate communicative behavior or artistic violations of communicative conventions, and by its variable applicability. In contrast, functional models are limited because they lack well-developed pragmatic principles for their development and use.

While Levinson faults all the pragmatic approaches outlined above, he nevertheless concludes that pragmatics needs to be a part of linguistic theory. He notes that a pragmatic theory can simplify semantic theories; indeed, the two theories working together can provide full lexical descriptions for a language. In addition, a pragmatic theory is needed to account for devices such as honorifics, and expressions such as "well," which have important pragmatic functions. Finally, and most importantly, a pragmatic perspective is necessary for an adequate theory of verbal communication. As Levinson (1983) cogently observes:

...we can compute out of sequences of utterances, taken together with background about language usage, highly detailed inferences about the nature of assumptions participants are making, and the purposes for which utterances are being used. In order to participate in ordinary language usage, one must be able to make such calculations, both in production and interpretation. This ability is independent of idiosyncratic beliefs, feelings and usages (although it may refer to those shared by participants), and is based for the most part on quite regular and relatively abstract principles. Pragmatics can be taken to be the description of this ability, as it operates both for particular languages and language in general. Such a description must certainly play a role in any general theory of linguistics. (p. 53)

Levinson's discussion leaves us with a useful working definition of pragmatics. However, as Levinson himself notes, this discussion of alternative approaches is likely to leave readers frustrated with the lack of direction and coherence in pragmatics. Yet this dissatisfaction arises *only* if one considers these approaches to be *competing* models, as they are in fact typically taken to be. Dissatisfaction with these approaches may also arise if any single approach is singled out as an overarching model for pragmatics.

It seems highly unlikely that any single theoretical model will adequately characterize the complexity of pragmatics. Levinson himself calls for complex, multi-faceted pragmatic approaches. Other scholars, particularly those working on language and communication development, note that any single theory is unlikely to adequately explain the richness and complexity of human communicative processes (see M.P. Atkinson, 1981; Bates, 1979; Sugarman, 1983 and Snow & Gilbreath, 1983 for excellent discussions of this point). Gumperz (1982) also calls for a new integrated theory of pragmatics; pragmatics needs to focus on what enables interactants to interpret particular configurations of cues, so that situated interpretations of utterances can be made.

It appears, then, that communicative phenomena call for complex, multi-faceted approaches. If the pragmatic approaches outlined previously are viewed as complementary ones, in the sense that each deals with a different *aspect* of pragmatics, then these approaches, when integrated, can provide an overarching framework for pragmatics. An integrated approach would also provide a more adequate analysis of communication since the weaknesses in one particular approach could be compensated for by the strengths of other approaches. Furthermore, such a framework can illuminate human verbal communicative processes, and provide a meta-theoretical basis for the study of human communication. Through this book, I hope to provide *a first, rough approximation* of this pragmatic synthesis and apply it to an analysis of human communication.

Toward an Integrated Pragmatic Perspective

In interpreting language use in context, we have three essential components: the utterances or text itself, the context, and the language user. The functional approaches to pragmatics deal primarily with language users' goals, which are being accomplished through the use of particular language forms. Pragmatic approaches centering on language appropriateness emphasize the context; any criterion for appropriateness must be measured against the communicative demands of the context. Finally, those pragmatic approaches emphasizing language form, often labeled as discourse analytic approaches or pragmalinguistics, focus on the language form itself and the inferences derived from a particular language form, irrespective of context or language user. While interpreting language, listeners use inferences derived from the text, the context, and the speaker. Thus it seems necessary, for any pragmatic perspective trying to account for language use in context, to incorporate inferences from all three bases—text, context, and language user.

When pragmatic approaches are reframed in this way, each approach contributes to a theory of discourse. Discourse analytic approaches, focusing on the form of language, deal with structural aspects of pragmatics. Structural aspects reflect universal features of text interpretation. These features apply to any text, whether written or spoken, irrespective of the language used. For example, deixis or clear identification of referents is necessary for understanding a communicative message, and thus it is a universal, structural feature of any communicative message.

Pragmatic approaches emphasizing the appropriateness of language use focus upon inferences about the context. Contextual inferences, it should be noted, need *not* involve all the tacit, commonsense knowledge that may characterize a social encounter. Pragmatic approaches need deal *only* with those aspects of context that constrain the communicative processes in an interaction. Pragmatic approaches will need to carefully link contextual features directly to the alleged communicative constraints.

Functional approaches, as previously mentioned, deal with the goals of the language user. It is assumed that the functions that utterances perform express the language user's goals. There is considerable debate, however, over the extent to which language users are aware of their goals (Bowers, 1981). Considerable research has demonstrated that some encounters require very little active monitoring of the encounter by the participants (Langer, 1978; Nisbett & Ross, 1980; Ross & Flavell, 1981). Such encounters are viewed as routines, or encounters that are well-scripted (Goffman, 1970, 1981; Nelson, 1981; Tannen, 1979). A related issue has been that of intentionality—the degree to which communicators consciously select their communicative strategies (see, for example, Searle, 1983 for a lengthy treatment of this issue).

Careful analysis of these approaches reveals their interrelationships. The context, for example, provides certain types of communicative opportunities while restricting others. Legal settings prescribe certain types of communicative behaviors while job interviews provide different communicative options. However, while the context establishes the potential for certain types of communicative options, the characteristics of the language user—motives, purposes, social status, experience, age, sex and the like—will determine what options are selected. Many may participate in a marriage ceremony, but only a judge, minister or other legally recognized authority can *perform* a binding ceremony. Anyone can tell a joke or story, but regardless of who tells the joke and whatever the context, most jokes and stories require a punch line or central point. Jokes without punch lines, or stories without a point are ineffective and thus unsuccessful. The structural form of a joke or story must be maintained, although the language user and context characteristics may influence the type of joke or story told. For example, social norms may prohibit women from telling off-color jokes or stories, or prohibit funny stories being told at a funeral.

From these brief examples, and undoubtedly many more that readers can provide, it seems clear that, during communication, the elements of text, context, and language users interact and influence one another. These interrelationships exist on multiple levels and operate in diverse ways. Any theory of human communication must account for these interrelationships in a systematic, principled manner. Furthermore, these interrelationships may be universal in some respects (i.e., existing in all natural languages) and language-specific in other respects (i.e., existing only in certain languages). It seems reasonable to assume that structural aspects of pragmatics are the most likely candidates for universal pragmatic principles, while contextual aspects may frequently be found to be language specific.

Despite the debates about the precise nature of pragmatic theories, it seems clear that such theories would be very useful in analyzing human verbal communicative processes. Clearly, speaking is an action that accomplishes social goals; while theories of action are too general to be useful, pragmatic theories focus on the social accomplishments of interaction itself. Cognitive theories generally deal with the mental processes involved in human thought, whereas pragmatic theories deal with how language is processed in terms of real-world time constraints. Theories of social interaction generally discuss how people interact, whereas pragmatic theories focus on *verbal* communication as a means of interaction. Thus pragmatic theories offer valuable insights into verbal communication, but must be integrated to reflect the rich diversity and complexity of verbal communication.

While this book focuses on verbal communication, clearly any adequate modeling of human communicative behavior must also incorporate nonverbal communication as well. Nonverbal communication, especially prosody, intonation, and eye gaze, plays a central role in interpreting interaction (Duncan & Fiske, 1977; Gumperz, 1982; Scheflen, 1974). Of particular interest here is research analyzing the interaction between the verbal and nonverbal communicative systems (Beattie, 1981; Bull, 1983; Goodwin, 1981; Scheflen, 1972).

While I attempt to reframe and to integrate pragmatic approaches in order to provide a basis for examining human communication, a synthesis of these approaches can be suggested on another level of analysis. When one surveys these approaches, they appear to rely upon common underlying assumptions about human communication. Common assumptions about intentionality, inferences, commonsense knowledge shared by speaker/ hearers, contextual cues, and the like, permeate these approaches. We now turn to an examination of these underlying assumptions, which provide a conceptual basis for the integration of these approaches.

III. UNDERLYING CONCEPTUAL ASSUMPTIONS

All the major pragmatic approaches—the appropriateness model, the functional model and the language form model (or as I have reframed them, the contextual, functional and structural approaches)—have common underlying assumptions. All view language interpretation in context as:

- inferential

- intentional

- conventional

- jointly negotiated between speakers and hearers

- varies according to context and language user

- involves commonsense knowledge

- sequential

- accomplished in real time and space

- systematic

- interpretive, and

- varies according to the participants' social relationships

Many of these underlying assumptions are interrelated. For example, our taken-for-granted commonsense knowledge frequently provides a basis for inferences and for interpretive procedures used in evaluating interaction. Furthermore, commonsense knowledge itself is a function of the context in which the interaction occurs. Taken together, these assumptions present a stable, coherent perspective on communication. While not exhaustive, these shared assumptions are significant conceptual foundations of a pragmatic approach to verbal communication. In what follows, each assumption is discussed in more detail. Various research approaches are briefly discussed under each concept to demonstrate its broad base of support. By citing a number of different scholars, however, I am *not* suggesting that these researchers use these concepts in identical ways. Rather, I am suggesting that these scholars view the concepts in similar ways and that these concepts play an important role in their approaches to communication.

Inferences

In general, inferences can be viewed as the implicit meanings humans assign to objects and events. We derive these meanings on the basis of what is said (e.g., through presuppositions, conversational implicatures, etc.), on the basis of the context, and on the basis of commonsense knowledge. Cicourel (1980) defines inferences as the "tacit ways in which we link information from different sources to create coherency and relevance in our speech acts and nonverbal and paralinguistic actions" (p. 117). Speech act models rely on inferential processes since an utterance's illocutionary force is inferred from the social action that utterance accomplishes by being spoken. Grice (1975) refers to the interpretive, inferential nature of communication when he suggests that interactants construct arguments that support one interpretation over another by using conventional meanings, the Cooperative Principle, conversational maxims, and contextual knowledge.

Intentionality

Most communication scholars agree that communication, as a social act, is inherently intentional (Berger & Bradac, 1982; van Dijk, 1981; Grice, 1975; Kreckel, 1981). Grice (1975) views talking as an instance of purposive, rational behavior. While communication is commonly viewed as intentional, there is little agreement on how to conceptualize or measure intentionality. Implicit in any discussion of intentionality are unresolved questions such as the degree to which individuals consciously plan their communication, the degree of cognitive monitoring humans are capable of, the degree to which humans can accurately report their intentions, and the like.

Three recent approaches to intentionality appear to have important implications for communication research. One approach, taken by Searle

(1983), Shotter (1984) and others, views communicative behavior as motivated by the need for social communion and cooperation. Our intentions, from birth, are driven by these basic social needs. Another approach views communicative intentions from the standpoint of social control. Here our communicative purposes are tied to issues of social control and influence, whether over our own behavior (Langer, 1983) or over a relationship (Rogers, 1983).

The third approach, taken by researchers in artificial intelligence, views intentionality as goal-seeking; when we act, we act to accomplish some goal. Douglas (1970), following in the tradition of Schutz and Husserl, argues that "it is primarily intentions at any time—*our purposes at hand* —that order human thought, that determine the relevance of information and ideas about the world and ourselves" (italics mine, p. 26). Parisi and Castelfranchi (1981) define a goal as a state that regulates an individual's behavior. A communicative goal is one that involves a listener's acknowledgement and adoption of this goal. In conversation, speakers and hearers must adopt at least one goal in common. At a minimum, their mutual goal may be merely to engage in a conversation with one another.

As we can see from the brief comments made here, while intentionality is a taken-for-granted characteristic of communication, there is considerable debate over its conceptualization and measurement.

Conventionality

Ventola (1979), following Firth and Corder, argues that much of interaction, especially conversation, is more routinized than commonly realized. Underlying these interactional routines are conventional rules and stereotyped patterns of behavior. Heritage (1984) notes that utterances are interpreted in light of the normal, conventional patterns of interaction that operate in a given setting. Communication behavior, then, can be viewed as conventional; guided by shared lexical meanings, shared commonsense knowledge, and shared social rules of behavior.

Tacit, Commonsense Knowledge

Ethnomethodologists, with their focus on understanding how social order is established, assume a common, largely tacit, vocabulary of symbols (Denzin, 1970). Communication is not possible without such shared knowledge, but communication itself also enables us to share knowledge. When interacting, participants assume that they share some common definitions of the situation, and they act on the basis of these shared definitions. These shared assumptions reflect taken-for-granted, commonsense knowledge about communication behavior and everyday life (von

Raffler-Engel, 1977). Douglas (1970) suggests that interpreting messages depends, in part, on common-sense understandings of everyday communicative behavior (pp. 30–31). Although scholars utilize tacit, commonsense knowledge in varied ways in their accounts of communicative behavior, all agree that its role is vital.

Joint Negotiation of Interaction

Interaction requires coordinated communicative behavior between at least two participants. In conversations, taking turns, responding to the talk of other participants, and the like, require joint management by participants. Interpreting utterances is also jointly managed, since hearers must ratify, disconfirm or otherwise respond to the speaker's utterance. Speakers must secure uptake on the part of their conversational partners (Dore, 1983, 1985; Good, 1979; Levinson, 1983). As Kreckel (1981) notes, speakers provide potential sources of information that listeners act upon. In addition, Franck (1981) argues that the jointly negotiated nature of interaction allows for the indeterminacy of utterances; this indeterminacy is necessary for maintaining face and for allowing interaction to flow smoothly. Franck does not deny that literal meanings can be attached to utterances, but argues that interpretation relies on both negotiated meanings and literal meanings.

Variability as a Function of Context and Language User

One of the most widely shared assumptions about communicative behavior is that it varies across different contexts and different language users. Van Dijk (1980) suggests that communicative models need to incorporate multiple levels of context (the cultural level, the organizational level, and the immediate social setting) as well as language-user characteristics such as age, sex, motivation, personal values, and so on. Dascal (1981), after Bar-Hillel, differentiates two types of contextual influences. The *co-text* refers to the background provided by the utterances themselves, while the *context* refers to the physical and sociocultural environment surrounding the interaction.

That language use varies as a function of the context and the participants is clearly well-established. Here again the basic controversy focuses on how the context and user characteristics are conceptualized and measured. Ethnomethodologists, for example, focus predominantly on contextual determinants of meaning, while many in the communication discipline focus on how interactants' characteristics influence their communicative behavior.

The Sequencing of Communicative Behavior

Schutz (1967), Cicourel (1980) and others note that communication is both retrospective and prospective. Ongoing talk can retrospectively recast the interpretation of preceding turns as well as prospectively shape opportunities for future interaction. Dore (1985) notes that the sequencing of utterances determines, in part, what is accomplished in interaction, and reflects its planned nature.

The sequencing of utterances influences the interpretation of utterances as well as the general format of interaction. For example, conversations are sequenced structurally; they begin with greetings, then the conversational topic is introduced, and finally, closings end the conversation. Analytic units within conversations, like questions and responses, may be considered both structural as well as interpretive units.

Most researchers would agree that communicative behavior is sequenced. However, important differences exist about how sequencing units are defined, measured and interrelated. Some scholars suggest that sequencing rules are similar to those found in generative grammars. Others argue that conversations are sequenced by participants' strategies for achieving particular goals. Still others suggest that formal sequencing structures will not be found in conversations (Levinson, 1983). While sequencing in conversations appears to exist, the nature of the principles governing such sequencing is not fully understood.

Communication Occurs in Real Time and Space

Adequate models of language use must reflect real-world time limitations and spatial references since interactions are limited by humans' ability to process language. Psycholinguists have been particularly concerned with the analysis of language in terms of human perceptual and processing limitations. Van Dijk and Kintsch (1983), for example, in their model of discourse comprehension, emphasize the importance of time constraints on comprehension. In addition, time and spatial constraints have different effects on different mediums. Ricouer (1981) notes that writing is not subject to the time and space considerations that speaking is. Any modeling of interaction should acknowledge the time and processing limitations under which it occurs.

Systematicity

The systematicity of communication reflects both its sequential and structured nature. Brief mention has already been made of the sequential aspects of communication, particularly the debate over what are the most appropriate means for analyzing such sequencing (Goodwin, 1979; Heritage, 1984; Levinson, 1983). Wilson (1970) notes that both normative and interpretive approaches to social behavior (including communicative behavior) assume that social behavior is systematic. Normative approaches stress the organized, socially sanctioned expectations individuals have about their social behavior. In contrast, interpretive approaches emphasize the cultural patterning of social behavior and individuals' recognition of those patterns.

Many different types of structural communicative units have been suggested. Discourse analysts have identified overall structural formats that characterize jokes, narratives, conversations, news reports and the like (Gumperz, 1981a, b; Schenkein, 1978; Tracy & Craig, 1983). Within conversations, scholars have identified structural pairs like compliment/response; greeting/greeting; question/answer and the like. And from another perspective, Wilder (1979), characterizing the Palo Alto Interactional work, suggests that communicative behavior should be viewed as a cybernetic system, with its structural properties of feedback, redundancy, homeostasis, and equifinality. Thus, the systematicity of human communication appears on many levels of analysis. Depending upon the researcher's purposes, different aspects of the systematic nature of communication will be of interest.

Interpretiveness

The text, context, interactants, and their mutual interrelationships determine how communicative behaviors are interpreted. The relative influence of each factor appears to be a function of the task and goals of the interaction. Additional complexity in interpretation is apparent when one considers that a text may have multiple meanings (Franck, 1981; Haslett, 1984b; Levinson, 1983).

Ethnomethodologists and phenomenological sociologists have been particularly concerned about the interpretive procedures individuals use to make sense of everyday social behavior. Cicourel (1980), Douglas (1970) and others argue that interpretive procedures must be analyzed independently of the decontextualized (literal) meanings of lexical items. These interpretive procedures are based upon taken-for-granted, commonsense knowledge about everyday life (Wilson, 1970). These interpretive procedures are characterized by (1) the reciprocity of perspectives, (2) the et cetera assumption, (3) the presence of normal forms of interaction, (4) the retrospective-prospective nature of talk, (5) the reflexivity of talk, and (6) the indexicality of talk (Cicourel, 1970).

In general, several important conclusions can be drawn from this brief survey of interpretive procedures. First, interpretations of communicative behavior vary as a function of text, context, communicator and/or their interrelationships. Second, contextualized meanings must be analytically separated from decontextualized meanings. And finally, communicator characteristics and the social relationships among participants appear to play a central role in the interpretation of on-going interaction.

Relational Influences on Communication

The most fundamental purpose of communication is to develop and maintain social relationships among individuals. Only through communication are individuals able to share information and coordinate their activities. Scholars from a wide range of disciplines have acknowledged the fundamental role of communication in establishing social order, cooperation, and social relations with one another (Cicourel, 1980; Douglas, 1970; Goffman, 1974, 1976).

IV. CONCLUSIONS AND IMPLICATIONS

The three perspectives on pragmatics briefly outlined in this chapter—the structural, functional, and contextual approaches—all make important contributions to the analysis of human verbal communication. Since each approach focuses on different aspects of communication, their integration into an overall analytic framework should provide a more adequate basis for studying communication. A solid basis for this integration can be seen in the common underlying assumptions regarding communicative behavior found in these approaches. In addition, many scholars support the integration of separate perspectives into a general theory of communication.

In building this synthesis, I first discuss each broad pragmatic approach—the structural, functional, and contextual approaches—in more detail. Within each general approach, scholars have employed different theoretical models, different methods of analysis, and different levels of analysis. For each general approach, I discuss these different models, their strengths, their weakness, and their implications for analyzing communication.

In the next section of the book, I propose an integrated pragmatic approach to communication. This approach emphasizes the interpretive processes involved in human communication. In brief, I argue that participants' goals govern their interactions with others. In pursuing their conversational goals, interactants rely upon commonsense knowledge relevant to accomplishing their goals. This relevant commonsense knowledge includes knowledge of the appropriate norms of behavior in a particular social situation, expectations concerning the other interactants and their goals, and so forth. The text—the utterances of the interactants—express the relevant norms of interpretation for this interaction, and signal their mutual recognition of what is going on in the interaction.

As can be readily seen, the underlying pragmatic assumptions outlined in this chapter play a significant role in the model of communication being developed here. Individuals intend to accomplish conversational goals through their interaction with others. The strategies they pursue in achieving these goals vary as a function of the context, the other participants, and the social relationships among the participants. To select the most effective communicative strategies, participants activate portions of their common-sense knowledge *relevant* to their purposes. These strategies guide the production and comprehension of the text. Through the text, participants signal their meanings and interpret others' meanings.

The text expresses, through its sequencing and the inferences derived from the text, the speaker's intended meaning. In turn, listeners, relying on their relevant commonsense knowledge about the ongoing interaction, signal their interpretation of and reaction to the speaker's utterances through their own responses. Through their utterances, which constitute the text of the interaction, speakers and listeners jointly negotiate and publicly signal their mutual understanding of the interaction.

Taken together, these assumptions suggest that communication is a *strategic* activity. That is, interactants choose what to say from among a wide range of alternative possible utterances. Their choices are strategic in that, as interactants, they try to maximize their effectiveness in achieving their conversational goals. And interactants attempt to maximize their effectiveness despite the limitations imposed by fragmented, incomplete knowledge about the context, other interactants, and their goals. Thus communicative strategies are "best estimates" about what utterance maximizes effectiveness at a given point in time.

The most important principle for determining our communicative strategies is that of *relevance*. Communicators activate their relevant commonsense knowledge about the interaction in order to maximize the probability of achieving their goals. In addition, since listeners assume that the speaker's utterances are relevant to the conversation at hand, they try to relate the speaker's utterances to some inferred goal of the speaker. In other words, listeners rely on the principle of relevance in trying to interpret a speaker's utterances. For both participants, the text signals the mutually understood interpretation of what is going on in the interaction. If speakers and listeners disagree on their interpretations, the text also reveals that through utterances like "No, that's not what I meant at all! Weren't you listening?" In short, interactants try to select the most effective communicative behaviors; and the most effective behaviors are those perceived to be the most *relevant* for achieving their conversational goals.

The strategic model of communication outlined here suggests that, in order to understand the full complexity of communication, scholars must analyze communication as it occurs in everyday encounters. Only in such situations can we view the strategic choices interactants actually make and assume that these choices have real consequences for the interactants. Although the view presented in this book relies heavily on naturalistic data collection and observation, nevertheless controlled empirical testing of communicative behavior is necessary. Under carefully controlled conditions, experimental studies can test significant variables uncovered in naturalistic studies; thus the two methods of analysis complement one another. The complexity and richness of human communicative behaviors are most adequately examined through the use of multiple perspectives and methods of study. These issues are more thoroughly discussed in part II of the book.

With this general overview in mind, let us now turn to a more in-depth discussion of each major pragmatic approach—the structural, functional, and contextual perspectives.

2 Structural Approaches to Pragmatics

Structural pragmatic approaches focus on language form, and the inferences that can be drawn from the use of a particular linguistic form. In addition, structural approaches concern themselves with the coherence, or meaningfulness, of a text. Since achieving coherence is necessary for all texts, structural pragmatic approaches thus emphasize the universal dimensions of communication. However, while coherence must be established in any text, different languages and different cultures may use varied methods to achieve coherence.

Structural approaches also vary in their level of application; some structural approaches are broad in scope, while others are more limited in scope. Since a substantial research literature exists on structural pragmatic approaches, the discussion of these approaches encompasses two separate chapters. This chapter discusses more macro-level structural analyses, and those that apply to any text. Chapter 3 focuses on micro-level structural approaches that examine how conversations are organized.

The structural pragmatic approaches outlined here vary from an analysis of an entire text (van Dijk's theory of discourse) to analyses focusing on single utterances or utterance pairs (speech act analysis). Communicative rules are also analyzed since these rules are used to interpret and organize utterances in context. While communicative rules vary across cultures, and from context to context, nevertheless all social groups appear to use such rules. Finally, central issues in establishing coherence—deixis, presupposition, entailment, and implicature—are discussed. Again, while these issues are dealt with differently in different languages, cultures, and contexts, nevertheless they appear to be universal aspects of text coherence.

22

More specifically, the most inclusive, broadly-based structural model covered is that of van Dijk (1977a, 1981, van Dijk & Kintsch, 1983). In his model, van Dijk posits global units of meaning (macrostructures) and global structural units (superstructures) in texts; he argues that these structures play an important role in the processing and retrieval of complex information. (For a more complete review of van Dijk's work, see Haslett, 1986a). Although other scholars have developed similar cognitive models (see, for example, Mandler, 1984; Meyer 1975; Schank & Abelson, 1977), van Dijk's model focuses more on communicative issues and thus, for our purposes, provides the best exemplar of such approaches.

The next structural model discussed, that of the ethnography of speaking, focuses on a more restricted domain of communicative activity—namely, speech events. Speech events are social activities primarily governed by speaking. While this approach deals primarily with face-to-face interaction, analyses of speech events could be applied to any text. The next model, Burke's structural model of interaction, focuses on communication as social action, and reflects a dramaturgical approach.

Next, speech act analysis is discussed. A speech act is frequently suggested as the minimal unit of communicative analysis since it uses a single utterance as the basic unit of analysis. As Austin (1962) and Searle (1969, 1976) note, speech act analysis can be applied to any utterance. Some aspects of speech act analysis, such as adjacency pairs, reflect the structural connectedness of pairs of utterances.

The final structural model presented, communicative rules, may be said to determine choices from among competing utterances. These rules reflect the communicator's purposes and judgments about what particular utterance is most effective in a given social situation. The problem of choosing the most effective utterance is universal; however, the communicative rules for selecting the most effective utterance vary across cultures.

Finally, critical issues in achieving coherence—the problems of deixis, implicature, presupposition, and entailment—are discussed. All communicators need to have clear reference (deixis). In addition, all communicators appear to make inferences on the basis of the text (presupposition and entailment) and on the basis of the context (implicature). We now turn to a more detailed discussion of structural pragmatic models.

I. STRUCTURAL PRAGMATIC MODELS

van Dijk's Theory of Discourse

Van Dijk uses two different structures to explain how texts are processed and understood. Macrostructures (MS) represent the meaning of a text while superstructures (SS) represent the structure of different types of discourse like scholarly papers, narratives, and so forth. Macrostructures, superstructures, and their influence on discourse comprehension are discussed in more detail.

Global Structures in Texts: Macrostructures and Superstructures

Global structures are higher level, abstract semantic or schematic units used in discourse, interaction, and cognition. These global structures are flexible and vary as a function of three factors. First, these structures vary with respect to their level of analysis. That is, global structures, like a story's conclusion, can be distinguished from local structures, like a single utterance. Second, these structures vary with respect to point of view. Global structures may focus on the whole, a part, or on some stated perceptual viewpoint. Finally, global structures vary with respect to relevance. For example, the explicitness of detail in these global structures varies, depending upon what level of generalization is needed.

1. Macrostructures in Discourse. A macrostructure is a semantic representation entailed by a sequence of propositions in a text. Macrostructures are formed at different levels of generalization within the text, and organize semantic information for processing and storage. For any given discourse, the macrostructure of that entire discourse is its most general meaning structure. For example, the most global macrostructure of Pinnochio might be roughly stated as "A young boy discovers the unfortunate consequences of lying."

Macrostructures are formed through the application of macrorules. Macrorules act as semantic derivation or inference rules (van Dijk, 1980); they are

1. *deletion/selection macrorules* — these rules delete text propositions which are not relevant for interpreting other propositions in the text (or, conversely, these rules may be regarded as selecting all propositions that are needed for text interpretation);
2. *generalization macrorules* — these rules abstract a proposition that generalizes over sentential details;
3. *construction macrorules* — these rules group micropropositions into

a single proposition because the micropropositions are normal components, conditions or consequences of that single proposition. (pp. 46–48)

Macrorules are ordered in their application to a text; with construction, generalization and deletion/selection being applied respectively (p. 50). In addition, macrorules appear to operate differently in different types of discourse.

2. Superstructures of Discourse.   While macrostructures are global units of meaning, van Dijk posits superstructures as global structural units. Superstructures thus provide the structural form for the text's meaning. Rules specify what superstructure categories may combine and how they are sequentially ordered. For example, a narrative's superstructure represents the categorical structures (e.g., introduction, conclusion, complicating action, etc.) that organize the narrative's content. Superstructures thus play a critical role in discourse production and comprehension, and constrain the meanings contained in different aspects of the text (e.g., introductions contain different information than conclusions).

3. The Interrelationships Between Superstructures and Macrostructures. Superstructures influence macrostructures in several important ways. First, superstructures influence macrostructures through ordering their sequencing in discourse. Second, each superstructure has a conventional semantic content (macrostructure) assigned to it. For example, a story's introduction (a superstructure category) contains information about the story's characters, the setting and other semantic information that orients the reader/listener to the narrative. Finally, superstructures determine the formation of macrostructures by highlighting what information is most important in a given text. As van Dijk (1980) notes, "assumptions about the actual schema or schema-category provide the language user with expendient strategies in the hypothetical formation of respective text topics" (p. 128). More work, of course, is needed to fully detail these interrelationships: questions about the generality of superstructures, the nature of rules applying to macrostructures and superstructures, the recursiveness of superstructure categories, and so forth need more theoretical explanation and empirical testing.

Cognitive Processing of Texts

Now that we have briefly discussed van Dijk's model of text, we next consider the processing of text in context. Van Dijk's analyses of the cognitive processes of discourse comprehension and production emphasize the role of two factors: knowledge representation and the cognitive set of the individual.

1. Knowledge Representation. Commonsense knowledge, knowledge of the communicative context, and knowledge of interaction are semantically interrelated. In addition, they are pragmatically interrelated through inferences that are implicit in our commonsense knowledge of a given context. Thus, commonsense knowledge enables speakers and listeners to apply macrorules to texts since this knowledge reflects what events, properties, etc. are *most relevant* in a given context. Commonsense knowledge also represents the *normal conditions and consequences* of an action. In sum, knowledge representation appears to play a critical role in discourse comprehension and production (van Dijk, 1980, p. 229–233).

A. The Situational Model. Van Dijk and Kintsch's (1983) situation model represents a subset of commonsense knowledge that reflects events, actions, persons, etc. a text refers to. In short, situation models appear to capture *relevant* commonsense knowledge needed for discourse understanding.

> Using knowledge in discourse comprehension means being able to relate the discourse to some existing knowledge structure, which then provides a situation model for it. . . . Thus, each person has subjective experiential clusters about the town he or she lives in, the house, friends, place of work, and major life events. Similarly, each person shares, to some extent at least, other clusters of experiences about such items as countries, towns, historical events, political events, or well-known people. At the other extreme, as decontextualization sets in, these experiences become entirely general or almost so, such as one's knowledge of arithmetic or chess. (p. 337)

B. Strategies. Strategies enable interactants to choose the most effective utterances in a given situation. Strategies operate at different discourse levels, allowing at each level a choice of the "most effective or rational alternative" (p. 65). (I discuss strategies more thoroughly later in this chapter, and contrast them with communicative and linguistic rules). For our purposes here, it is important to note that

> strategies applied are like effective working hypotheses about the correct structure and meaning of a text fragment, and these may be disconfirmed by further processing. Also, strategic analysis depends not only on textual characteristics, but also on characteristics of the language user, such as his or her goals or world knowledge. . . .
>   Strategies are part of our general knowledge; they represent the procedural knowledge we have about understanding discourse. They are an open set. They need to be learned, and overlearned, before they can become automatized. New types of discourse and forms of communication may require the development of new strategies. (pp. 10–11)

2. Characteristics of Language Users.   Individual characteristics, such as one's motivations, purposes, beliefs, values, norms, and attitudes, influence how information is processed and understood. These characteristics partially determine how much attention is paid to particular topics, the importance of particular ideas, and the nature of further interpretations assigned to a particular discourse (van Dijk, 1980, pp. 247–248). In addition, the context and individual characteristics interact and subsequently influence discourse processing.

While van Dijk's work offers a cognitively-grounded structural model of discourse, his analysis needs to be further specified. The operation of rules forming macrostructures and superstructures; the relationship between macrostructures and superstructures, and the development of a situational model need to be further detailed. In addition, the nature of strategies, their interrelationships, their operation, and their influence on discourse needs to be further specified. Finally, although van Dijk's model is more oriented toward communication than other cognitive models of discourse, many significant communication variables, such as the social relationships among participants, are not sufficiently emphasized. (For a more in-depth review of van Dijk's work, see Haslett, 1986a.)

The next structural model discussed is that of the ethnography of speaking. In contrast to van Dijk's model, the ethnography of speaking emphasizes the immediate, contingent social context of interaction and assumes the necessary cognitive processing skills.

Ethnography of Speaking

In a set of essays, *Directions in Sociolinguistics,* Gumperz and Hymes (1972) set out a new approach to the study of human verbal communication, derived primarily from research and theory in anthropological linguistics. This approach, known as the ethnography of speaking, emphasizes the naturalistic collection of interactional data. In addition, they suggest that data analysis should be based upon participants' interpretations of their encounters. Hymes' research (1972) serves as a basis for much of the ethnographic work on communication in educational settings (see, for example, Mehan, 1979 and Wallat & Green, 1979). Gumperz and his colleagues (1977, 1982) have focused upon contextual constraints in interaction. (Their work is discussed in greater detail in subsequent chapters. See Chapter 5 for a detailed discussion of Gumperz' work, and Chapter 9 for a detailed discussion of Hymes' work).

The ethnography of speaking, hereafter referred to as ES, outlines a descriptive taxonomy of human verbal communication and offers a model for integrating these elements. ES elements are to be viewed as heuristic devices, rather than a priori categories. Since communicative analyses should rest upon the distinctions that participants themselves make in an encounter, these categories are suggested as useful departure points for analysis. The ES model closely parallels models of language analysis, but focuses upon the appropriateness of communication in particular settings—a concern ignored by traditional theories of language.

ES has five distinct components; one component, the *speech event,* is typically viewed as a model of a communicative encounter. According to Hymes, *speech acts* build up into *speech events,* which in turn constitute *speech situations.* Thus, we can analyze interaction on multiple levels, as we can with van Dijk's model, depending upon the researcher's particular focus. For example, we could focus on a particular joke (a speech act), in a given conversation (a speech event) at a particular party (the speech situation).

Although Hymes' conceptualization highlights salient features of inter-action, his view does not discuss how these features influence one another

TABLE 1
Hymes' Ethnography of Speaking

Goal: to provide a descriptive taxonomy and model for human verbal communication

ES Descriptive Units:

1. Speech community—individuals who share rules of language use and rules of language interpretation, and at least one linguistic code

2. Speech field—range of individuals beyond your speech community that one can communicate with in an understandable fashion

3. Speech situation—a bounded and recognizable activity, viewed as the social setting or context for interaction

4. Speech event—activities or aspects of activities that are governed by rules of communication; comprised of the following units:

   a. situation or context—the time, place, psychological and cultural setting

   b. participants—speaker and hearers

   c. ends or goals—the goals and purposes of the interaction, as well as the actual outcomes

   d. act characteristics—the message form and content

   e. key—attitude or mood of the participants

   f. instrumentalities—the channels (medium) and codes (language, dialect, accent, etc.) the participants use

   g. norms of interpretation—specific behaviors that accompany speech acts

   h. genre—categories of speech acts, like lectures, jokes, prayers, and so forth

5. Speech acts—a rule-governed, minimal unit of communication that reflects the kinds and occasions of speech

during interaction. That is, ES is a static rather than a dynamic model of communication. In addition, the larger sociocultural context that surrounds any interaction is not explicitly discussed.

The next structural model, that of Kenneth Burke (1969), focuses on communication as social action. His model, the *pentad,* is based upon a dramaturgical approach. Both Burke (1969) and Duncan (1962) argue that humans are social actors whose actions are interpreted in light of the situated activity in which they are involved. Burke's pentad involves five elements: the act, scene, agency, agent, and motive.

Burke's Pentad

The *act* involves what is done in a specific situations. According to Burke, meaning is always dependent on the situated activity in which participants are involved. Participants' acts are supported, in context, by a set of implicit, tacit rules and assumptions about how the interaction is to be interpreted (Brittan, 1973).

The *scene* refers to the situation in which the social activity takes place. People evaluate, interpret, define, and symbolize situations to themselves. Some situations permit certain actions to be performed, while prohibiting other actions. Thus, situations *direct* the activities that take place, but do not *determine* them. Situational definitions are also influenced by others' interpretations; participants' perceptions of the situation may be broadly or narrowly focused. Briefly then, scenes provide the symbolic frame through which actors construct their meanings. As such, scenes provide the necessary social support for everyday interaction.

Motives refer to an interactant's purposes; these motives guide an interactant's actions. Typically, motives are discussed in terms of socially defined, legitimated reasons for actions. In imputing motives, individuals are guided by situationally appropriate behavioral norms (Mills, 1940). Motives may also be provided by the interaction itself, as part of the participants' interpretations which develop during interaction.

Agency refers to the way in which people mutually construct their social worlds. Communication is the vehicle through which we construct shared social reality (Berger & Luckman, 1967; Brittan, 1973: Burke, 1969; Douglas, 1970; Schutz, 1967). In addition, new meanings can derive from interaction as well as simultaneously reinterpret past action (Brittan, 1973).

The *agent,* of course, refers to the individual actor. Actors evaluate their own acts and thus some degree of self-observation enters into any interaction (Burke, 1969). Agents have motives for entering into situations, yet interaction itself also provides additional motivation because every interaction involves establishing a personal identity. An individual's plans do not determine their subsequent acts, but act as filtering mechanisms for interpreting their interaction (Brittan, 1973, p. 100).

Thus far, the three structural approaches discussed have been very broad-based models. A model encompassing a wide-ranging breadth provides an overall view of some phenomena, but also typically suffers from a lack of detail and/or careful discussion of how various components of the model fit together. These structural models differ fundamentally in their underlying metaphors. Burke uses a dramaturgical metaphor that emphasizes the symbolic nature of situated activity; van Dijk uses knowledge representation and cognitive processing of texts as his basic metaphor, and Hymes relies on an ethnographic analysis of a situated speech event. The next structural model is speech act analysis, which deals with the utterance as a basic unit of analysis. As such, this model is very narrow in its focus when contrasted with other structural models. Of all the models concerned with pragmatic approaches to communication, it is perhaps the most widely researched.

Speech Acts

At the outset, it is important to note that different theorists conceptualize speech acts in varied ways. Here I use the conceptualization of speech acts developed by Austin and Searle. However, varying definitions of the concept exist, even among those who claim to be adherents of the Austin-Searle view (see, for example, Chapter 5 in Levinson, 1983).

Linguistic philosophers have long been concerned with the reference and implications of sentences. Both Austin and Searle base their analyses, in part, on earlier work done by Wittgenstein. Wittgenstein, in *Philosophical Investigations* (1958), suggests that utterances can only be explained in terms of the activities and purposes for which language is being used.

Felicity Conditions. Austin (1962), writing in *How To Do Things With Words,* further developed the view that meaning is tied to language use. He suggests that a set of words, called *performatives,* accomplish action simply by virtue of being uttered. Speech activities like promising, warning, apologizing and the like are performatives; their purposes are achieved through being spoken. Performatives are not true or false, but are either successful (felicitous) or unsuccessful (infelicitous). For utterances to be felicitous, four conditions must be met:

1. accepted conventional procedures must be followed—certain words must be uttered by specified individuals in a given situation (for example, a marriage ceremony must be correctly followed and performed by an official who has that particular legal authority);

2. an appropriate individual must state the specific utterance (for example, in the U.S., a child could not be married);
3. all participants must execute the procedures properly, and
4. the procedure must be completed.

The Force of an Utterance.   Austin also suggests that all utterances have certain forces—that is, they accomplish certain actions. Thus, any spoken utterance has a *locutionary force* (the content of what is said); an *illocutionary force* (the intent or conventional force of what is said); and a *perlocutionary force* (the effect of the utterance, including both intended and unintended effects). Any utterance, then, is simultaneously a locutionary, illocutionary and perlocutionary act.

Searle's Speech Act Analysis.   Searle (1969) extended the analysis of illocutionary acts. He suggests that any speech act (i.e., utterance) consists of a proposition and its illocutionary force. Searle's analysis specifies the necessary and sufficient conditions needed to successfully perform an illocutionary act, and the rules that govern the use of a particular linguistic expression.

Searle's speech act analysis can be exemplified by his analysis of "promising." In order for promises to be felicitous, Searle argues that:

1. the propositional content must be appropriate—for promises to be effective, the speaker must promise some future action;
2. preparatory conditions must be satisfied—e.g., the speaker must believe that the future action is important or desirable to do, the future action must *not* be what is expected, the speaker must believe s/he can perform the act, and the speaker must believe the listener wants the act performed;
3. the speaker must be sincere; and
4. stating the utterance implies an obligation to perform the action.

Such felicity conditions—the necessary and sufficient conditions required to perform a speech act—can be specified for any speech act. Roughly, these felicity conditions can be organized into four categories—the specification of propositional content, preparatory conditions, sincerity conditions, and the essential condition (respectively illustrated in the "promising" example).

Constitutive and Regulative Rules.   In addition to felicity conditions, Searle discusses the rules that govern the use of particular linguistic expressions, like apologies. He distinguishes between two types of rules, regulative and constitutive rules. *Regulative* rules refer to the conditions for performing various speech acts. These rules can be thought of as rules governing our verbal interactions; in brief, who can say what kinds of utterances under what circumstances. In contrast, *constitutive* rules define "what counts" or can be recognized as a particular speech act. Another way of viewing this distinction might be to say that regulative rules govern the performance of a speech act (e.g., a judge must sentence a prisoner) while constitutive rules govern the format of a speech act (e.g., a judge must follow specified legal processes in sentencing).

Several scholars (Austin, 1962; Bach & Harnish, 1979; Hancher, 1979, Searle, 1976) have classified speech acts into a more limited set of basic actions, like making requests or stating factual information. Although these categories reflect basic actions performed by a set of speech acts, such categories appear to be inexhaustible as well as culturally variable. Little seems to be gained by such classification schemes, even those based on communicative intentions (see Levinson, 1983, pp. 239–241 on this point). While such categories appear to be based on direct, explicit performatives, oftentimes the illocutionary force of an utterance is indirect, such as in hinting or bribing. To account for these inferential speech acts, Searle distinguishes between indirect and direct speech acts. It is to this distinction we now turn.

Indirect Speech Acts.   According to Levinson (1983), citing Gazdar's analysis of speech acts (1979a, b; 1981), speech act theorists are committed to the *literal force hypothesis* (hereafter cited LFH). First, the LFH assumes that explicit performatives specify their illocutionary force in the performative verb in the utterance's main clause. For example, if I say "I apologize," then the performative verb (apologize) expresses the illocutionary force of the utterance, namely the intent to apologize. And second, the LFH assumes that the three main sentence types, imperatives, interrogatives, and declaratives, have conventional illocutionary forces associated with them, respectively ordering or requesting, questioning, and stating. All other speech acts are indirect speech acts; such utterances have an additional inferred, indirect force associated with them. However, as Levinson notes, most language usage is indirect; and it is very difficult to derive illocutionary force from the variety of utterances used in interactions. There is, put succinctly, no simple correspondence between utterance form and utterance force.

Criticisms of Speech Act Theories.   In addition to the problematic connection between an utterance's form and its function, Levinson details other major difficulties with speech act models. First, there is difficulty in distinguishing between an utterance's illocutionary and perlocutionary force. Illocutionary acts have built-in consequences, some depending on uptake by the listeners (e.g., like a bet) while others have direct consequences (e.g., like declaring war). The boundaries between perlocutionary and illocutionary force are thus quite fuzzy, and the role of listener in determining the force of an utterance has been largely neglected (Levinson, 1983, pp. 236-237).

Second, indirect speech acts are very difficult to explain adequately. They often have syntactic features related to their surface structure form and their illocutionary force (Levinson, 1983, p. 265). For example, the restricted distribution of "please" in direct and indirect requests, and the placement of parenthetical clauses like "I believe" are cited as examples of the connection between an utterance's pragmatic force and syntactic processes. Some theorists have suggested that indirect speech acts may be idioms. However, Brown and Levinson (1978) argue that universality of indirect speech acts across cultures suggests that they are not idiomatic in nature, but rather reflect a more fundamental communicative process. Furthermore, other models, explaining indirect speech acts through inferences, fail to deal with the motivation for using indirect speech acts (Levinson, 1983, p. 274). Levinson (1983) concludes that

> There are some compelling reasons to think that speech act theory may be superseded by much more complex multi-faceted pragmatic approaches to the functions that utterances perform. The first set of these have to do with the internal difficulties that any speech act theory faces, of which the most intractable is probably the set of problems posed by ISAs. Note that any theory of speech acts is basically concerned with mapping utterances into speech act categories, however those are conceived. The problem then is that either this is a trivial enterprise done by *fiat* (as by LFH), or an attempt is made to predict accurately the functions of sentences in context. But if the latter is attempted, it soon becomes clear that the contextual sources that give rise to the assignment of function or purpose are of such complexity and of such interest in their own right, that little will be left to the theory of speech acts....
>
> In this way, speech act theory is being currently undermined from the outside by the growth of disciplines concerned with the empirical study of natural language use (as Austin indeed foresaw). (pp. 278-279)

Other objections to speech act analyses of utterances center on its neglect of the listener's role in interaction. Gazdar (1981) notes problems with the assignment of speech acts to utterances, arguing that there is no form/force parallel and that utterances alone do not determine illocutionary force. Like Gazdar and Levinson, Edmondson (1981) argues that illocutionary acts have been inadequately characterized. More importantly, Edmondson suggests that illocutionary force is a function of its treatment by a hearer: that is, the hearer's uptake is central to the illocutionary force of an utterance (1981, pp. 50ff). I have suggested elsewhere (Haslett, 1982) that speech act analysis is inherently problematic because it focuses only on the speaker's perspective, and ignores the negotiation of meaning between speakers and hearers.

Other scholars note that speech act models fail to adequately analyze communicative processes. Both Levinson (1983) and Edmondson (1981) suggest that the speaker's motives, beliefs, and intentions are not always clear from their utterances and that there could be a number of intents suggested by the speaker's utterance. In brief, utterances typically have more than one function. And finally, both Haslett (1982) and Levinson (1983) suggest that speech acts are not an appropriate unit of analysis for discourse, and that speech act analysis fails to consider the importance of background, commonsense knowledge possessed by both speakers and listeners.

One final structural approach remains to be discussed, that of communicative rules. Rules have been widely used in the study of language itself (Chomsky, 1965) as well as discourse (van Dijk, 1977a, 1980; Bach & Harnish, 1979). As Shimanoff (1980) notes, the conceptualization of rules is a complex issue, and has been vigorously debated over several decades. In discussing the notion of rules, I first discuss the communicative sense of rules (essentially prescriptive); then contrast this with linguistic rules (essentially descriptive); and finally, characterize the qualities of communicative rules.

Communicative Rules

As Shimanoff notes, for communication to be possible, interactants must share rules for using symbols (1980, p. 31). Hymes (1972) also notes that, in order to be competent communicators, members of a speech community must master both rules of grammar and rules of language use.

Chomsky's use of linguistic rules has been descriptive; these rules characterize the language user's knowledge of language. Linguists have not debated the nature of rules per se, but rather which rules best account for speakers' linguistic knowledge (Hymes, 1980). Furthermore, linguistic rules focus on productivity and creativity: that is, "from a finite system of grammar, the competent speaker can do an infinite number of things" (Hymes, 1980, p. 19). Thus, linguistic rules generally describe what speakers *can* do with language, not what speakers *actually* do or *should* do.

Linguistic rules offer a sharp contrast to the concept of a communicative rule. Harre and Secord (1972) view rules as guidelines for appropriate, situated actions (pp. 150–151). Similarly, Shimanoff, in her insightful analysis of communicative rules, defines a rule as a "followable prescription that indicates what behavior is obligated, preferred, or prohibited in certain contexts" (1980, p. 57). (While scholarly debate on the nature of rules is not covered in detail here, the reader is encouraged to read Shimanoff's *Communication Rules,* 1980, for an excellent discussion and synthesis of rules research.) For the purposes of our discussion, I follow Shimanoff's definition of a rule since her general criteria can subsume many of the other views on rules.

The Nature of Communicative Rules.   Shimanoff argues that rule-governed behavior is followable, prescriptive and contextual. Individuals can choose whether or not to follow a rule. Thus rules apply to controllable behaviors. Rules govern behavior that is prescribed and controllable, whereas laws describe noncontrollable phenomenon (Shimanoff, 1980, pp. 39).

Since communicative rules are prescriptive, they specify behaviors that *should* be done. As such, communicative rules also incorporate sanctions; failure to perform a prescribed behavior will be noticed and commented upon. Von Wright (1968) categorizes four types of prescriptive force; obligation, prohibition, permission, and indifference. Of these, Shimanoff suggests that neither permitted behavior (because of lack of sanctions) nor indifferent behaviors (because of implied neutrality) are rule governed behaviors.

The last major characteristic of communicative rules is that they are contextual. "Rules apply in all similar situations, but they may not be applicable under different conditions" (Shimanoff, 1980, p. 46). That is, rules have conditions that must be fulfilled before the rule can be applied. Because of their context-bound nature, communicative rules vary in their generalizability. Cushman and Whiting (1972) suggest that the more generalizable the rule, the less specific the behaviors prescribed.

As we have seen thus far, communicative rules are followable, sanctionable, prescriptive, and contextual. There are also other aspects of communicative rules that enhance our understanding of them. Rules appear to be of varying generalizability and of varying specificity. Communicative rules also have varying prescriptive force, ranging from obligation to prohibition. In addition, sanctions for rule-breaking also vary. Following a communicative rule is often viewed as demonstrating a commitment to one's social community (Collett, 1977; Harre, 1979; Scott & Lyman, 1968). Rule-following may also vary as a function of its salience and its degree of consensual validation (Shimanoff, 1980, p. 97). And finally, rules may be explicit or implicit.

One quality of communicative rules deserves special consideration. Shimanoff argues strongly that the appropriate domain for communicative rules is behavior, not cognitions. She notes that since we cannot observe cognitions, we therefore cannot prescribe them in any meaningful way nor can we sanction them. Thus Shimanoff concludes that inferences are not communicative rules.

However, she seems to contradict this when she subsequently suggests that communicative rules can function as interpretive rules: "rules may be utilized to interpret behavior by assuming that an actor follows a particular rule in producing an utterance" (1980, p. 86). Regardless of how a listener interprets a speaker's utterance—whether by implicature, presupposition, or other inferences—clearly such interpretations seem rule-governed: they are controllable, criticizable, and contextual. Furthermore, since speakers plan their utterances on the basis of the listener's anticipated interpretation, both the production and interpretation of utterances appear to be rule-governed. Both speakers and listeners appear to share an understanding of these communicative rules. Finally, one could measure whether or not an inferential communicative rule has been followed by examining a listener's interpretation. Interactants routinely examine listener's interpretations in order to correct misunderstandings and the like. For these reasons, I would argue that cognitions (i.e., inferences) can be viewed as communicative rules. I discuss this point at some length because of the importance of inferences in accounting for communicative behavior.

Based on her analysis of communicative rules, Shimanoff proposes the following taxonomy of rule-governed behavior:

1. Rule-absent behavior—behavior that fails to meet any of the three criteria are termed rule-absent;
2. Rule-fulfilling behavior—behavior that fulfills the rule, but the actor has no knowledge of the rule (the rule may be fulfilled by accident or imitation);
3. Rule-conforming behavior—one's behavior corresponds to the rule, and one has tacit knowledge of the rule, but does *not* refer to the rule while performing the behavior;
4. Rule-following behavior—one knowingly and consciously performs the prescribed behavior;
5. Positive rule-reflective behavior—same requirements as rule-following behavior, but also requires one to evaluate the rule itself;
6. Rule-ignorant behavior—one fails to fulfill the rule because of lack of knowledge of the rule;
7. Rule-error behavior—one fails to comply with the rule because of inadequate knowledge or inadvertent noncompliance like forgetfulness, etc.;
8. Rule-violation behavior—conscious noncompliance; and
9. Negative rule-reflective behavior—one decides the rule is not valuable, and thus rejects and violates it.

Shimanoff criticizes other taxonomies of rules because of overlapping categories and inconsistent applications (Toulmin, 1974), and the lack of a distinction between compliant and noncompliant behaviors (Ganz, 1971; Toulmin, 1974).

One major issue remains: how do we decide when to apply rules? Bach and Harnish (1979), for example, argue that interactants know rules and their applicability, and assume that others do as well. Other scholars (Bruner, 1983; Dore, 1983; Haslett, 1984b) suggest that early interactional experience and commonsense knowledge enable individuals to acquire interactional rules. Still others argue that the tacit, commonsense knowledge interactants possess enables them to identify and apply various communicative rules (Cicourel, 1973; Garfinkel, 1967b; Heritage, 1984; Hopper, 1981; Shotter, 1984).

As we have seen, communicative rules vary along a number of important dimensions, such as prescriptive force, generalizability, contextual conditions, awareness of the rules, and so forth. Communicative rules also have varied functions: Shimanoff notes that communicative rules regulate, interpret, evaluate, justify, correct, predict, and explain behaviors.

Scholars have often used the terms "rule" and "strategy" interchangeably. Van Dijk and Kintsch (1983) added a new level of analysis to their theory of discourse, that of strategies, using the term strategy in a fashion similar to that of Shimanoff and other scholars working with communicative rules. To further illustrate the nature of communicative rules, van Dijk and Kintsch's concept of strategy will be more thoroughly discussed.

Discourse Strategies.   Van Dijk and Kintsch (1983) regard strategies as involving "actions, goals and some notion of optimality: Intuitively, a strategy is the idea of an agent about the best way to act in order to reach a goal" (p. 65). Although some actions do not involve strategies, strategies are used when the goal is very important or the means are costly or risky. As they note:

> strategic analysis depends not only on textual characteristics, but also on characteristics of the language user, such as his or her goals or world knowledge. . . .
>
> Strategies are part of our general knowledge; they represent the procedural knowledge we have about understanding discourse. They are an open set. They need to be learned, and overlearned, before they can become automatized. New types of discourse and forms of communication may require the development of new strategies. (pp. 10–11)

Strategies appear to be flexible, ordered hierarchically, context-sensitive and to operate both inductively and deductively (1983, p. 77).

Van Dijk and Kintsch (1983) outline several different types of strategies. Each set of strategies is related to some overall goal of the speaker/listener (pp. 65–67). *Tactics* denote an organized system of strategies; these systems characterize one's life-style (p. 66). *Cognitive strategies* are problem-solving strategies that enable humans to act on the basis of incomplete, limited information. *Language strategies* are a subset of cognitive strategies dealing with discourse production and comprehension. *Cultural strategies* enable speakers and listeners to utilize relevant cultural information in interpreting utterances. *Social strategies* reflect information about a group's social structures, values, and conventions. *Interactional strategies* reflect the use of specific interactional strategies in a given context and inferences about the other interactant's beliefs and values, etc. *Pragmatic strategies* refer to speech acts; that is, they reflect what social action is being accomplished by specific utterances in a given context. *Semantic strategies* enable individuals to infer global meanings while *schematic strategies* allow us to anticipate what is forthcoming in a discourse. *Stylistic* and *rhetorical strategies* enable interactants to assess discourse effectiveness. Finally, *metastrategies* refer to strategies that control subsets of strategies, and define the "general principles underlying such sets of strategies" (1983, p. 152). As can readily be seen, these strategies operate at different levels of discourse and at different levels of social structure. Taken together, these strategies enable participants to appropriately adapt their communication to different participants and in different settings.

Contrasting Rules and Strategies. Rules and strategies can be compared in several ways. First, both rules and strategies appear to rely on the same discourse units and categories (like words or sentences). However, strategies also use information from the communicative context. Second, a strategy is the best course of action to follow on the basis of limited information. However rules, at least linguistic rules, guarantee success when they are followed. For example, following grammatical rules enables one to produce acceptable sentences. Third, rules appear to reflect general norms whereas strategies are often very specific and individualized. As van Dijk and Kintsch (1983) note, rules "define the possible moves, whereas strategies determine which choices are made among the possible moves so that the aims of the agent are realized optimally" (p. 67). Finally, strategies enable individuals to act and make choices in light of human limitations on time and resources. In contrast, rules appear to work in principle, but not necessarily in real time. On the whole, strategies appear to be primarily cognitive processes while communicative rules reflect social processes. Quite clearly, however, both strategies and communicative rules appear to play important roles in human interaction.

An Overview of Linguistic Rules, Communicative Rules, and Strategies. Thus far, each structural principle—linguistic rules, communicative rules, or strategies—reflect processes used to interpret and produce discourse. Each structural principle is also pragmatic; that is, they deal with the use of language in context. For example, even very traditional views of linguistic rules include the concept of acceptability and hence, issues of language usage. Each structural principle deals with issues of *relatedness* as well: linguistic rules deal with the relatedness of units within sentences or across sentences; communicative rules relate communicative behavior to the context; and strategies relate actions to their anticipated effectiveness in accomplishing a goal. These structural principles can be violated, and all appear to vary as a function of different contexts. Finally, these structural principles allow for tacit, out-of-awareness processing as well as overt, conscious processing.

Despite these similarities, there are subtle differences among them. In terms of overall goals, linguistic rules describe what speaker/listeners can do in a given language; communicative rules prescribe what should be done, and strategies deal with making the most effective choice among alternative communicative behaviors. Following a linguistic rule insures that a speaker will be grammatical; following communicative rules guarantees that one's behavior is acceptable (i.e., will not be sanctioned), and following strategies does *not* necessarily insure a successful outcome for one's efforts. Linguistic rules deal with obligatory force; communicative rules deal with variable forces, and strategies reflect a strong force to choose the most effective action (to act otherwise would be acting against one's own self-interest). While van Dijk and Kintsch argue that strategies can be very personal and specific, linguistic and communicative rules appear to reflect norms and conventions. Not following linguistic rules may produce language errors and perhaps incomprehensibility. The sanction for strategies would appear to be failing to achieve one's goal, and communicative rules appear to have a variety of sanctions.

While all theorists allow for the possibility of meta-rules or meta-strategies, there is a conspicuous lack of discussion about how such meta-level structural principles might operate, how they might be organized, and the like. Both linguistic rules and strategies allow for hierarchical ordering, but communicative rules do not seem to be hierarchically ordered. (Of course, conflict over communicative rules, such as whether one should be clear or polite, are possible, but here again we could simply have a rule that *prescribes* a rule choice in those special cases). While linguistic rules may change as a language changes (e.g., a language becomes more complex, etc.), strategies and communicative rules appear more flexible and changeable. Although it is tempting to suggest that strategies (e.g., cultural, rhetorical, social, etc.) are merely subsets of Shimanoff's interpretive rules, it should be kept in mind that *strategies determine one's choice among rule-governed options.* For instance, given a set of compliance-gaining strategies, these strategies could be ranked in order of their probability of success. (In fact, young children seem to go through this ranking as they try one strategy after another to persuade an adult to comply with their request)!

Many scholars (Cushman & Whiting, 1972; Hymes, 1980; Pearce & Cronen, 1981; Shimanoff, 1980) note the utility of rules for theory construction in communication. However, as this brief overview has shown, such structural principles need to be much more carefully specified. Many researchers who invoke rules as explanatory principles fail to adequately discuss *the particular sense in which they are invoking rules.* For example, what are the sanctions, what is the force, what is the intensity, and so on, of a particular rule or strategy? If anything is to be clearly concluded from this overview, it is that scholars must carefully characterize their use of rules.

The final section deals with the most micro-level structural units—such as single words (like pronouns) or single clauses—that connect the surface structure of a linguistic form to its immediate context. These units, as do the other structural units or principles discussed in this chapter, apply to any text. We now turn to a discussion of these micro-level, interpretive, structural units—deictic units, presuppositions, entailment, and conventional implicature.

II. INTERPRETATIVE MICRO-STRUCTURES IN TEXTS

Four key structures are discussed: deixis, presupposition, entailment, and conventional implicature. Each structural device plays an important role in accurately interpreting texts, whether the texts are written or oral (Levinson, 1983). All these structural devices are inferential in the sense that they connect utterances to the context and to participants.

Deixis

Deictic elements provide a very direct link between context and language. Demonstratives, pronouns, verb tense, place adverbs, and other deictic elements serve to anchor the utterance to a particular context. The importance of deictic elements is clear. Utterances, to be accurately interpreted, must clearly and explicitly refer to specific events or objects in a given context.

Levinson (1983) posits five categories of deictic elements. Person, place, and time deixis refer to linguistic elements that identify the individuals, the location and the time respectively in a particular context. Discourse deixis refers to a particular part of a text, or relates one part of a text to another. Social deixis refers to the encoding of social distinctions relevant to participants, their roles and their relationships. Each of these is discussed in turn.

1. Person Deixis.   The assumed deictic focus in interaction is the speaker; as the speaker changes, or a particular person is addressed, this focus shifts. Person deixis includes such things as specific forms of address, honorifics, and kinship terms. Languages, of course, vary in the extensiveness of deictic terms for persons. For example, some languages mark sex of the speaker while others do not.

2. Time Deixis.   Deictic time references reflect the way in which a particular culture semantically organizes time and its measurement. Fillmore (1971) distinguishes between coding time (the time at which the message is sent) and receiving time (the time at which the message is received). Some deictic time units, like "yesterday" or "tomorrow," mark a very precise temporal unit. However, other deictic time elements, like "then" or "recently," refer to more imprecise time boundaries. Levinson notes that time deixis is complex because it interacts with other deictic elements. For example, greeting someone in the morning is governed by time deixis (i.e., it is morning) as well as discourse deixis (i.e., greetings appear in the beginning of conversations or texts).

3. Place Deixis.   Place deixis locates objects and events in space; these distinctions reflect the spatial distinctions and orientations made by a given culture. According to Levinson, locatives like "this/that" and "here/there" serve to indicate proximity to or distance from the speaker. "This/that" distinctions can also signal emotional distance from the speaker. Motion verbs, like "come" and "go," usually specify motion with reference to the speaker. For example, "Come here please" indicates that the addressee is to approach the speaker. (This example also illustrates that the speaker is typically assumed to be the focal point of person deixis.) Levinson (1983) also mentions "home-base" deictic references, which use an individual's home or base of operations as a spatial reference point.

4. Discourse Deixis.   Discourse deictic units refer to a specific part of a text containing a particular utterance, or relate portions of the text to one another. Expressions such as "this story," "that issue" or "the next chapter" illustrate discourse deixis. Levinson (1983) carefully distinguishes this from anaphora (i.e., a pronoun used to refer to someone or something already mentioned in the text), and argues that anaphora rests upon deictic notions.

Some discourse deictic units act as structural markers, which indicate the relationship of one part of the text to other parts. For example, the expression "in conclusion" or "but" requires one to process the text units in relation to one another.

5. *Social Deixis.*   These deictic elements mark the social identities of participants, or their social relationship. *Relational* deictic elements mark the relationship between the speaker and referent, between the speaker and listener, between the speaker and bystander, or between the speaker and setting (e.g., level of formality, etc.). In contrast, *absolute* deictic elements indicate authorized speakers or listeners (e.g., "Mr. President, Members of the Press," etc.).

This brief overview of deixis illustrates its fundamental importance for pragmatics. As Bruner (1983) observes, the basic deictic distinction between speaker and listener is at the heart of any human communicative endeavor. Several complex issues still remain in this area of study. All deictic categories need further research, since we have a very limited understanding of cross cultural variation in deixis. Additional complexity arises when we consider the interaction among deictic elements themselves, and the necessity to anchor these deictic distinctions with independent theories of spatial, temporal and gestural systems. A final critical issue appears to be the degree to which individuals must be aware of the surrounding environment in order to understand deictic elements. For a very insightful, detailed discussion of deixis and its relationship to semantics and pragmatics, see Levinson (1983).

Pragmatic Inferences

Pragmatic inferences are assumptions that participants use to guide their interactions with others and that enable them to understand utterances. These inferences have been divided into two categories: presupposition and conventional implicatures. As we shall see, the distinctions drawn between these inferences vary from theorist to theorist.

1. *Presupposition.*   Presuppositions are inferences that represent the background assumptions in a particular communicative context. These background assumptions enable us to interpret utterances in context. Levinson (1983) suggests that although presupposition has been defined in varied ways, two key conditions—appropriateness and mutual knowledge— underlie most approaches to presupposition. However, Levinson argues that the appropriateness criterion is too vague and imprecise to be theoretically useful and that the mutual knowledge condition (i.e., that presuppositions are to be known to both speaker and hearer) is too strong a condition.

Levinson suggests that presuppositions have two important characteristics: they are defeasible and tied to surface structure aspects of a language. *Defeasibility* refers to the way in which presuppositions may be "cancelled" or negated in certain contexts. Presuppositions may be negated by background contextual conditions, by evaluating the evidence in support of a presupposition (i.e., the interactants are debating whether a presupposition might apply in that situation), or by other factors (Wilson, 1975; Levinson, 1983).

Presuppositional-triggers are those surface-structure linguistic features which signal that a particular background inference is being assumed. In his review of presupposition, Levinson (1983, pp. 181-184) lists thirteen types of presuppositional-triggers:

1. Definite descriptions — Example: Jill saw an old horse} presupposes that an old horse exists.
2. Factive verbs — ex: Jane regrets her rudeness} presupposes that Jane was rude.
3. Implicative verbs — ex: Bill forgot his wallet} presupposes that Bill ought to have remembered his wallet.
4. Change of State Verbs — ex: Dave finished his book} presupposes that Dave had been working on his book.
5. Iteratives — ex: Rick has been break dancing again} presupposes that Rick had been break dancing before.
6. Temporal clauses — ex: While Heidi was sleeping, she fell out of bed} presupposes that Heidi was sleeping.
7. Cleft sentence — ex: It was not Kip who kicked the dog} presupposes that someone kicked the dog.
8. Implicit clefts with stressed constituents — ex: Bill didn't kidnap Christina} presupposes that someone kidnapped Christina.
9. Comparisons and contrasts — ex: Rick is a better batter than David} presupposes that David is a batter.
10. Non-restrictive relative clauses — ex: The Bonniwells, who settled in the Midwest, sailed from Bristol in 1832} presupposes that the Bonniwells sailed in 1832.
11. Counterfactual conditionals — ex: If Dave had any sense, he'd leave town!} presupposes that Dave has no sense.
12. Questions — ex: Who is the author of this book?} presupposes that someone wrote the book.

While other linguistic expressions may be added, depending upon how presuppositions are defined, Levinson suggests that these be viewed as core presuppositional expressions.

Levinson also contrasts presuppositions with entailment and conversational implicatures. Entailments are *logical* inferences that can be derived from a linguistic expression and are a part of a truth-conditional semantic theory. For example, the statement "Jim is a bachelor" entails that Jim is an unmarried male. One contrast between presupposition and entailment is that negating a linguistic expression will change entailment, but not presupposition. Levinson further argues that presuppositions are not a special case of entailment since presuppositions are defeasible. Finally, he notes that since presuppositions do not have the context-independent, stable meanings required for a semantic theory, they most appropriately belong in a pragmatic theory.

The nature of presupposition needs further clarification (Karttunen & Peters, 1979; Levinson, 1983; Wilson, 1975; Wilson & Sperber, 1979). For example, specifying the relationship between semantics and pragmatics within presupposition seems necessary. Of special concern is the presuppositional nature of complex sentences: how do we derive presuppositions in such sentences and how do we specify general pragmatic principles used to predict presuppositions?

2. Conventional Implicature.   Grice (1975) separates conversational implicature from conventional implicature. Since conversational implicatures deal with face-to-face interaction, we discuss those in Chapter 3 and restrict our discussion here to conventional implicature.

Conventional implicatures are non-truth-conditional inferences that are conventionally linked to specific lexical items. Some examples of conventional implicature are "therefore," and "even" (Karttunen & Peters, 1979); a number of discourse-deictic items (however, moreover, besides, etc.) and socially deictic items (sir, madam, etc.) (Levinson, 1983, p. 128). Levinson characterizes conventional implicatures as non-cancellable, detachable, given by convention, and having a "relatively *determinate*" content (p. 128). In contrast to other theorists, Levinson argues that conventional implicatures can not be subsumed under presuppositions because presuppositions are cancellable while conventional implicatures are not. He notes that conventional implicatures reflect "one of the clearest areas where pragmatics impinges deeply on grammatical processes" (p. 130).

As we have seen, these structural, interpretive units play an important role in text comprehension and reflect significant aspects of meaning that extend beyond truth-conditional requirements. Furthermore, these pragmatic inferences closely connect linguistic expressions to the context; or, in the case of entailment, connect linguistic expressions to their logical implications. Since pragmatic inferences add to the meaning signalled by a linguistic expression, they make a significant contribution to text interpretation.

III.   CONCLUSIONS

As we have seen, the structural units discussed in this chapter play a vital role in the production and interpretation of discourse. We may say, in one sense, that these structural features are universal since they apply to any text. For example, any text has an overall structure; any text relies on deictic elements, presuppositions, etc., for its interpretation; and so forth. These structural features also vary in their scope: some provide organization for an entire text (e.g., superstructures govern the overall form of a text, like narratives, scholarly papers, etc.), or for an element within the text (e.g., deictic elements, pragmatic inferences, etc.).

Communicative rules, linguistic rules, and strategies are structural principles that relate subparts of the text to one another, or relate the text to the context. The structural units (like macrostructures, superstructures, or speech acts) and structural principles (like linguistic rules, communicative rules, or strategies) vary in their breadth, specificity, level of abstractness, variability, generalizability, and applicability (i.e., force). In addition, some structural units and principles are cognitive in their orientation, while others place more emphasis on social factors.

However, these structural approaches offer relatively static, rather than dynamic, interactive views of communicative processes. First, a more process-oriented view is needed so that a given structural approach can begin to deal with the interconnectedness of various aspects of that approach. For example, both van Dijk's discourse theory and Hymes' ethnography of speaking need to focus more on the interrelationships among the different features of their models. Second, more focus on process in these structural approaches provides a more dynamic, interactive view of the interrelationship between the text and the context. At present, the text is related to the context in a static manner: little attention is given to the way in which text and context mutually influence one another.

The text itself is the focal point of structural approaches. Of the three key elements in a pragmatic perspective on communicative processes— text, context, and language user—the text is stressed; the context is presented as an assumed given; and the language user is virtually ignored.

Of the common, underlying pragmatic assumptions outlined in Chapter 1, those assumptions dealing with the text are emphasized in structural approaches. That is, the inferential, conventional, sequential, interpretive, and systematic aspects of communicative processes are emphasized in structural approaches. In fact, some structural models detail more completely a single assumed underlying feature of communication. For example, pragmatic inferences focus exclusively on the inferential nature of human communication. Other structural approaches, like the ethnography of speaking, rely on a number of these underlying assumptions.

As I argue in Chapter 6, the text provides an essential departure point for analyzing human communicative processes. The text publicly signals what participants are willing to be held accountable for. In addition to this, however, we need to examine the influence of the context and language user on human communicative processes. An adequate analysis of the text itself is not possible without looking at the relationships between text and context, between text and language user, and among text, context, and language user. In short, structural approaches fail to adequately explain the interactional nature of human communication.

A particular type of structural approach—conversational analysis—overcomes some of these weaknesses through its emphasis on the structural form of conversations. Since conversation is, by definition, a dialogue between at least two participants, conversational analyses must explain, at least in part, how speakers and listeners adapt their messages to one another. However, as we shall see, conversational analysis, like other structural approaches, focuses on the text and fails to adequately assess the influence of context and language user characteristics. We now turn to a more detailed discussion of conversational analysis and the varied approaches taken to analyzing conversations.

3 Structural Pragmatics: Managing Conversations

Face-to-face interaction profoundly influences the development of an individual's self-identity and relationships with others. From our earliest adult/infant interactions and peer/peer interactions, we learn communicative skills that enable us to both cooperate and compete with others. The primary communicative context in which these skills develop is conversation.

In Chapter 2, the structural approaches and principles used to organize coherent texts were discussed. While those structures apply to both oral and written texts, in Chapter 3, we shall focus on a specific form of interaction, casual conversation. The structural issues here, as in Chapter 2, involve issues of coherence and of organization. Managing conversations successfully enables us to interact effectively with others, and thus to grow and develop as individuals.

The basic structural features of conversation enable speaker/listeners to plan, interpret and coordinate their conversations. Turn-taking, the exchange of speaking and listening roles among interactants, is viewed as a fundamental characteristic of conversation. Generally, speaking turns are exchanged smoothly. However, instances of simultaneous talk, interruptions, noticeable gaps, and overlaps do occur between talking turns.

A number of diverse structural features are used by participants to manage their conversations. Turn-taking is accomplished, in part, by the use of other structural units. For example, in *adjacency pairs,* one utterance (a first-pair-part) requires a second utterance (a second-pair-part). These adjacency pairs, like question/answer, summons/reply, and greeting/greeting are often interpreted as global units. Another structural conversational unit, a *pre-sequence,* is often used to foreshadow subsequent requests,

47

announcements and the like by checking whether the necessary preconditions are present. For example, a friend might ask if you have any plans for the evening, before she asks you to go to a movie. Conversational strategies that enable participants to introduce new issues, to make repairs and so forth are termed *side* or *insertion sequences.* Some *overlaps* and *interruptions* may represent strategies for clarification or correction of the on-going talk. Our final structural unit, *topicalization* — how we initiate and maintain conversational topics — serves to organize talking turns as well as to provide an opportunity to talk.

While these structural units help interactants organize and interpret their conversations, sometimes conversations do not proceed smoothly. To handle problematic aspects of conversations, such as a misunderstanding or mishearing, interactants need structural devices to help remedy these problems. A set of *alignment strategies* help participants adapt their talk to one another by signalling how talk is to be interpreted. Alignment strategies include: *disclaimers, licenses, formulations,* and *meta-talk.* In addition, *repairs* and *topicalization strategies* help keep the conversation flowing smoothly. Alignment strategies try to prevent conversational miscues, while repairs correct such miscues.

In sum, then, interactants organize and interpret conversations by using various structural features, repairs, and alignment strategies. We discuss each of these areas in turn.

I. THE NATURE OF CONVERSATION

Before discussing how conversations are managed by participants, we first must specify the characteristics of conversations. While I am not suggesting a specific definition here, nevertheless it is possible to specify a number of generally agreed upon features that characterize conversations. First, of course, conversations occur between at least two individuals. While it is possible for three or four individuals to participate in a conversation, with that number of participants not every participant's attention may focus on the common conversational topic. Goffman (1971) labels such interactions as unfocused. Second, participants act so as to maintain a conversational topic. Third, there is role reciprocity: participants exchange speaking and listening roles. Fourth, conversational activity appears to be relatively unplanned. Individuals plan speeches and lectures, but do not generally plan conversations in much detail. Fifth, conversations occur in a wide variety of social settings. Sixth, conversations appear to be relatively informal as opposed to being formally planned or conducted. And finally, conversational meanings are jointly constructed by the participants. Listeners respond to the speaker's utterances and thus co-manage the conversation.

Conversations: A Turn-Taking View

Sacks, Schegloff, and Jefferson (1974) outline several characteristics of conversations. Their view emphasizes turn-taking as the basic organizational structure of conversation. Conversational characteristics include:

1. speaker change;
2. only one speaker talks at a time;
3. transitions between speakers are usually of short duration;
4. turn-taking is negotiated, not fixed;
5. turn length varies;
6. the content of turns varies;
7. the length of conversations is flexible;
8. the number of participants in a conversation varies;
9. the number of talking turns a participant takes varies, but generally no single participant dominates talking time;
10. conversational talk can be continuous or discontinuous;
11. conversational repair strategies can be used; and
12. talking turns may be allocated.

The turn-taking system advocated by Sacks et al. (1974) allows for the joint management of conversations; each participant's contribution can be coordinated with that of others.

Conversations can also be examined through the background assumptions participants have about conversations. These background assumptions are referred to as conversational maxims (or conversational implicatures). For the purposes of clarity, I shall only use the term conversational maxim. This background, situated knowledge about conversations enables participants to evaluate and judge what is going on in the conversation. While these maxims may not operate in every culture, they appear to be valid with respect to the United States and Great Britain. The Cooperative Principle, with its maxims of Quality, Quantity, Manner, and Relevance can thus be viewed as characteristics that help define conversational activity (Grice, 1975, 1978). It should be noted, however, that conversational maxims provide guidelines for evaluating the on-going exchange. When these maxims are violated, Grice (1975) suggests that they are usually purposefully violated (e.g., to indicate sarcasm, irony, etc.).

Conversational Maxims

Grice's maxims are rational principles or means for conducting co-operative exchanges. While Levinson (1983) suggests that such maxims may apply to any co-operative exchange, such as nonverbal exchanges, here we consider only their conversational implications. These conversational maxims are summarized in the Cooperative Principle. This Cooperative Principle and its underlying conversational maxims are outlined below:

Cooperative Principle:
make your conversational contribution as is required, when it is needed, in accordance with the accepted purpose of the conversation in which you are participating

Maxim of Quality
make your contribution truthful; do not state that which is false or that for which you have inadequate support

Maxim of Quantity
give as much information as needed for the purposes of the exchange, and only that information

Maxim of Manner
be perspicuous, avoid ambiguity and obscurity, and be orderly and brief

Maxim of Relevance
make your remarks relevant

Grice suggests that communicators assume other participants are either following the maxims or are deliberately violating them. For example, deliberately lying or reaching an unwarranted conclusion violates the maxim of Quality. A violation of the Relevance maxim would be for a speaker to make an irrelevant, "off the wall" remark. A speaker who gives more information than necessary violates the maxim of Quantity. Violating the maxim of Manner is exemplified by someone is rude or abrasive. Nofsinger's analysis of indirect answers (1976) contains good examples of violations of the Manner maxim (e.g., "Is it hot out today?" "I always sweat like this on a cold day," etc.).

The Politeness Maxim. Other scholars have suggested additional conversational maxims. The most important of these, in my view, is the Politeness maxim. Bach and Harnish (1979) suggest politeness, or preserving face, as an additional maxim. According to Brown and Levinson (1978), face is the "public self-image that every member of a society wants to claim for himself" (p. 66). While interacting, participants try to preserve face for all participants.

Brown and Levinson (1978) suggest that politeness is the major reason for use of indirect utterances. They suggest that interactants avoid face-threatening acts, unless the demands for clarity and goal-accomplishment are of greater importance. Positive face is the individual's maintenance of a worthy self-image, while negative face refers to an individual's ability to choose actions without coercion or interference from others. From a speaker's perspective, actions like confessing or apologizing reflect a threat to his/her positive face, while asking for help or accepting an offer reflects a threat to the speaker's negative face. Orders threaten a listener's negative face, while accusations and contradictions would threaten a listener's positive face.

Although participants try to maintain face (i.e., act politely), it is sometimes necessary to state unpleasant, threatening facts or opinions. Brown and Levinson suggest that the communicative strategies participants follow are based on estimates of the strategy's riskiness (i.e., the degree to which face-threats might be needed). The riskiness of a strategy varies according to the comparative status of the participants, their relationship, and the extent of the imposition or threat. Speakers can mitigate the riskiness of face-threatening acts by adding negative or positive politeness strategies. A positive politeness strategy would be something like emphasizing one's in-group membership, complimenting the listener on something else besides the behavior being discussed, and the like. A negative politeness strategy might mention the listener's relative autonomy or control over his/her actions.

Additional Maxims.   Bach and Harnish (1979) suggest two other maxims. According to the Morality maxim, speakers may not ask speakers to perform immoral acts. For example, speakers do not ask for confidential information, or request listeners to lie. Their Charity maxim requires that listeners, unless advised to the contrary, interpret the speaker's utterances as violating as few maxims as possible. The Charity maxim seems to parallel Clark and Clark's (1977) reality principle, which states that "speakers expect their listeners to assume they will talk about comprehensible events, states and facts" (p. 226). All these principles compel listeners to search for coherence and relevance in the utterances they hear, and thus listeners are being cooperative.

Supporting the maxim of politeness may be another maxim, that of reciprocity of responses. In general, interactants' communicative behaviors tend to parallel one another. For example, if I am rude to you, you are likely to be rude to me in return. [Reciprocal response patterns have been found in a wide variety of behaviors, including interpersonal bonding (Bochner, 1984; Duck, 1976); speech style (Giles, 1977; Giles & Powesland, 1975); dialogue rhythm (Cappella & Planalp, 1981; Jaffe & Feldstein, 1970); and parent-child interaction (Bruner, 1983; Dore, 1983).] While the reciprocity norm may support politeness, clearly the politeness maxim exists as a strong underlying assumption for interactional behavior.

Clark and Clark's Interactional Principles. Although not presented as maxims, Clark and Clark (1977) suggest that speakers follow these guidelines when determining what they want to say:

1. *Knowledge of the listener* — speakers make adjustments in their talk on the basis of their judgments about what listeners know;
2. the *Cooperative Principle;*
3. the *Reality Principle;*
4. the *Social Context* — different contexts call for different styles of speaking;
5. the *Linguistic Devices Available* — the linguistic features a particular language makes available to speakers of the language. (The perspective in this book would also include not only the language features themselves, *but also interactants' abilities to use those features.)* (pp. 225-226)

Clark and Clark (1977) point out that, in many cases, speakers have conventional solutions to these considerations. That is, speakers follow conventional *communicative rules.* However, these rules

> go only partway toward specifying what they should say at any particular moment, and they may even want to flout the rules for their own devious purposes. The point is, speakers always have choices and they resolve them on the basis of their goals in talking plus the side considerations just listed [the five considerations cited above] (p. 226)

We should add to this that listeners have choices as well. Listeners choose whether to confirm, disconfirm, ignore, challenge, or otherwise respond to the speaker's utterances.

Evaluating Conversational Maxims. One difficulty with conversational maxims is that they may interact and conflict with one another. For example, Levinson (1983) suggests that a maxim, termed the *principle of informativeness,* may contradict the maxim of Quantity. The principle of informativeness requires that one "read as much into an utterance as is consistent with what you know about the world" (p. 146). The Quantity maxim, in contrast, suggests that speakers present only that information needed for purposes of the interaction. Does one follow the Politeness maxim or the maxim of Quality, if telling the truth will significantly damage the other's face? Are there preferences, then, as to what maxim to follow when maxims are in conflict with one another? The point here is that the interrelationships among maxims, and their implications for how we converse with one another, need to be more fully worked out. It may be, as I suggest later, that the maxim of Relevance is the most fundamental maxim and underlies all the other maxims.

As you recall, it is generally assumed that a speaker/listener is following conversational maxims unless the context suggests otherwise (Grice, 1975). For example, one might suspect another of lying in order to escape being punished for some misdeed or accident. (Note that this assumption presupposes that the maxims can be consistently followed and that none conflict with one another. However, as previously pointed out, this seems unlikely). In addition, although these maxims seem applicable to British and North American conversational encounters, their applicability to other societies remains in dispute. Philips (1974, 1976) suggests that conversational maxims provide a basis for ethnographic studies of conversations in other cultures (1976, p. 89). Her study of the Malagasy demonstrated that following the maxim of Quantity depended upon the significance of the information, the interactants' relationship, and their sex. Similar situational constraints seem to operate in Western cultures as well. For example, bad news does not readily travel up the organizational ladder, certain occupations require discretionary uses of information, and the like.

In summary, conversation can be characterized as a dialogue between at least two people, in which each participant contributes to the conversational topic. Thus conversations are jointly produced, relatively informal occasions for talk. Underlying this coordinated communication is a set of maxims that participants assume are being followed, unless circumstances suggest otherwise. These conversational maxims provide a basis for the interpretation of utterances and a guideline for the production of utterances. When we converse with others, we expect them to be relevant, informative, truthful, and so forth: as communicators, we act on these assumptions until circumstances indicate otherwise. While these principles seem quite useful in characterizing our communicative expectations, they nevertheless need to be more precisely conceptualized and their interrelationships more carefully examined.

With these assumptions about the nature of conversation in mind, let us now examine how conversations are organized. Organizing conversations requires a set of management strategies that enable speakers and listeners to coordinate their talk.

II. CONVERSATIONAL MANAGEMENT:
A STRUCTURAL ANALYSIS

Conversational organization focuses on two key issues, coherence and order. Coherence, the process of making sense of utterances, is one major issue facing conversational participants. The other major issue confronting participants, that of order, is the task of producing utterances that contribute clearly to the conversational topic, and mesh with the contributions made by other participants. In general, issues of coherence and order cannot be neatly separated. For example, to make a conversational repair, participants make judgements about coherence (i.e., some mistatement or misunderstanding has occurred) and about order (i.e., how and when can the repair be made). Conversational analysis reveals some of the systematic ways in which participants cope with problems of coherence and order, and it is to these processes we now turn. First, we consider the overall organization of conversation; then examine conversational structures such as turn-taking, adjacency pairs, and pre-sequences; and finally, discuss alignment strategies, such as the use of metalanguage, and repairs.

Overall Conversational Organization

According to Levinson (1983), conversations have an opening section, a topic discussion section, and a concluding section. Openings allow participants to become mutually accessible to one another and thus, further interaction becomes possible. Topic discussion allows topics to be introduced, maintained, and changed. Closings allow conversationalists to smoothly conclude their interaction.

Conversational openings proceed in three stages. In the first stage, *cognitive recognition,* a participant is recognized as a member of a particular group (e.g., "Nurse!") or as a specific individual (e.g., "Dr. Spock"). In the second stage, *identification displays,* participants acknowledge one another either verbally or nonverbally. In the third stage, that of *recognition displays,* participants exchange mutual greetings and make themselves more accessible for continued interaction. If one or both of the participants are unable to give full attention to the opening sequence, this sequence may be shortened so that identification displays and social recognition displays are completed simultaneously (Schiffrin, 1977). Conversational openings are frequently initiated by adjacency pairs; either greeting/greeting pairs (e.g., A: "Hello," B: "Hi, how are you" etc.) or summons/answer pairs (e.g., A: "Bob?" B: "Yes.").

After this opening sequence, conversational topics are introduced. Establishing a conversational topic requires that participants share a set of concepts or a superordinate category for discussion; this develops across a number of talking turns (Levinson, 1983, pp. 312–315). Participants may gain longer talking turns by announcing a particular topic, and then elaborating upon it. Or still other topics can be introduced, when appropriate, during the conversation. If topics do not readily fit into the conversation, a new topic can be introduced by explicitly marking it as a departure from the current topic (e.g., a new topic could be introduced by using an expression like, "Oh, by the way, that reminds me, have you . . . ?").

Terminating a conversation needs to be carefully negotiated by both participants. Topics and conversations must not be closed down prematurely. Frequently, participants use *pre-closings* to signal their willingness to end the conversation. An example illustrates these pre-closings:

A: Well, I guess that about does it.
B: Yeah, it looks okay.
A: So long then.
B: See you.

The first two turns are pre-closings, tentatively indicating that the participants view the conversation as completed. Since both participants signal their willingness to end the conversation, final closings (e.g., "So long then," and "See you") follow and conclude the conversation. Pre-closings are important since they give interactants an opportunity to continue the conversation if desired (Levinson, 1983, pp. 315ff).

McLaughlin (1984) suggests that closings and openings mirror one another. Openings have the following sequence: salutation, reference to the other, personal inquiry, external reference, and finally, topic initiation. Closings are sequenced as follows: summary, justification, positive statement, continuity statement, and well-wishing (good-bye). As McLaughlin (1984) points out:

the last act in the opening sequence and the first act in the closing sequence both have to do with bracketing *topic*. Similarly, the next-to-last opening act and the next-to-first closing act both have to do with the *reason* or occasion for the impending increase or decrease in access. A further parallel is that the next act in the opening sequence, inquiry about the *other's welfare*, is mirrored in the closing sequence by corresponding other-orientations represented by positive statements, continuity statements, and well-wishing. Finally, the first act of the opening sequence, the salutation, has a corresponding "slot" in the optional good-bye at the end of the closing sequence. (p. 179)

Organizational Structures for Managing Conversations

Organizational structures for managing conversation facilitate coordinated turn-taking as well as the interpretation of utterances. In this section, a number of structural devices, such as turn taking, adjacency pairs, pre-sequences and so forth, are discussed. Perhaps the most well-known organizational structure is turn-taking.

Turn-Taking

Turn-taking refers to the exchange of speaking turns between speakers and listeners in conversations. The most systematic, well-known system of speaker exchange rules has been developed by Sacks, Schegloff, and Jefferson (1974).

A turn-taking system explains a speaker/listener's ability to identify when a turn has been taken, when a turn has been completed, and when others can speak. Sacks et al. (1974) define a turn as a speaker's utterances at a single time. Talking turns can be of variable length, involving just a single word or a lengthy argument.

1. The Turn-Taking Unit. A turn is comprised of *turn constructional units,* which are usually marked by prosodic and intonational features (e.g., like a clause, sentence, etc.). Turn constructional units are separated from one another by transition-relevance places (TRPs); each TRP marks a possible completion point at which speakers *may* change. For example, in the utterance, "John, come here please" (which represents a single talking turn), there are two TRPs (one after "John" and one after "please"). TRPs are points at which another speaker may smoothly take a turn.

2. Turn Completion Points. Jefferson (1973) suggests that conversational participants recognize the potential endings of speaking turns. This recognition is demonstrated by participants' ability to complete utterances for one another, or when both speaker and listener complete an utterance at the same time. These completion points may be signalled by the use of fillers (e.g., Uh, yeah, uhmmm, etc.), lowered intonation, averted eye gaze, completion of a grammatical clause, the use of sociocentric sequences like "you know," and/or a terminating hand gesture (Duncan & Fiske, 1977). Duncan and Fiske suggest that speakers and listeners coordinate their conversational activities through the use of back-channel information. Back-channel information refers to the paralinguistic, nonverbal, and linguistic cues which interactants use to provide feedback to one another and to help regulate conversational exchanges.

3. Speaker Selection Rules. Sacks, Schegloff, and Jefferson (1974) outline the procedures through which the current speaker can select the next speaker. First, the current speaker may identify the next speaker directly (e.g., "John, do you have the information on the Coors order?"). Second, the current speaker may select the next speaker by identifying a particular issue that must be addressed (e.g., "I think we need to discuss the legal issues next;" the company counsel is the next speaker since she alone has the necessary knowledge for responding to these issues). Finally, the current speaker may leave open the next speaking turn (e.g., "Is there any further discussion?"). In formal or institutionalized settings, speaking turns may be prescribed and thus controlled by speech exchange systems. Each of the speaker selection options are preferentially ordered: selecting the next speaker directly takes precedence over limiting the issue to be discussed, and limiting the issue takes precedence over leaving the speaking turn open. These speaker selection rules operate on an utterance by utterance basis. Next speakers begin speaking at potential completion points—those points at which the current speaker signals his/her remarks are completed (e.g., lowered intonation, etc.).

Speakers also use structural devices to extend their talking turns through possible completion points (Sacks et al., 1974). One device is to indicate that remarks are incomplete (through the use of structural markers like "but," "since," "however," "and," "if" and the like). Another structural device is to initiate a talking turn by indicating that the turn is likely to be somewhat lengthy (e.g., "Say, did you hear what happened to John yesterday? It was really something."). Finally, paralinguistic and nonverbal cues, like prolonged stress, can also signal a speaker's unwillingness to stop speaking (Duncan, 1973; Duncan & Fiske, 1977; Goodwin, 1981).

Sacks et al. (1974), note that participants relate their talking turn to the ongoing topic of conversation.

> It is a systematic consequence of the turn-taking organization of conversation that it obliges its participants to display to each other, in a turn's talk, their understanding of other turns' talk. More generally, a turn's talk will be heard as directed to a prior turn's talk, unless special techniques are used to locate some other talk to which it is directed. (p. 728)

Turn-taking, then, appears to be a fundamental, context-free characteristic of conversations.

While this overview of turn-taking appears to suggest that the speaker is in complete control of the turn-taking system, this is not the case. Listeners, through varying types of back-channel feedback—like head-nodding, or making comments like uhm-hmm—may encourage speakers to take longer turns (Duncan & Fiske, 1977, pp. 94–98). Turn-taking appears to be jointly controlled since each turn gives a response to the preceding turn, and invites a further response. These responses, of course, can also ignore the speaker's preceding comments.

4. Limitations of the Turn-Taking System.   Some scholars note that turn units and turn-transition points are not well-defined (Edmondson, 1981; Goodwin, 1981). For example, participants may define turn-units differently than do observers (Edelsky, 1981). In addition, she suggests that there are different types of speaking arrangements (an orderly versus a relatively informal arrangement) and turn-taking may vary across both types.

A final issue concerning turn-taking systems is the difficulty in determining whether or not back-channel cues are really turns. Some argue that back-channel cues serve as feedback, and cannot be regarded as turns because no explicit claim for a talking turn has been made (Edelsky, 1981). In contrast, McLaughlin (1984) argues that back-channel cues are legitimate turns since they have functional significance in the interaction, and can be regarded as a symbolic request for a talking turn (pp. 102–103). Since signals for turn-taking include paralinguistic and nonverbal cues (Duncan & Fiske, 1977; Goodwin, 1981; Sacks et al., 1974), it is tempting to argue that back-channel cues (like head-nods, postural shifts, etc.) are indeed legitimate turns. On the other hand, they do not, as Edelsky points out, specifically request a talking turn.

It might be most helpful to simply regard these back-channel cues as transition-relevance-places since they may, on some occasions, represent initial actions in starting to take a turn. For example, Goodwin (1981) suggests that a listener's eye gaze focuses on the current speaker in anticipation of the speaker's turn completion. This, in effect, signals the listener's desire to speak. Other times, the presence of back-channel cues may not be used to initiate a turn. For example, a listener's head nod may encourage the speaker to continue. This seems a plausible position to take since there is some evidence that turn-taking may be signalled by multiple cues. In the absence of multiple cues, a listener may indicate that she is foregoing her turn at talk (see Duncan & Fiske, 1977; and DeLong, 1974). For example, Duncan (1973) discusses claim-suppressing behavior in which speakers signal their unwillingness to relinquish the floor by their hand gestures (for example, by putting a hand up with the palm facing toward the listener, etc.).

The controversy surrounding turn-taking illustrates two major underlying themes in this book. First, any explanations of communicative behavior that rely solely on *what* is said are inherently indefensible. Every analysis based solely on *what* is said has been shown to be limited in significant ways, regardless of whether the analysis is a Chomskyan view of grammar, Searle's speech acts, or a turn-taking system based primarily on syntactic features, as is the Sacks et al., system. Second, communicators make a global assessment of the on-going interaction. They simultaneously balance and evaluate the utterances, the context, and their relationships with other participants in interpreting an encounter. Any analytic model that systematically excludes any of the features participants use to interpret interaction will be seriously limited. In Chapter 6, I suggest a descriptive model that integrates the influence of text, context, and participants.

Clearly, scholars need to examine the syntactic, paralinguistic, and contextual constraints on turn-taking. Only then can the contribution each makes in organizing and interpreting discourse be adequately understood. However, scholars also need to analyze the interactions among these constraints. Considerable evidence demonstrates that such interactions do, in fact, influence turn-taking. For example, Goodwin's (1981) very detailed analysis of eye-gaze behavior reveals its influence on turn-taking behavior.

As we have seen, conversational turn-taking is a complex process. It seems much simpler to actually take a turn during a conversation than to explain how it is done! Some of the objections to the Sacks et al. (1974) model may be removed with the consideration of turn cues like eye gaze, head nods, body shifts, and the like. Further research could also explore the issue of different types of access to turn-taking. For example, Ciolek and Kendon (1980) found that spatial arrangements among conversationalists varied as a function of the surrounding environment and the presence of others. The relative "tightness" or "looseness" of the conversational groups could influence turn-taking options and accessibility.

Managing turn-taking smoothly and efficiently may also depend on speaker allocation rules. That is, coordinating turns may be done by pairing the utterances of the speakers and listeners. These paired responses are called adjacency pairs: in adjacency pairs, the first-pair-part requires a second-pair-part for a meaningful exchange to occur. We now look more closely at the structure of adjacency pairs in conversations.

Adjacency Pairs

Several commonplace communicative behaviors can be classified as adjacency pairs: question/answer, summons/response, greetings, closings, compliments and accept/reject, request and accept/reject, and so forth. Each pair is incomplete unless the appropriate reply is given: questions call for answers, a greeting calls for a reciprocal greeting, etc. Most scholars characterize adjacency pairs as follows: (1) they are two utterances long; (2) they are uttered in succession by two different speakers; (3) the two utterances are ordered into first-pair-parts and second-pair-parts; (4) a first-pair-part is followed by an appropriate second-pair-part; and (5) the first-pair-part usually sets up the next speaker and the next action. For example, someone who asks a question expects an answer from a listener. In brief, the first-pair-part sets up an expected second-pair-part, which is provided by the next speaker. Put another way, the first-pair-part sets up a *transition relevant place* and thus calls for the appropriate second-pair-part.

Coulthard (1977) notes that some pairs are reciprocal (like greetings); other first-pair-parts have only one appropriate response (like questions and answers), and yet other first-pair-parts have more than one appropriate response (like complaints and apologies or justifications). Levinson (1983) also notes that second-pair-parts are more variable than previously assumed. For example, a question can be ignored, challenged, re-routed to someone else, and so on. Because of this, he suggests that adjacency pairs are related to one another by *conditional relevance.* As Levinson (1983) observes

> What the notion of conditional relevance makes clear is that what binds the adjacency pairs together is not a formation rule of the sort that would specify that a question must receive an answer if it is to count as a well-formed discourse, but the setting up of specific expectations which have to be attended to (p. 306)

Levinson (1983) suggests that possible second-pair-parts are preferentially ordered; that is, at least one response is preferred and one is dispreferred. This preference is not some psychological preference by the speaker/listener, but rather parallels the concept of markedness in linguistics. Dispreferred second pair parts are *marked* in that such responses are typically delayed, prefaced with remarks indicating their dispreferred status (like "well" or "but"), or some explanation for the dispreferred response is given (p. 307).

In the following example, Joe marks his dispreferred response in several ways.

Moe: Hey, Joe, want to go bowling tonight?

Joe: *Well,* I'd really like to, but I have to study for my communication exam. It's tomorrow and I really need a good grade.

Accepting an invitation is the preferred response. Declining an invitation is behaving in a socially unsupportive way, regardless of *why* a refusal may be necessary. Joe's response marks its dispreferred status through the use of "well" and "but," and a professed desired to go coupled with the justification for his refusal.

Why are some responses preferred over others? Heritage (1984) suggests that preferred responses are those that support social solidarity (i.e., the maintenance of face). Levinson suggests a speech production rule that indicates dispreferred actions are to be avoided. Accordingly, Levinson (1983) outlines a set of preferred responses listed below (p. 336).

First-Pair-Part	Second-Pair-Part	
	Preferred	*Dispreferred*
requests	accept	refusal
offer/invite	accept	refusal
assessment	agree	disagree
question	expected answer	unexpected or refusal
blame	denial	admission

These preferences not only apply to adjacency pairs, but also to less tightly-knit utterance pairs, such as Pomerantz' (1978a) action chains. Action chains are discourse units in which there may be competing preferences, and thus a compromise response may be given. For example, in compliments, one should avoid self-praise, yet there is a preference for agreeing with a compliment.

In sum, conditional relevance occurs when an immediately prior utterance provides an implied relevance for a subsequent comment. If the second-pair-part is not forthcoming, its omission is noticed and may be commented upon (Heritage, 1984).

In a similar vein, Jefferson (1978) argues that every utterance has implications for subsequent utterances. That is, every utterance has *sequential implicativeness* for subsequent utterances. In their strongest form, these positions support the concept of adjacency pairs. In their weakest form, these positions may be subsumed under the maxim of Relevance; that is, utterances are assumed to be relevant, in some way, to the topic at hand. In general, strict sequential relations between any set of paired utterances appear difficult to establish. In fact, as we have seen, adjacency pairs allow for a number of possible second-pair-parts.

Another type of structural device that appears in conversations is a *pre-sequence*. Pre-sequences often foreshadow a specific type of action. In particular, pre-sequences check whether or not necessary preconditions for some forthcoming request or action have been fulfilled. In some instances, these pre-sequences "act as" the request or action itself. Many types of actions can be foreshadowed in this way, and we now turn to an analysis of the ways in which pre-sequences operate in conversations.

Pre-Sequences

A major motivation underlying the use of pre-sequences is that by foreshadowing upcoming actions, participants can evade the upcoming action. An example will help clarify this point:

1. A: Did you have any special plans for dinner?
2. B: I really haven't thought about dinner.

3. A: Well, how about going out for a pizza?
4. B: Sounds good.

In line 1, A foreshadows the proferred invitation in line 3. Speaker B, in line 2, has the opportunity to circumvent the forthcoming invitation (e.g., "I'm working through dinner to finish this project"), or leave open the possibility of an invitation (which B does offer).

Levinson (1983) outlines the following generalized structure for presequences. The preceding example illustrates this general sequence with the utterances in lines 1–4 respectively being positions 1–4 as outlined by Levinson below:

1. In position 1 (or turn 1), a question checking if a necessary precondition obtains is asked;
2. In position 2, the request on the precondition is answered, often with a question or request to proceed to position 3;
3. In position 3, the prefigured action is completed, contingent upon the supportive response in position 2; and
4. In position 4, the response to the action proposed in position 3 is given. (p. 347)

To this formulation, Levinson adds a distributional rule so that positions 1 and 3 are uttered by one speaker, and positions 2 and 4 by another. If the speaker in position 2 indicates that the specified precondition does not apply, then the specific action in position 3 is usually withheld. Thus our example might have gone as follows:

1. A: Do you have any special plans for dinner?
2. B: Yes, I'm going out with Herb tonight.
3. A: Oh, I was hoping we could go out for pizza.

Thus, in position 3, speaker A now offers an explanation of what would have been forthcoming. The presence of "Oh" indicates that the speaker now has information previously unknown and thus indicates that the question was a legitimate query (Heritage, 1984).

Another type of pre-sequence, pre-requests, deserves special attention. Pre-requests appear to obviate the need for indirect speech acts. As Levinson (1983) observes:

> One major reason for utilizing a pre-request is, then, that it allows the producer to check out whether a request is likely to succeed, and if not to avoid one in order to avoid its subsequent dispreferred response, namely a rejection. Given which, in cases of doubt, pre-requests are to be preferred to requests. (p. 357)

Conditions questioned in pre-requests ask about the recipients' ability to comply with the request (as in line 1 in the preceding example). Another motivation for using pre-requests is to avoid requests altogether (p. 359). Levinson concludes that there may be preferred responses to pre-requests such that:

> if you can see that someone wants something, and a pre-request may be an effective clue to that, then it may be most preferred to provide it without more ado, next most preferred to offer, and third in preference to simply solicit the request (p. 360)

As Edmondson (1981) observes, these pre-requests invite the hearer to complete the request.

Frequently, conversations contain other communicative acts within them. For example, a conversation may contain the communicative acts of story-telling and joking. Structural devices are needed to place these communicative acts at appropriate places in the conversation, and to do so without disrupting the flow of conversation. It is to these structural devices we now turn.

Inserting Communicative Acts into Conversations[1]

Communicative acts are distinct forms of communicative behavior such as lectures, prayers, sermons, jokes, and so on (Hymes, 1972, 1974). Each communicative act has a unique structure and related semantic constraints (van Dijk, 1977a, 1981). Some acts, like jokes, stories, arguments, telling troubles (Jefferson, 1984b), blamings (Pomerantz, 1978b), and the like are forms that occur frequently in conversations. Schiffrin (1980) refers to these acts as discourse units embedded in talk (p. 225).

Communicative acts need to be smoothly interjected into the ongoing dialogue. *Insertion* or *side sequences* can accomplish this task (Jefferson, 1972). These sequences immediately suspend the on-going conversational activity so that new topics can be incorporated, or conversational repairs can be made. For example, a listener might initiate a talking turn by saying something like, "that reminds me of a story . . . " which serves to introduce the story.

---

[1]Although we will not discuss these genre in detail, it is necessary to note the presence of these communicative genre and their entrance into conversations. Readers are encouraged to explore in more detail research on arguments (Jacobs & Jackson, 1982; Maynard, 1985); on narratives and stories (Beach & Japp, 1983; deBeaugrande & Colby, 1979; Chafe, 1978; van Dijk, 1977a; Haslett, 1983b; Polanyi, 1979, 1985; Stein & Glenn, 1979; Tannen, 1982); on dueling games or rapping (Abrahams, 1970), jokes and teasing (Drew, 1986; Sacks, 1974), compliance-gaining (Brenneis & Lein, 1977; Eisenberg & Garvey, 1981; Haslett, 1983a; McLaughlin, Cody, & Robey, 1980), and account-giving (Cody & McLaughlin, 1985; Morris, 1985).

While, from an ideal point of view, turn-taking proceeds smoothly and without noticeable gaps or overlaps, we know from our own everyday conversational experience that gaps, interruptions and overlaps occur. It is to these structural features we now turn.

Hesitations, Overlaps and Interruptions

Although these devices can be disruptive, nevertheless they accomplish particular conversational goals. A speaker's hesitation may reflect discomfort with the topic of the conversation or with one's conversational partner. Interruptions may be used to make necessary conversational repairs, and overlaps may occur when two speakers simultaneously try to take a turn.[2]

Interruptions occur when the current speaker's talking turn is broken into by another conversational participant. Jefferson (1973) suggests that interruptions must occur prior to a transition-relevant place so that the interruptor's contribution is relevant and applicable. How the interruption is viewed by participants appears to influence how it is handled (Bennett, 1981; Mishler & Waxler, 1968; Zimmerman & West, 1975). McLaughlin suggests that (1) conversational participants are able to judge when overlaps and interruptions are disruptive and (2) participants are "modestly

---

[2]Frequently, overlaps and interruptions are defined in ambiguous ways as are hesitations and silences. Rosenstein and McLaughlin (1983) investigated overlaps (simultaneous talk), forced interruptions (the interrupted speaker gave up the talking turn) and interruptions (the speaker retained the talking turn). Speakers who overlapped were rated as more competent than speakers who used forced interruptions. They suggest that overlaps were more positively viewed since the speaker's turn was not discontinued and did reflect any loss of face. Forced interruptions were rated as the most domineering technique; however, judgments of interruptions were mitigated by whether or not the speaker had good reason for the interruption (e.g., perhaps an essential clarification, etc.).

Silences in conversations may occur within and between talking turns. Silences within a turn are termed *hesitations* and silences between turns are called *switching pauses* (McLaughlin, 1984, p. 111). The time elapsing during switching pauses is a function of the complexity and predictability of responses for children (Garvey & Berninger, 1981). McLaughlin and Cody (1982) argue that switching pauses are dyadic because (1) such pauses appear to be subject to interactional synchrony; (2) heavy encoding demands may have been placed on the listener; (3) the speaker's statement may have been very weakly implicative, and (4) if a section of talk is being "closed down" a subsequent turn may be problematic since new topics may have to be introduced.

McLaughlin and Cody viewed switching times of 3 seconds or more as *lapses* and argued that they indicate that the current topic of talk is no longer sustaining the conversation. They found that formulations and minimal responses often preceded lapses, and suggest that this sequence (e.g., minimal response followed by a lapse) indicates topic failure.

This brief note indicates some of the complexity regarding research on overlaps, hesitations and interruptions. Unless standard definitions are adopted, confounded results will continue in this area of study.

sensitive to the issue of the precision timing of interruptions" (McLaughlin, 1984, p. 126; see also, McLaughlin & Cody, 1982; Rosenstein & McLaughlin, 1983).

Topicalization

Topicalization, or the ability to introduce, change, and maintain conversational topics is another fundamental organizational issue. For example, to make their remarks relevant, participants need to know the topic or main gist of the conversation.

Generally, in conversations, new information provides more details about the topic which is already understood or given (Chafe, 1977; Reinhart, 1981). Utterances are assumed to be relevant and participants search for the connections between the speaker's utterances and the topic at hand (Sperber & Wilson, 1986; Strawson, 1979). Participants typically maintain the topic by talking about the same event or class of events. Shifts from these topics are usually marked by specific disclaimers (e.g., "By the way, I don't mean to change the topic, but . . . " or "That reminds me . . . ," etc.) (Reichman, 1978). Topics may also be limited by the participants' relationship or by the situation (e.g., situation informality or formality, etc.) (Coulthard, 1977). Finally, topics seem to be "chunked" into issue context spaces or event context spaces (Reichman, 1978); and preferences for topic switches center on the ease of processing those switches (Planalp & Tracy, 1980; Tracy, 1982).

Topics may also be discontinued. Weiner and Goodenough (1977) discuss passing moves (like "ok" and "hmm"), which do not elaborate on the topic. If these passing moves are matched by the speaker, then the topic is terminated and a new topic may be introduced. However, Jefferson and Schenkein (1978) note that passing moves may also act as *processing moves* in which the response is passed along to a more appropriate respondent (e.g., "I really can't answer that, but maybe Tom can") or *conference passes* in which one transfers the response to someone else by consulting them (e.g., "Well, guys, whadda ya think?").

Thus far, we have explored the structural devices that organize conversations: these structural devices also provide a basis for interpreting the interaction (Atkinson & Heritage, 1984; Garfinkel, 1967b; Heritage, 1984). Conversations have an overall structure consisting of openings, topic development and closings. Within conversations, the smooth coordination of speaking turns appears to be structured by a turn-taking, speaker allocation system. The phenomenon of turn-taking, it has been argued, must incorporate nonverbal, paralinguistic, and linguistic cues. Other interpretive structures (those used by speakers to plan their utterances and by hearers to comprehend utterances) consist of adjacency pairs, pre-sequences, interruptions, topicalization, and embedded communicative acts like jokes, stories, and the like.

The structural devices previously discussed make possible and facilitate the smooth coordination and interpretation necessary in conversation. However, not all conversations proceed smoothly because speakers and listeners make errors, perhaps through stress, inattention, mistatements, mishearings, and the like. It is necessary, therefore, to have devices that (1) help maintain the conversation in its intended direction and (2) allow for the repair of conversation when breakdowns occur. Such breakdowns may be anticipated (e.g., a speaker is discussing a very technically involved point and "warns" his audience that the information is quite complex) or repaired after the fact (e.g., a speaker self-corrects a mistatement).

Generally, I use the term "alignment strategies" for discourse strategies that signal how talk is to be interpreted. As such, these strategies mark how an utterance is to be heard and thus help keep the conversation flowing smoothly. These strategies include disclaimers, licenses, formulations, and meta-talk. In contrast, repairs serve as devices that re-align the talk after some error has occurred.

Both alignment strategies and repairs are structural procedures for coordinating and interpreting talk. Alignment and repairs are distinct from one another. Alignment strategies are part of the routine "accomodative work" in conversation, whereas repairs actually *correct* a failure in alignment. That is, repairs allow participants to re-align their talk after some breakdown has occured. Thus, alignment is routine and preventative while repairs are marked and treat some failure to coordinate talk. Such failures can reflect organizational problems in coordinating talk, comprehension problems or both. Since alignment and repair have been used in a very inconsistent, confusing fashion in conversational research, I want to be very clear about how these terms are used here.

III. STRUCTURAL PROCEDURES FOR MANAGING CONVERSATIONS

Alignment Strategies

Several different alignment strategies are used to signal how participants mean their utterances to be taken. These devices, as you recall, facilitate the listener's interpretation and help prevent misunderstandings. Each alignment strategy is discussed in more detail.

Metalanguage.   Metalanguage provides speakers with a way of explicitly framing how their talk is to be viewed, or how the interaction is proceeding.

Metalinguistic comments such as "Oh, I didn't mean it that way," "I was teasing," or single words like "well," "really" and "but," indicate the way in which talk is to be taken. Bateson (1972) suggests that metalanguage may also be complemented by metacommunication. Metacommunicative messages signal how the message is to be taken *as well as signalling the relationship among the participants*. Metacommunicative comments may imply how utterances *should* be viewed as well as commenting on relational issues. (These relational issues are discussed more fully in Chapter 8.) For our purposes here, we focus on metalinguistic comments, although it is difficult to separate metalinguistic (an interpretation issue) and metacommunicative issues (a relationship issue).

Disclaimers. Disclaimers allow speakers to state potentially face-threatening utterances, while disclaiming personal responsibility for the utterances. Thus, disclaimers provide speakers with a way of avoiding negative judgments about themselves. Hewitt and Stokes (1975) suggest the following five categories of disclaimers.

a. *hedging* — used to "preface statements of facts or opinion, positions in arguments or expressions of belief" (e.g., "I'm not a lawyer or anything like that, but . . . ");
b. *credentialing* — used "when the individual *knows* the outcome of his act will be discrediting but is nevertheless strongly committed to the act" (e.g., "I hope you won't be offended, but . . . ");
c. *sin licenses* — used "when the actor is committed to a line of conduct and is certain of negative responses, but does not fear some specific undesired typification" (e.g., "This may be slightly illegal, but . . . ");
d. *cognitive disclaimers* — used when "the possibility that the words or deeds of one participant will be construed by others as lacking sense, as out of touch with empirical reality, as somehow indicating the individual's failure to perceive the situation adequately and correctly" (e.g., "This may seem completely off the wall, but . . . "); and
e. *appeals for the suspension of judgment* — used when "individuals appeal to their fellows to suspend judgment until the full meaning of the act can be made known" (e.g., "You really need to hear the whole story . . . "). (p. 3ff).

Generally, disclaimers also act to qualify the forcefulness of utterances (Beach & Dunning, 1982). Some studies have related the use of disclaimers to subsequent judgments of speakers and found mixed results (Bell, Zahn, & Hopper, 1984; Bradley, 1981).

When one surveys the wide variety of disclaimers, some overlapping categories and examples are apparent. It seems likely that disclaimers are based on the more general underlying conversational maxims. For example, a cognitive disclaimer may be viewed as a request that the listener allow the speaker sufficient time to make the relevance of the speaker's utterances clear. As such, cognitive disclaimers are following the maxim of Relevance. Grice (1975) notes that violations of maxims provides very useful strategic devices for both speakers and listeners.

Formulations.   Formulations, as developed by Garfinkel and Sacks (1970), are ways of saying what we are doing in our talk. Examples of formulations would be summaries, conclusions, reporting the "gist" of the conversation, and so forth. Heritage and Watson (1979) suggest that formulations are ways of interpreting and preserving the on-going talk. These formulations can be confirmed or disconfirmed, and given from the perspective of the speaker or listener (p. 124ff). Formulations thus provide "benchmark" statements for the status of the on-going talk, or may recast prior talk in some way (e.g., "I thought he meant we were to . . . ," etc.).

Meta-Talk.   Meta-talk refers to structural features that signal how specific parts of the text are to be interpreted and/or evaluated. Schiffrin (1980) includes three linguistic devices or strategies in her discussion of meta-talk: meta-linguistic referents, operators, and verbs. *Meta-linguistic referents* include deictic elements (e.g., tense), words like "former" and "latter," and demonstrative pronouns when they refer to items in the text (e.g., "That's a big joke") (p. 202). *Meta-linguistic operators,* like "true," "right," and "wrong," are viewed as marking the status of arguments made in the text itself. And finally, *meta-linguistic verbs* also indicate how utterances are to be taken (e.g., argue, joke, lie, etc. as in, for example, "They were only joking").

Schiffrin (1980) also discusses *discourse brackets* and *evaluative brackets.* Discourse brackets indicate what is coming up in subsequent talk, or mark the end of a given discourse segment. For example, expressions like "You see, it happened like this . . . " or "the final point" serve as markers indicating "where we are in the talk." In contrast, evaluative brackets are utterances which reflect one's assessment of utterances (e.g., "I don't agree with that," "That is not the point," etc.) (p. 218). While these discourse brackets and meta-linguistic expressions can be used to organize talk, they also serve to evaluate and to mark interpretations of on-going talk (Schiffrin, 1980, p. 231).

As we have seen, conversationalists signal how their utterances are to be taken in a variety of ways. These alignment strategies serve to clarify the intended uptake for listeners, or to establish preconditions that insure successful uptake. However, these varied alignment strategies do not seem mutually exclusive. Future research in this area could focus on the underlying principles for these devices and build a systematic taxonomy on that basis.

Alignment strategies, as a group, clarify talk and keep the conversation going in its intended (or planned) direction (Stokes & Hewitt, 1976). In this sense, alignment strategies are *feedback* strategies that try to prevent misalignment and help repair it when it occurs. Alignment strategies are of critical importance for conversations because participants follow the Cooperative Principle by using such strategies, even when conversations break down. The use of alignment strategies are governed by the demands of the text itself (i.e., what kind of alignment is needed?), the context (i.e., what is the appropriate alignment strategy?), and the relationship between participants (i.e., is it necessary to maintain face and if so, to what degree?).

Despite adherence to conversational maxims and the use of alignment strategies, communication breakdowns in the form of misunderstandings and mishearings do occur. Thus, strategies to *repair* conversations are needed. It is to these repair mechanisms that we now turn.

Conversational Repairs

The repair system operates to correct a wide variety of conversational problems, and can be characterized along several basic dimensions. Repairs may be self-initiated or initiated by others, and may be done by the speaker (self-repair) or by the listener (other-repair) (Schegloff, Jefferson, & Sacks, 1977). Levinson (1983) notes that preference rankings occur across repairs as well. Types of repairs, listed in order of their preference (and also in terms of their usage) are: (1) self-initiated, self-repair in the speaker's own turn; (2) self-initiated, self-repair in the transition relevant place between the speaker's turn and the next turn; (3) other-initiated, self-repair in which the listener requests the speaker's correction in the next turn; and (4) other-initiated, other-repair (p. 341). Remler (1978) suggests that other-initiated repairs follow three basic steps: a request for a repair, a remedy, and then an acknowledgment of the repair. Side-sequences can frequently be used to initiate needed repairs (Jefferson, 1972; Jefferson & Schenkein, 1978).

Schonbach (1980) suggests that repair sequences are failed events. In failed communicative events, there is (1) a failure event (e.g., a misunderstanding or mishearing); (2) a reproach; (3) an account of the failure; and (4) an evaluation of the account. This structure is used in concessions, excuses, justifications, and refusals. For example,

A:	Hey, come here a minute! ⎫	*failed*
B:	What? ⎭	*event*
A:	Come here. Good grief, don't you ever listen?	*reproach*
B:	Sorry, guess I'm tired.	*account*
A:	Well, pay more attention. Now we need . . .	*evaluation*

As we have seen, conversational repairs take a variety of forms. These repairs not only address a specific conversational problem, but also address the implied relational issues as well. For example, participants' feelings of guilt were found to influence their choice of repair strategy (McLaughlin, Cody, & O'Hair, 1983). Repair structures, as conceptualized by different theorists, seem to overlap with one another. However, a standard format for repairs appears to be (1) a failed event of some sort; (2) a repair of that failure; and (3) a subsequent acknowledgment.

IV. CONCLUSIONS AND IMPLICATIONS

Structural approaches to conversational analysis reveal the systematic ways in which participants sequentially order their conversational activity and are thus able to coordinate their talk. Conversations are viewed as goal-directed, planful interactions between at least two participants who alternate speaking and listening roles. In Anglo-American societies, conversational activities are apparently based on several deep-seated assumptions about how talk should be conducted: namely, the Cooperative Principle, and the maxims of Quality, Quantity, Relevance, and Manner. To this, we have added the maxims of Charity, Morality, Informativeness, Politeness, and perhaps most importantly, the Reality Principle.

One of the major goals in any interaction is achieving coherence. Participants achieve coherence, in part, through the use of organizational devices and procedures outlined in this chapter. We have divided these structural features into two categories. First, structural units for organizing and interpreting conversations were discussed, including turn-taking, adjacency pairs, pre-sequences, embedded communicative acts, topicalization, and interruptions/overlaps. Secondly, a set of structural procedures—side-sequences, alignment strategies and repairs—were discussed. These procedures enable participants to coordinate their talk, to maintain or change the conversational topic, to introduce new information, and to clarify the intended direction of the conversation. Taken together, these structural devices and procedures make possible participants' coordinated management of their conversations.

As previously suggested in Chapter 1, structural models are inherently limited. Conversations appear to vary as a function of the participants' purposes, the context, and the relationship between participants, but structural approaches are not sensitive to these variations.

In addition to extending the analysis of structural aspects of conversations by reference to context, purposes and relationships, attention must be focused on three issues. First, there is the issue of cross cultural variability. For example, utterances and maxims may be marked and applied differently in different cultures. The concept of politeness, and by implication, the conduct of conversational alignment and repair strategies, appear to vary significantly across cultures. Exploring cross-cultural variation in conversational behavior will make a significant contribution to pragmatic theories of human communication. As previously noted, our views on the nature and conduct of conversations are grounded in Western philosophic assumptions about time, man's capacity for action and thought, rationality, and so forth.

A second issue concerns the need to integrate the verbal and nonverbal dimensions of conversational analysis. Ample evidence exists concerning the importance of paralinguistic features, like intonation and stress, in the interpretation of conversation. The work of Scheflen (1974), Birdwhistell (1972), Hall (1969), Beattie (1978b, 1981, 1983; Beattie & Stephens, 1986), Bull (1983) and Goodwin (1981) provides clear theoretical and empirical support for their mutual interaction in human communication. One of the most recent and elegant arguments in support of these interrelationships in conversation is Goodwin's work on turn-taking and eye gaze behavior. While unarguably increasing the complexity of our research, it nevertheless must be a part of our accounts of communicative behavior.

Finally, there is the issue of what the basic unit of conversational analysis should be. Generally, the researcher's basic unit of analysis depends upon his/her purpose in doing the analysis. The weaknesses of turn-taking systems and adjacency pairs are readily apparent. However, some of them may be overcome by focusing on a triadic unit of analysis.

Goffmann (1976) suggests that a three-part interactional unit is most appropriate for conversations. There is a mentionable event, a mention, and comment on the mention.[3] Significantly, he notes that the first part (a mentionable event) may not involve speech (p. 200). He concludes

> that our basic model for talk ought not to be dialogic couplets and their
> chaining, but rather a sequence of response moves with each in the series

---

[3]Like Goffman, I would argue that the analytic unit of interaction should be a tri-part unit. One might extend Goffman's argument to adjacency pairs and suggest that the third response is often nonverbal as well. For example, take the following question and answer adjacency pair:

A: What's the time please?
B: Three o'clock.
A: Thanks mate.

A's response of "Thanks mate" might well have been nonverbal, like a smile, head nod or hand wave. What I am suggesting here is that, given the sequential implicativeness of utterances, we need to recall that conversation is jointly negotiated: hearers respond, but for the conversation to proceed, the speaker must *subsequently respond to the listener's uptake by confirming, disconfirming or ignoring it.* Thus, I would argue that analyses which ignore the speaker's subsequent response to the listener's uptake are inherently insufficient.

carving out its own reference, and each incorporating a variable balance of function in regard to statement-replay properties. In the right setting, a person next in line to speak can elect to deny the dialogic frame, accept it, carve out such a format when none is apparent. This formulation would allow us to give proper credit to the flexibility of talk—a property distinguishing talk, for example, from the interaction of moves occurring in formal games—and to see why so much interrupting, nonanswering, restarting, and overlapping occurs in it. (p. 294)

A triadic interaction unit has also been assumed in the analysis of teacher/student dialogues (Bellack, Kleiman, Hyman, & Smith, 1966). The basic format is: the teacher's inquiry; the student's response; and the teacher's evaluation of the student's response. Triadic units have also been suggested for organizations (Weick, 1979); for bargaining and conflict (Rogers, 1983); and for therapuetic interviews (Labov & Fanshel, 1977). It appears necessary, in interactional analysis, to have the speaker—as well as the listener—confirm or disconfirm the direction of the conversation. The advantage of the triadic unit is that it incorporates uptake from both speakers and listeners, and thus seems truly interactional since both participants are allowed the opportunity to negotiate the conversational direction.

Structural analyses of conversations focus on how conversations are managed. But the *how* of communication needs to be complemented by the *why* of communicator behavior. Our next chapter deals with the purposes communicators fulfill through using language. We are speaking here of the broad communicative functions that languages perform, like informing or expressing, rather than a very precise analysis of a participant's specific communicative intent. We now turn to an analysis of these functions.

4 Functional Approaches to Communication

CONTRASTING STRUCTURAL AND FUNCTIONAL APPROACHES

The structural approaches previously discussed focus on the organization of texts and conversations. Such approaches stress the format in which communication occurs, rather than its content or purpose. In contrast, functional approaches emphasize the varied purposes communication serves. Before analyzing various functional approaches, however, I wish to briefly contrast structural and functional approaches in order to provide a frame of reference for our subsequent discussion.

Zimmerman and Whitehurst (1979) suggest some important differences between structural and functional approaches to language and cognition. First, functional explanations and structural explanations must complement one another: neither explanation can contradict the other. However, both resolve different problems and differ in the type of explanation given. Second, they note that structural and functional approaches represent a continuum: most approaches will fall somewhere between those two poles. Third, functional and structural approaches are not independent. They suggest that structural explanations depend upon well-developed functional explanations.

According to Zimmerman and Whitehurst (1979), structural approaches, while very diverse, "all stress understanding the general organization of knowledge" (p. 4). Structural approaches explain consistencies in behavior and assume a single, encompassing, underlying cognitive structure. These assumed underlying structures are sets of principles or mental operations that explain the observed behavioral consistency (p. 9). Structural approaches thus emphasize the rule-governed aspects of language and thought (p. 8).

In contrast, functional approaches explore individual differences and situational effects upon human behavior. Functional approaches analyze the interdependent linkages among private thought, public behavior, and environmental features (p. 11). Thus functional approaches do not separate cognitive processes from situational cues and from the individual's personal history.

In addition, Zimmerman and Whitehurst argue that several distinctive issues separate the two approaches. Functional models stress prediction and control, whereas structural approaches focus on deductive explanations of observed behavioral regularities. Second, structural models can be entirely mentalistic whereas functional explanations must be grounded in context and reflect participants' goals in that context. Finally, structural models emphasize structural consistency while functional approaches emphasize situational and individual variation. The approach ultimately found most appealing will reflect the researcher's general satisfaction with a particular type of explanation.

It should be kept in mind, however, that most theories will fall somewhere between these two extremes, or may also combine both functional and structural explanations. Zimmerman and Whitehurst note that Piagetian theory, for example, provides both functional and structural explanations. Speech act models provide structural explanations (i.e., all utterances have an illocutionary, locutionary, and perlocutionary force) as well as functional explanations (i.e., speech act taxonomies outline the functions of language use—see for example, Bach & Harnish, 1979).

With this brief overview in mind, we now turn to an analysis of the functions performed by communication. These functions vary depending upon the participant's goal, the context, the social relationships among participants, and the culture. Several functional models are reviewed including those of Halliday, Tough, speech act analysis, and compliance-gaining strategies.

I. ANALYZING FUNCTIONAL APPROACHES

Scholars advocating functional approaches suggest that *function determines form* (Halliday, 1973). Functionalists assume that linguistic variation exists; that language variation is related to co-occuring nonlinguistic events; and that some properties of language covary with the communicator's purpose. All functionalists argue that humans learn linguistic meanings in *context*—that is, within a concrete conceptual domain (Baron, 1981). Structural theorists, with their assumption of an idealized speaker/listener, emphasize the standard formats of texts, and thus have underestimated the influence of the communicative context (Baron, 1981).

One of the earliest functional theories of communication was that of Bühler (1934). He suggests that there are three major functions of language: the *emotive* (corresponding to the speaker); the *conative* (corresponding to the listener); and the *referential* (corresponding to the person/thing being spoken about). Jakobson (1960) subsequently expanded these functions into six categories: the emotive function (speaker), conative function (hearer), referential function (context), poetic function (message), phatic function (interpersonal contact), and metalingual function (code).

The most prominent functional theorist today is M.A.K. Halliday. His work reflects the anthropological tradition of Firth, Malinowski, and other functionalists. It is to his work that we now turn.

Halliday: Language as Social Semiotic

Malinowski's fieldwork (1923) clearly demonstrates that language reflects societal demands and social contexts. As such, the meaning of a word or utterance is based upon how it functions in a particular culture. In following Malinowski's work, Halliday acknowledges the multifunctional nature of language (Kress, 1976).

Firth (1957) formally describes meaning as how language functions in context. To fully describe utterances, Firth includes (1) an analysis of the participants (including their relevant verbal and nonverbal actions); (2) the relevant objects and nonverbal events in the context; and (3) the effect of the utterance itself. Following Firth, Halliday further extends the description of the situational context. He suggests that general types of situations call for different language techniques (i.e., different language registers). (Since the emphasis here is on the functional analyses of language rather than a formal theory of language, I shall not discuss Halliday's systemic grammar. For an overview of Halliday's systemic grammar, see Halliday and Martin, 1981.)

Language: Its Role in Constructing Social Reality. In Halliday's view, communication and language play central roles in how humans socially construct their reality. According to Halliday (1978), the construal of reality is inseparable from the construal of the semantic system in which one's experience is encoded (pp. 2–4). That is, an individual's experiences are conceptualized and expressed in terms of that individual's language. Social reality is an "edifice of meanings"—a social semiotic—and language is the semiotic system that encodes these meanings. Through everyday interaction, people act out their perceived social reality; confirming their own identity, and establishing and transmitting a shared system of values and of knowledge (pp. 2-3). Thus, language is viewed as *meaning potential,* which is *actualized* in particular settings through communication.

Halliday (1973) suggests that language derives from its social functions. As he observes:

> The essential feature of a functional theory is ... that it provides a basis for explaining the nature of the language system, since the system itself reflects the functions that it has evolved to serve. ...
>
> Those of the first set, the *ideational,* are concerned with the content of language, its function as a means of the expression of our experience, both of the external world and of the inner world of our own consciousness—together with what is perhaps a separate sub-component expressing certain basic logical relations. The second, the *interpersonal,* is language as the mediator of role, including all that may be understood by the expression of our own personalities and personal feelings on the one hand, and forms of interaction and social interplay with other participants in the communication situation on the other hand. The third component, the *textual,* has an enabling function, that of creating text, which is language in operation as distinct from strings of words or isolated sentences and clauses. It is this component that enables the speaker to organize what he is saying in such a way that it makes sense in the context and fulfils its function as a message. (pp. 65-66; italics added)

In Halliday's view, the social functions of language are important in interpreting language as a system. Meaning is defined as function; as such, language represents a potential set of alternative meaning choices for speakers. Speakers select their meaning choices at the semantic, grammatical, and phonological levels (p. 29). Every speaker/hearer has a set of meaning options within a specified setting: that is, in a given environment $x,$ there are meaning options between choices $a, b,$ or $c,$ and a speaker selects from those alternatives. Individuals can also choose a setting. Thus any utterance reflects the set of choices made within the systemic network of a language.

Language Structure and Function. According to Halliday, any utterance has three different structural aspects, each reflecting a different language function (i.e., the ideational, interpersonal, or textual functions mentioned above). *Transivity* represents the agent of action, the action itself, and the end result; as such, it expresses content and reflects the ideational function. *Mood* expresses the interpersonal function by specifying both the speaker's and hearer's roles in the interaction. Finally, the textual function is realized by an utterance's *theme* (the given information) and *rheme* (the new information). Any utterance reflects these three functions simultaneously. For example, in the utterance "I had a cat," the ideational function is a relational one indicating possession; the interpersonal function is a non-modalized declarative, and the textual function has an unmarked theme ("I") with the rheme or new information being the possession of the cat (Halliday, 1973, p. 45). (For a more thorough discussion of his system, see Halliday, 1973, especially Chapter 2.)

Halliday views language as a set of systems embedded in one another. The lexicogrammatical system actualizes the semantic system; the semantic system, in turn, actualizes the culture's meaning system. Thus lexicogrammatical elements, like clauses, must be linked to the culture's social meaning system, and aspects of the culture's social meaning system must be expressed in the lexicogrammatical system. For example, a participant's social status can be signalled by forms of address, intimacy can be signalled by use of nicknames, and the like.

In sum, a culture's social system is reflected in the semantic system of its language; language thus embodies a culture's semiotic system. During communication, information about the social system is conveyed and presented in highly context-specific ways (Halliday, 1978, p. 79). Through their talk, individuals express meanings and the talk itself, in turn, signals how the context is being interpreted (pp. 135–145).

The Functions of Language.   Halliday (1973, 1975) suggests that the social functions of language evolve over time. A young child's utterance expresses a single function directly, whereas an adult's utterance expresses multiple functions simultaneously. Halliday argues that, for children, there is a direct correspondence between content and form. Children's language expresses the following functions: (1) an *instrumental* function provides a means to accomplish things; (2) a *regulative* function serves to regulate others' behavior; (3) an *interactional* function serves to mediate relationships between the self and others; (4) a *personal* function mediates the development of one's personality; (5) a *heuristic* function explores the environment; and (6) an *imaginative* function creates a private world for the self (Halliday, 1973, pp. 11–15). The instrumental, regulatory, interactional and personal functions appear between 10.5 to 16.5 months. Around 18 months, children develop heuristic and imaginative language functions. An informative function does not develop until the child has mastered the reciprocal exchanges necessary in interpersonal communication. The instrumental and regulatory functions merge into a broad pragmatic function that reflects the child's responses to the environment. The personal and heuristic functions merge into a general mathetic function that reflects the child's observations of the environment.

By adulthood, these functions have merged into three metafunctions: the *ideational, interpersonal,* and *textual.* The ideational function reflects the content or idea contained in an utterance; the interpersonal function expresses the relationships among the participants, and the textual function reflects the assumed old information (theme) and the new information presented (rheme). Adults accomplish these three functions simultaneously in their utterances. As Halliday (1973) points out:

> The innumerable social purposes for which adults use language are not represented directly, one by one, in the form of functional components in the language, as are those of the child. With the very young child, "function" equals use; and there is no grammar, no intermediate level of internal organization in language, only a content and an expression. With the adult, there are indefinitely many uses, but only three or four functions, or "macro-functions" as we are calling them; and these macro-functions appear at a new level in the linguistic system—they take the form of "grammar." The grammatical system has as it were a functional input and a structural output; it provides a mechanism for different functions to be combined in one utterance in the way the adult requires. But these macro-functions, although they are only indirectly related to specific uses of language, are still recognizable as abstract representations of the basic functions which language is made to serve. (pp. 36–37)

The development of the grammatical system enables adult utterances to be multi-functional, or, in Halliday's (1978) terms, to have "functional plurality" (pp. 53–55). Halliday's model of language, systemic grammars, connects these functions with language structure (see, for example, Halliday, 1978, and Halliday & Martin, 1981).

Thus, Halliday's work integrates function with structure, and suggests that language structure evolved in terms of its social functions. Three functions—the ideational, interpersonal, and textual—are expressed in every linguistic utterance. Halliday does not order these functions in any hierarchy of relative importance, but rather views all three as essential. Other more specific social purposes, like promising, informing, or threatening, derive from one of these metafunctions.

The breadth of Halliday's functional view, language as social semiotic, is more inclusive and grammatically-based than other models of language functions. Other scholars concerned with language functions view them as specific social purposes, whereas Halliday regards functions as reflecting a culture's social meaning system. As such, Halliday's work can serve as an overarching frame of reference for the other functional approaches discussed in this chapter.

We first look at the work of Joan Tough (1977), who applies Halliday's work within a Piagetian cognitive framework. Next, we consider some functional approaches based on speech act analysis, and finally, we consider work viewing language functions as performing very specific social purposes, like persuasion or compliance-gaining.

Tough's Functional Model

Tough's research examines young children's use of language, which reflects their construction and expression of meaning. As the child's conceptualization of the world develops, so too does the child's use of language (Tough, 1977, p. 44).

Each language function is expressed in a different way; these distinct ways of performing a particular language function are termed *uses* of language. In turn, each use can be accomplished by different devices called *strategies*. Thus, different *strategies* reflect different *uses* of language; different *uses* of language reflect different functions. Outlined below are the four language functions and their uses.

Functions	*Uses*
1. Directive—directs actions and operations	1. self-directing 2. other-directing
2. Interpretive—communicates the meaning of events and situations the child witnesses	1. reporting 2. reasoning
3. Projective—projects and explores situations the child is not actually experiencing	1. predicting 2. empathy 3. imagining
4. Relational—establishes and maintains relationships	1. self-maintaining 2. interactional

Tough's work emphasizes the cognitive as well as social functions that language performs. Her research and that of Haslett (1983b) demonstrate that as children's cognitive abilities grow, they also develop increasingly complex uses and strategies in their language.

The next functional approach we consider focuses on the social actions accomplished by particular utterances. Within speech act analysis, the illocutionary force of an utterance can be viewed as the *function(s)* that utterance performs. It is to this perspective we next turn.

Speech Acts: Illocutionary Force as Language Function

Austin and Searle both propose taxonomies of speech acts; each speech act category reflects a different social function of language. Austin (1962) suggests five major classes of illocutionary acts:

1. Verdictives—giving a judgment or verdict; for example, to acquit, judge, etc.
2. Excercitives—exercising rights, power or influence; for example, advising, warning, etc.
3. Commissives—committing the speaker to doing something; for example, promising, etc.
4. Behabitives—expressing attitudes; for example, apologizing or criticizing, etc.
5. Expositives—clarifying how an utterance fits into on-going talk; for example, debating, etc.

Bach and Harnish (1979) developed a comprehensive speech act taxonomy based on an utterance's illocutionary force. The four communicative functions of illocutionary force are: (1) *constatives* (which express the speaker's desire that the hearer have a similar belief); (2) *directives* (which express the speaker's attitude toward a pending action by another); (3) *commissives* (which express a speaker's obligation to carry out some act) and (4) *acknowledgments* (which express the speaker's feelings about the listener or expresses the speaker's intention to fulfill his/her face obligations) (pp. 40–41). Two other classes, *effectives* and *verdictives,* are considered conventional rather than communicative.

Some examples of constatives are describing, confirming, asserting, predicting, and the like. Directives are acts such as making requests, asking questions, prohibiting some act, giving advice, and so forth. Commissives are acts like promising, offering, and the like. Finally, acknowledgments include acts like apologizing, greeting, congratulating, and so forth.

Using illocutionary force to describe how language functions appears to be useful. However, even with this brief overview, it is easy to see that a multitude of speech act taxonomies can be developed. And indeed, that has occured. The relative merits of each taxonomy appear to depend upon the researcher's purposes. One could, of course, following Searle, take the position that every utterance can be restated as a performative, and thus an infinite number of illocutionary acts are possible as well as an infinite number of functional categories. Whatever particular category of speech acts is being proposed, all schemes appear to collapse into Halliday's three macro-functions—the ideational, interpersonal, and textual.

Thus far, the functional approaches discussed focus on very general social functions that language, used as a communicative tool, can accomplish. However, such approaches appear to have limited value. The language functions specified are so general in scope, and the potential set of utterances that serve a given function so large, that it seems pointless to relate functions to utterances—at least at this level. The multitude of speech act taxonomies that have been developed illustrates this problem.

Some scholars have taken an alternative approach, and analyzed how very specific communicative purposes, like persuading or arguing, are accomplished. The strategies participants use to accomplish their purposes are categorized and their linguistic features analyzed. We turn now to a brief examination of compliance-gaining research as an example of this type of approach.

Compliance-Gaining Research

Social scientists have a long tradition of studying the communicative processes by which people persuade and influence one another (Cody, Woelfel, & Jordan, 1983; Falbo, 1977; French & Raven, 1960; Pondy, 1977). Marwell and Schmitt (1967) suggest that people spend much of their time trying to influence others through the use of varied strategies. Attempts to influence others seem to be a fundamental feature of any communicative situation (Watzlawick, Beavin, & Jackson, 1967). These control or influence strategies have been studied under the general rubric of compliance-gaining strategies.

According to Smith (1984), compliance-gaining research focuses on persuasion as a context-dependent phenomenon. She notes that:

> researchers have attempted to determine how influence and resistance strategies vary systematically as a function of context variables such as the nature of the relationship between communicators and the different predispositions communicators bring to persuasive encounters. (p. 490)

A wide range of contexts and persuasive strategies have been explored: for example, among children (Brenneis & Lein, 1977; Delia, Kline, & Burleson, 1979; Eisenberg & Garvey, 1981; Haslett, 1983b); in different relational contexts such as marital partners (Falbo & Peplau, 1980; Fitzpatrick & Winke, 1979; Sillars, 1980); and in differing social settings (Cody & McLaughlin, 1980; McLaughlin, Cody, & Robey, 1980; Miller, Boster, Roloff, & Seibold, 1977).

However, most compliance-gaining strategies are descriptive, rather than explanatory (Smith, 1982, 1984). Such taxonomies are derived from a priori assumptions about persuasion, rather than from strategies developed in on-going persuasive contexts. These a priori categories are then used to classify the strategies that individuals say they would be willing to use in a specified situation.

Smith (1984) proposes a contingency rules theory of compliance-gaining. She suggests that persuasive behaviors are selected in terms of their anticipated consequences. She argues that five self-evaluative and adaptive rules govern the selection of persuasive strategies in varied persuasive contexts:

self-identity rules link persuasive strategies to personal values; *image-maintenance rules* link persuasive strategies to impression-management concerns; *environmental contingency rules* relate persuasive strategies to concerns about the physical well-being of the self and significant others; *interpersonal relationship rules* relate persuasive strategies to maintaining good relationships with others; and *social normative rules* link persuasive strategies to norms of appropriate behavior. As such, her model attempts to relate persuasive strategies to underlying social concerns that may operate in a given context. Such theory building models will be necessary to integrate the diverse range of compliance-gaining studies. Although our review of such strategies has been very brief, it nonetheless demonstrates the utility of a micro-level analysis of communicative strategies in persuasive contexts.

II. CONCLUSIONS AND IMPLICATIONS

Functional approaches to language vary widely in their level of analysis (from macro to micro-level); in their generality (from being relatively decontextualized to being context-dependent); and in their focus (social, cognitive, or a combination of the two). Halliday's view of language as a semiotic system presents the most macro-level, general approach. He derives language structure, in part, from the three social macrofunctions of language (the ideational, interpersonal, and textual), and argues that all three functions are simultaneously realized in any utterance.

In contrast, other functional analyses are more micro-level. Speech act taxonomies focus on the action performed by utterances in context. Tough's model suggests that language performs important cognitive and social functions. Finally, we have briefly examined a functional analysis of a specific social purpose, that of persuasion, as it occurs in diverse settings. Here, too, we have numerous taxonomies of persuasive communicative strategies. Generally, these approaches are descriptive.

Functional approaches, taken together, produce various taxonomies reflecting the communicative functions that language performs. These approaches focus more on communicative purposes, rather than on the form of the text as do structural approaches. However, these communicative functions are potentially infinite. That is, in any taxonomy, there can always be more fine-grained analyses or alternative distinctions drawn. And it is difficult to judge whether the taxonomies developed—especially those developed by a priori schemes—accurately reflect the strategies participants would actually choose in a given situation.

All functional approaches try to connect an utterance's function to its form and content. However, such connections are inherently problematic since any utterance can have multiple functions, even in a well-defined context. An utterance's function may also vary across different contexts and language users. Finally, as mentioned earlier, general functional analyses, like Halliday's, seem too broad in scope to be of value.

While functional analyses assume that language use varies across different contexts, these contextual influences have not been adequately investigated. Some functional approaches, such as those using an utterance's illocutionary force or a macro-level analysis like Halliday's, seem to be almost context free. Others, such as the compliance-gaining strategies, provide a clearly defined social setting and ask subjects to select the strategies they would use in that context. Using context in this simplistic way, however, does not adequately assess the complexity of selecting the most effective strategy.

Communicative functions need to be analyzed in their appropriate communicative contexts. First, researchers need to establish what particular functions may be accomplished in a given context. For example, the context of a college lecture to 5,000 students does not facilitate any interpersonal functions, although it may factilitate ideational functions. Second, the links between linguistic form, linguistic function, communicative context, and language users need to be developed in terms of the standards for appropriate communicative behavior in a given context. Given that an utterance may have multiple functions assigned to it, what function is most appropriate for a particular context? Or, put another way, what is the best context for achieving a particular communicative function? Finally, different individuals will have different functions they wish to accomplish, and different evaluations of the context and its importance. As such, the interrelationships among function, form and context appear to vary according to the participants' purposes.[1] For these reasons, functional analyses need to be accompanied by more detailed analyses of the other features of communicative processes, most especially adequate descriptions of the communicative context.

Thus, to fully appreciate a functional approach to language, we need to explore the concept of the communicative context and its influence on communicative behavior. Halliday (1978) notes the close relationship between communicative context and social function when he observes:

> language *actively symbolizes* the social system, representing metaphorically in its patterns of variation, the variation that characterizes human cultures. This is what enables people to play with variation in language, using it to

---

[1]See the voluminous literature on "naive psychology" and action theory for interesting discussions of the issues of awareness and action. See, for example, Brenner, 1980; Clarke, 1983, in press; Nisbett & Ross, 1980; Nisbett & Wilson, 1977; and von Cranach & Harre, 1982.

create meanings of a social kind: to participate in all forms of verbal contest and verbal display, and in the elaborate rhetoric of ordinary daily conversation. It is this same twofold function of the linguistic system, its function both as expression of and metaphor for social processes, that lies behind the dynamics of the interaction of language and social context; which ensures that, in the microencounters of everyday life where meanings are exchanged, language not only serves to facilitate and support other modes of social action that constitute its environment, but also actively creates an environment of its own. . . . The context plays a part in determining what we say and what we say plays a part in determining the context. As we learn how to mean, we learn to predict each from the other. (p. 3)

It seems quite clear that an adequate conceptualization of context is an essential prerequisite for adequate description and theory-building in communication. It is to this matter we now turn. And as we shall see, the concept of context is a very complex, multi-faceted concept.

5 Contextual Approaches to Communication

Although scholars agree on the importance of contextual influences on discourse comprehension and production, there is little agreement, however, about how communicative contexts should be described and studied (Brown, 1984; Magnusson, 1981c). Despite the diversity of views on the nature of communicative contexts, most scholars characterize them in terms of the knowledge that humans have about how to interact in a specific setting. That knowledge may range from background commonsense knowledge in a given culture to very specific, personalized knowledge about a particular type of context, which reflects an individual's extensive experience in that context. While it is commonly assumed that background knowledge plays a role in interpreting utterances, Gumperz (1982) notes that

> still very much a matter of dispute are the questions of what form the background knowledge, in terms of which we react to what we see and hear, takes; to what extent it is shared; how it enters into situated meaning assessments, and how the relevant cognitive processes are to be represented. (pp. 204–205)

These questions are the focus of our investigation of contextual influences in communication.

In what follows, some general definitions of communicative context are considered. Next, we examine approaches that view context as an *antecedent* variable. When the communicative context is viewed as an antecedent variable, it is defined as the participant's prior knowledge about the social setting in which the interaction will occur. These approaches

85

include systems of knowledge representation dealing with (1) commonsense knowledge, (2) situational knowledge, and (3) the perceived relationship between goals and situations. These knowledge bases provide interactants with *expectations* about what a forthcoming interaction might be like. Such expectations might include who is likely to be present, what are appropriate topics and remarks to make, and so forth. Those approaches viewing context as an antecedent variable include scripts, frames, situational models and prototypes, and social episodes.

Finally, we examine approaches that view context as an *emergent* variable. These approaches argue that, as the interaction proceeds, text and context mutually define and influence one another. As such, viewing the communicative context as an emergent variable focuses on the evolving interplay between text and context. Such approaches include Gumperz' contextualization cues, conversational analysis, and "speech marker" research.

I. DEFINING THE PARAMETERS OF CONTEXT

Why is a Theory of Context Needed?

Magnusson (1981a) cogently argues that environmental influences on an individual's behavior are always mediated by situations (contexts). A clear theory of situations is necessary to adequately account for human behavior. In particular, Magnusson (1981b) points out that a theory of situation (context) is required because: (1) different situations offer different opportunities for action, growth, and feedback; (2) situations influence human behavior; and (3) understanding situational influences enables us to modify situations so that interaction is facilitated.

Some Alternative Views of Communicative Contexts

Germain (1979), tracing the concept of context as it developed in linguistic theories, notes that context usually refers to the total linguistic setting and situation. As such, the context includes social knowledge about the situation, the text itself, and paralinguistic and extralinguistic features associated with the text. According to Germain, the *explicit* context includes the text and extralinguistic features of the text (e.g., pitch of voice, accompanying gestures, etc.). The *implicit* context incorporates the speaker/hearer's knowledge of the situation and his/her purposes.

Wentworth (1980), van Dijk (1977b) and Forgas (1978) offer situational definitions that emphasize interaction in situations. Given their interactional focus, such approaches represent the most useful views of context for our purposes. Forgas (1978) views knowledge of social episodes (situations) as a cognitive representation of recurring, stereotypical sequences of social interaction. These sequences are embedded within a broader cultural environment, with consensually defined boundaries and with a set of specific rules and norms relating to appropriate and inappropriate behavior (p. 435). Similarly, Wentworth (1980) argues that communicative contexts require participants to orient toward each other; this orientation rests upon participants' purposes, and their knowledge of the context. Communicative contexts, as such, are *mutually defined* by participants.

Van Dijk (1977b) notes that the concept of context is a cognitive, theoretical abstraction from an actual situation. Since not all features of the situation are relevant for interpreting ongoing interaction, contextual models need to rely on strategies and schemata that provide fast, functional, relevant interpretations of the communicative context.

Some Common Underlying Assumptions about the Communicative Context

Despite these contrasting views, several common assumptions guide research on contextual influences in communication. One common assumption is that individuals are active, intentional agents in situations (Magnusson, 1981b, p. 21). This assumption suggests an interactionist perspective, since the constant interplay between person and situation is acknowledged in both interpreting and planning action (Endler, 1981; Giles & Hewstone, 1982; Magnusson, 1981b; Monson, 1981). Second, most scholars distinguish the *perceived context* (as construed by the participants) from the *actual context* (the objective, verifiable aspects of the context such as the number and type of objects, the temperature, number of participants, etc.) (Craik, 1981; Magnusson, 1981a; Nystedt, 1981). Third, most scholars acknowledge that communication plays a vital role in defining the context (Argyle, Furnham, & Graham, 1981; Carswell & Rommetviet, 1971; Forgas, 1983; Furnham, 1986; Giles & Hewstone, 1982; St. Clair & Giles, 1980).

Fourth, contextual effects are assumed to be bi-directional. The context itself influences interaction, while simultaneously being defined by that ongoing interaction (Furnham, 1986; Giles & Hewstone, 1982; Magnusson, 1981b). Similarly, Craik (1981) notes that the context serves as both an independent and dependent variable. As an independent variable, the context may (1) change the environment for subsequent interactions; (2) modify a participant's personality and thus subsequent actions, and (3) through its construal by participants, modify their subsequent behavior. As a dependent variable, the context is determined by the participants, the physical environment, and the sociocultural environment.

Finally, the effects of context on interaction appear to vary both in application (e.g., as a function of how rigidly prescribed the context is, how inappropriate behavior may be sanctioned, etc.), and in intensity. In addition, Dascal (1981), Furnham (1986), and others have suggest that different contexts influence different aspects of interaction.

Although various taxonomies for describing contextual influences have been set out (see, for example, Argyle et al., 1981; Furnham, 1986; Giles & Hewstone, 1982), it seems useful to discuss contextual influences along two dimensions: *antecedent influences* (those present *prior* to the actual inter-action in context) and *emergent influences* (those *developing during* the encounter). Antecedent variables include participants' cognitive represen-tations of context (e.g., frames, scripts, etc.), their goals, and their consen-sual definitions of the context (i.e., definitions of the actual situation that most members of a group would agree upon). Emergent variables include the text itself, and the interaction between the text and context. We turn now to a fuller discussion of these categories of contextual effects. For purposes of our discussion, the term "situation" refers to the immediate, relatively well-defined social setting, whereas context refers to the more global, abstract representation of particular types of social settings, like "cocktail parties," "political conventions," or "going shopping."

II.   ANTECEDENT CONTEXTUAL INFLUENCES: COGNITIVE REPRESENTATIONS OF CONTEXTUAL KNOWLEDGE

Scripts, Plans and Frames

The problem of how humans acquire, represent, and apply knowledge has intrigued scholars for centuries. In recent years, knowledge representation has become an important issue in the study of human learning and memory. Knowledge representation concerns communication scholars because mes-sage comprehension rests, in part, upon participants' representations of the context (Carswell & Rommetveit, 1971; Forgas, 1978; Garfinkel & Sacks, 1970; Giles & St. Jaques, 1979; Magnusson, 1981a, b; St. Clair & Giles, 1980).

Other scholars, working in Artificial Intelligence, have developed com-puter programs that attempt to model human use of natural language. Through this research, scholars can presumably describe the cognitive processes people use in processing natural languages (Lehnert, 1979). As Lehnert observes, this modeling is difficult because the cognitive processes involved in language skills are inextricably intertwined with the processing and storing of information in general.

Tannen (1981) argues that the notion of "expectation" underlies current research on the structure of knowledge representation (see, for example, research on scripts by Schank & Abelson, 1977; on schemas by Bartlett,

1932; and on frames by Goffmann, 1974, and Minsky, 1975, 1977, 1979). As Tannen (1981) puts it, "based on one's experience of the world in a given culture (or combination of cultures), one organizes knowledge about the world and uses this knowledge to predict interpretations and relationships regarding new information, events, and experiences" (p. 138). Humans represent knowledge about how the world operates in general (i.e., commonsense knowledge) as well as about very specific settings and activities.

Scripts. According to Lehnert (1979), commonsense knowledge about the world is critical for processing language in four different areas: in understanding the communicative context, in using pronominal reference, in completing causal chains, and in establishing focus. Commonsense knowledge bases, Lehnert argues, are represented in scripts, which she defines as conventional situations identified by highly stereotyped sequences of events. As such, they provide a frame of reference for natural language processing. Scripts can be described from different points of view (e.g., from the viewpoint of a waiter as well as that of a consumer in a restaurant script, etc.) and represent both cognitive and behavioral features. While scripts are generalized situational representations (e.g., like eating at a restaurant), a *track* represents a particular version of a script (e.g., like eating in a Greek restaurant).

Scripts depend upon an underlying meaning system that expresses basic events and upon a systematic procedure for selecting scripts (Lehnert, 1979). When discourse covers a broad range of topics, as frequently occurs in ordinary conversation, participants need a mechanism which chooses and coordinates multiple overlapping scripts. The SAM program (Schank, 1979) is capable of handling 20 overlapping scripts, but that is obviously far fewer than humans would typically have. The problem, more simply put, is to explain how participants activate the most *relevant* script(s) for an ongoing interaction. In addition, as participants' roles change in an encounter, different scripts become relevenat.

Plans. Plans may be invoked when there are no clear-cut scripts to follow. A *plan* is a schema underlying intentional action. In interpreting behavior, individuals judge whether or not the performed action fits situational expectations. If the actions seem appropriate, then the script interpretation is confirmed. If participants' expectations are violated, they then try to hypothesize a plan that would treat the performed action as being relevant to some goal. If a goal is being inferred, then individuals also evaluate how well it fits in with the superordinate goal (most global, encompassing goal) in the situation (Wilensky, 1978).

Frames. Minsky (1975) uses the term *frame* to refer to a knowledge structure that represents a stereotyped situation. Frames incorporate typical actions in a given situation, and suggest what to do when expectations are not fulfilled (i.e., default instructions). Frames are hierarchically organized with the most abstract, top-level slots being fixed, while the lower-level slots are variable. For example, the top-level slots in a restaurant script would contain fixed features (like ordering) that are part of *any* restaurant frame. In contrast, the lower-level slots would specify the particular restaurant, the food selection, other participants, etc. for a particular dinner.

Frames can be related to one another and change over time. Frame-systems are a collection of related frames that often have important thematic structures organized around participants' goals. Transformations refer to important actions that may alter frames, such as a shift in emphasis or attention. As we represent ongoing action in frames, they build into ongoing scenarios, which are conceptually rich representations of goal-directed actions.

Applying Scripts, Plans, or Frames in Particular Situations. Given these alternative conceptualizations of contextual knowledge, how do participants activate this knowledge and apply it to their immediate social setting? A number of alternative models for explaining how contextual knowledge is activated have been formulated.

Activating Contextual Knowledge

Lindley (1983) argues that contextual knowledge is activated by information contained in the input text. Once this knowledge is activated, it is able to incorporate new information, both explicit and implicit. She notes that the relationship between contextual knowledge and text interpretation may be conceptualized in three ways. One approach reflects a *syntactic* relationship in which the text's content provides input for a pre-existing structure; an example of this approach is Chomskyan generative grammars. For example, a specific utterance is processed by having its constituent parts fill in pre-existing grammatical slots. A second approach reflects a *semantic* relationship in which the format for text representation is derived from the content of the text; van Dijk's work on macrostructures exemplifies this approach. A text's meaning structure (macrostructures) is built up from the specific propositions found in the text. Finally, the third approach reflects a *pragmatic* relationship in which previously stored knowledge (such as commonsense knowledge or scripts) is used to interpret and represent texts. Although all approaches tacitly acknowledge the others, both syntactic and semantic models deal with fairly restricted texts (Lindley, 1983). Since pragmatic models deal with more flexible texts as well as incorporate contextual influences, they seem most appropriate for describing communicative processes. We now turn to a brief discussion of some pragmatic processing models.

Pragmatic Models of Discourse Processing. Many differences exist among the pragmatic models describing discourse processing. I outline three alternative models here to highlight some critical differences (more models are, of course, available). First, the *bridging hypothesis* of Haviland and Clark (1974) suggests that individuals relate texts to their prior knowledge. During interaction, speakers present new information and relate it to old information, and the listeners relate new information to previously known information.

In contrast, Sanford and Garrod (1981) suggest that the text is broken down on the basis of its verb content and then stored as a set of primitive semantic acts. A text's structure (a scenario) is created during the following process: first, the initial input text is decomposed into semantic primitives; second, the explicit text—its sentences and phrases—is processed; third, acceptable alternative meanings are suggested; and fourth, a topic is produced by processing the initial noun phrase. A series of scenarios are linked by the topic. Primary processing occurs when an input text can be directly mapped onto a scenario. Secondary processing occurs when direct mapping does not occur; then either bridging occurs or a new topic is generated. Both the bridging hypothesis and the scenario model argue that the text serves as input to pre-existing knowledge bases.

A third approach argues that the text is integrated with knowledge bases to produce meaning. This integration is actively constructed by participants. As such, this view contrasts with other models in which the text "slots into" pre-existing frames. Bransford and his colleagues (Bransford & Franks, 1971; Bransford & Johnson, 1972, 1973) suggest that people use linguistic information in constructing semantic descriptions of the situation. People subsequently use that situational description to interpret and recall information. This situational description also contains extralinguistic situational assumptions that are partially based on participants' prior knowledge.

It seems likely that some aspects of text processing involve matching text input against pre-existing knowledge structures. However, since the context is partially determined by the ongoing interaction in an encounter, it also appears that some aspects of discourse processing result from the interplay between the evolving text and context. Discourse processing thus appears to involve static, pre-existing knowledge structures as well as dynamic, developing text and contextual structures. Some communicative contexts may emphasize the static structures rather than the developing structures for discourse processing. For example, very clearly defined contexts, such as legal settings, may rely most heavily upon static, pre-existing knowledge structures for discourse processing. In contrast, the introduction of new technological changes in an office may create entirely new patterns for processing and interpreting discourse.

A relatively recent approach, that of Artificial Intelligence (AI), also models discourse processing. Although AI scholars were initially concerned with modeling how knowledge is represented in memory, some scholars are now beginning to explicitly represent knowledge about how to conduct conversations (Brown, 1984). Knowledge about how to perform particular tasks has also been explicitly modelled since dialogues depends on this type of knowledge.

Artificial Intelligence Processing of Natural Language.   Brown (1984) suggests four basic utterance types in her processing model: *initiators* (determining the main tasks and introducing it); *standard path successors* (outlining the necessary conditions/procedures to complete a task); *recovery discussion* (remedying errors) and *metadiscussion* (clarifying the interpretive process). As can readily be seen, such a model parallels the units of conversational and discourse analysis discussed earlier. For example, initiators could be questions or greetings; standard path successors could be adjacency pairs or a narrative structure; recovery discussion parallels numerous alignment devices, and finally, metadiscussion closely approximates metatalk (or frames, as used by Bateson, 1972).

Information processing is viewed as both a top-down as well as bottom-up process. In top-down processing, one starts with the most global information and works down to finer details; this is primarily a deductive process. In contrast, bottom-up processing is inductive; one starts with a number of specific details and then forms a general conclusion. Considerable debate continues over what processes are involved in particular comprehension tasks (see, for example, Carpenter & Just, 1977; Frederiksen, 1977a, b; Lindley, 1983).

Most AI models incorporate knowledge representation—and these representations typically include a specification of the context. Lindley's experiments (1983) found that text interpretation relied primarily upon commonsense knowledge. She also concludes that three sources of information seem essential in text comprehension: the participants' goals, their relevant knowledge base, and the text itself. Similarly, Kintsch and Kintsch (1978) found that comprehension relies on general schemas and readers' world knowledge. Given the interactive nature of conversation in human interaction (as opposed to the comprehension of a written text by a reader), the pragmatic models, with their emphasis on the *construction* of meaning, seem most useful for human interaction.

A model that incorporates frames and their processing, yet adds other distinctive features, is the situational model of van Dijk and Kintsch (1983).

In addition to commonsense knowledge, scripts, and frames, they suggest that humans need relevant situational knowledge that provides specific, personalized, and detailed representations of situations. We now discuss this model in fuller detail.

Van Dijk and Kintsch's Situational Model.   Situational models provide the experiential basis for scripts and frames (van Dijk & Kintsch, 1983). The situation model

> is an integrated structure of episodic information, collecting previous episodic information about some situation as well as instantiated general information from semantic memory. . . . in discourse comprehension, the situation model should allow updating,. . . . the situation model is different from a frame or script in that it is much more personal, based on one's own experiences, and therefore it will feature all kinds of details. . . . a situation model will mainly be formed—and updated by previous macropropositions (from perception, action or discourse) plus some occasional details. (p. 344)

Thus, situational models provide interactants with relevant, activated knowledge structures that enable them to comprehend discourse. As such, situational models contain both macropropositions (e.g., that identify the social activity going on, like "eating dinner with a friend," etc.) and micropropositions (e.g., that supply specific details, such as which friend you were dining with, where you ate, etc.).

Strategies are also needed to access the situational model. Van Dijk and Kintsch (1983) argue that higher levels of abstracted knowledge are accessed first, and that processing continues until the appropriate level of knowledge representation is reached. They suggest that individuals rely on the following processing strategies:

1. General context dependence—limits semantic searches to the speaker's general cultural context;
2. Actual situation dependence—limits topic search to the situation's general properties;
3. Interaction dependence—decides which topics are functional for the speaker's interactional and pragmatic goals;
4. Discourse type—decides what topics are expected for this interactional context;
5. Referential freedom—decides who can talk about what with reference to the ongoing discourse. (pp. 200–1)

According to van Dijk (1983), situational models thus incorporate naive models of persons, actions, and social situations.

Finally, the actual communicative situation is also represented in the situational model (van Dijk, 1983). The actual communicative situation reflects the *immediate* social setting of the ongoing discourse and includes an assessment of the hearer (e.g., the hearer's level of knowledge, attitudes, goals, etc.). The active communicative situation is thus a *particular type* of situational model and is referred to as the *context* model.

> The context model is also constructed, on-line, during the understanding of the discourse, although language users will of course be able to represent part of it already *before* actual speaking begins. They have presupposed knowledge about *similar* communicative situations, about the same or similar speech participants, or about the same or similar settings or circumstances. . . .
>
> . . . a context model is about the actual fragment of the world constituted by the complex speech event, and hence is a pragmatic and, more generally, an interactional model. (p. 37)

Van Dijk (1983) argues that both text representation and situation models (including the more specific, detailed context model of the actual interaction) need to be integrated. (See Figure 1 for a diagram of situational models).

FIGURE 1

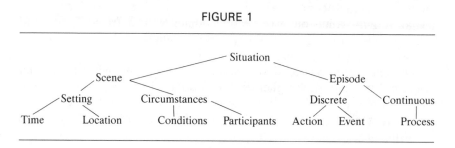

Through the use of the situational model, only *relevant* knowledge is activated for discourse comprehension and production (van Dijk, 1983, 1984). Many of those elements contained in the situational model (see Figure 1) parallel those contextual analyses advocated by other scholars (see, for example, Argyle et al., 1981; Giles & Hewstone, 1982).

Critical Issues in Knowledge Representation

Significant disagreements exist among artificial intelligence scholars and cognitive scientists about the nature of knowledge representation and its use. As noted previously, one important issue concerns the application of models of knowledge representation: some argue they are models for memory representation and thus distinct from actual interpretation of ongoing interaction (Berger, personal communication, 1985). However, others argue that they are used in both storing and processing of information generally (van Dijk, personal communication, 1985; Kintsch, personal communication, 1984; Winograd, 1977).[1] Given the efficiency and economy of the human mind, it seems reasonable to assume that units of knowledge representation—whether scripts or some other format—are used for both storage and ongoing interpretation.

Another disputed issue concerns the power of the claims made by AI researchers. Searle (1982) contrasts strong AI positions with weak AI positions. Strong AI positions claim that the mind is like computer software systems that are self-updating and self-designing. As such, computer simulation is a *replication* of cognitive processes. The weaker AI position is that the analogy between programming computers and cognitive processing is useful, but no stronger claims are made. As Searle puts it, the computer has syntax, but no semantics. The weak AI position has been presented in this chapter since stronger claims, at this point in time, seem unwarranted.

Finally, the work on scripts and frames has been criticized as being unscientific since general principles can be applied only within its narrow conceptualization (Dresher & Hornstein, 1977). Critics suggest that generalization to other areas is not possible. A related issue here is that it is difficult to empirically test among the competing models of knowledge representation. While considerable attention has been given to developing such models, equal attention must now be given to thoroughly testing and evaluating these models. It seems quite plausible that humans use multiple systems of knowledge representation, which vary as a function of the individual's goals, situational constraints, and the task involved.

In summary, models of knowledge representation appear to operate at different levels of abstraction, ranging from global, commonsense knowledge to specific social settings. These knowledge structures are *antecedent* variables because they represent expectations about what we anticipate will occur. However, these knowledge structures must be activated in a particular setting in order to influence the ongoing interaction. In addition, to be activated in a particular setting, these knowledge structures must be *relevant* to the encounter at hand. How to specify *relevant* contextual knowledge is a critical problem for approaches assessing contextual influences in discourse comprehension, particularly because these influences may be indirect and tacit (Cantor, 1981). *Although contextual knowledge is*

---

[1]There is considerable controversy over whether or not the structural features of long-term memory represent the structures used in the active processing of information. There does not seem any clear-cut way to determine this matter. Most scholars appear to *assume* that structures for knowledge representation are the same as those structures used in the processing of information. At a minimum, scholars should carefully articulate their positions on this matter (see, for example, Winograd, 1980 and van Dijk & Kintsch, 1983).

an antecedent influence, it is simultaneously an emergent influence since one's contextual knowledge must be activated and relevant to the ongoing encounter.

There is also the related issue of whether or not the structure for knowledge representation is the same structure used for interpreting discourse. While most scholars carefully state that their models refer only to knowledge representation, the underlying assumption seems to be that representation and interpretation utilize the same knowledge structures. While these and other thorny issues need resolution, nonetheless it is quite clear that contextual knowledge, as represented in scripts, frames, and the like, provide essential information for interpreting interaction.

The previous discussion of context undoubtedly seems very global and abstract, yet these overarching perspectives provide a background for more specific models of social situations. Thus far, the approaches discussed focus primarily on the cognitive structure of knowledge representation and processing. We turn now to social psychological models of context: these models focus on the social dimensions and features that characterize the interactional environment.

III. ANTECEDENT CONTEXTUAL INFLUENCES: SOCIAL PSYCHOLOGICAL APPROACHES TO THE COMMUNICATIVE CONTEXT

The most general model of interactional settings is that provided by Argyle et al. (1981). In their book, *Social Situations,* they outline the "generic" or universal properties of social settings. As such, it provides a very useful guide for the description and analysis of contextual effects on interaction. From this more general model of social setting, research focusing on specific social settings such as doctor/patient settings, therapist/client settings, and legal settings can be examined. Other social psychological approaches focus on particular features of the communicative context. Such approaches have discussed the contrast between perceived vs. actual situations, situational prototypes, and situational/personality interactions. The most specific contextual analysis focuses on social episodes, which are viewed as sequenced, structured social activities which, taken together, constitute an interaction.

The Global Structure of Social Situations. Argyle et al. (1981) outline the structure of social situations. They suggest that the key components of social situations are:

1. *Goals/Purposes* — social situations provide opportunities to accomplish certain goals; goals may vary and change over time as well as

come into conflict with one another; social behavior is governed by goals and thus are critical for understanding social behavior;

2. *Social Rules* — rules (shared beliefs and conventions) regulate and coordinate social behavior; rules prescribe appropriate behavior in a given social situation;

3. *Social Roles* — roles encompass the duties and rights of a particular social position such as father, son, judge, etc.; social roles help accomplish situational goals; are often interdependent;

4. *Repertoire of Elements* — a range of acceptable behaviors (speech acts) in a given social situation;

5. *Sequences of Behavior* — reflects the sequence of actions that must occur; some sequencing may be part of a ritual while others may reflect the order in which sub-tasks must be accomplished;

6. *Situational Concepts* — shared concepts that define the social construction of that situation;

7. *Environmental Setting* — the physical objects present in the social situation; the symbolic aspects of physical objects may have important implications for interaction;

8. *Skills and Techniques* — refers to specific skills that a participant needs in order to function effectively in a given social situation (e.g., good speaking skills for an interviewer, etc.).

These features appear to be important components of a social situation, irrespective of the culture or social group being analyzed. However, the relative importance of each component will undoubtedly vary across cultures, individuals, and tasks.

Perceived Versus Actual Situations.   Another typology of social situations distinguishes between the environment (i.e., context) "as is" and the environment "as perceived" (Magnusson, 1981a, p. 4). The actual environment refers to the physical and biological properties of the environment that are capable of being verified. Actual situations can be measured along several dimensions: complexity, clarity, strength, task, rules, roles, physical settings, participants, and the promotion/restriction of certain behaviors (Magnusson, 1981b). In contrast, the perceived situation—what Magnusson refers to as the person-bound properties of a social situation—includes the participants' goals, expectancies, needs, emotions, and their perceived control of the situation.

Magnusson, like Argyle et al., views goals as underlying the perceived structure of situations. Humans' perception of a specific momentary situation is determined by their "persistent, integrated system of abstractions and conceptions of the world" (Magnusson, 1981b, p. 22). These integrated conceptions determine what situations individuals seek or avoid; what situational characteristics an individual focuses upon, and how those characteristics are interpreted. He concludes that no single taxonomy of situational features is likely to adequately characterize a social situation because different people may construe the same situation in different ways. Simply put, there are marked individual differences in the social construction of reality. (This fact, in addition to the controversial research done in attribution theory, has led many to advocate an interactionist perspective regarding contextual influences. On this view, the most accurate way to predict human behavior is to look for situation-person interactions. We discuss this issue in greater detail later. However, as Magnusson points out, even if one takes an interactionist perspective, one still needs an adequate theory of situation to develop an interactionist position.)

Situational Prototypes. Cantor (1981) focuses on individuals' shared beliefs about the nature of everyday social situations. Humans possess relatively extensive knowledge regarding situations:

> that is, people expect certain kinds of behavior to occur in certain kinds of situations, certain types of people to be found in particular situations, and certain physical and social structures to be encountered in specific situations. (p. 230)

Categorical knowledge about situations is contained within situational prototypes that represent a set of abstract features commonly associated with the situation. To produce situational prototypes, subjects were asked to develop categories for everyday social situations, and then produce prototypes for each category. For example, a "party" is a common everyday social situation and is characterized as being a group activity, being a form of entertainment, etc. These situational prototypes were then analyzed to produce a consensual prototype. That is, the consensual prototype reflected high consensual agreement as to how the prototype was characterized.

Four broad categories of situations were analyzed: *ideological situations* (e.g., being at a religious ceremony), *social situations* (e.g., being at a party), *stressful situations* (e.g., being at an interview) and *cultural situations* (e.g., being at a performing art). Within each category, there were varying levels of specificity: for example, being at a party could be further specified as to the type of party—for example, a birthday party, cocktail party, etc.

Consensual prototypes are produced quite readily and reflected a rich set of beliefs about situational characteristics. Cantor found that the mid-level of detail in situational prototypes reflected the most distinctive situational features and contained fewer redundant features. Typical situations were more easily described than typical persons; this suggests that situational images may be richer than person images (Cantor, Mischel, & Schwartz, 1982).

Cantor suggests that situational knowledge may be used more in planning behavior than in interpreting behavior. For example, one may try to be a "prototypical" person for a particular situation. In interpreting behavior, however, an individual's judgments are made against a background of situational knowledge and thus situational knowledge influences interpretation in an indirect, implicit manner. Techniques for developing situational prototypes offer a very promising line of research for characterizing situational knowledge and evaluating its role in interpreting and planning communicative behavior.

As is readily evident, language itself both determines and reflects situational definitions. Language plays yet another important role in interaction: at both an interpersonal and intergroup level, language is a potent source of attributions (Giles & Hewstone, 1982). In part, attribution research focuses on the interaction between situation and person; these interactions are believed to determine subsequent human behavior. As Furnham (1986) points out, social psychologists have had a strong interest in defining situations because of the debate over trait (personal) versus situational influences on behavior. We are concerned about these attributions because they influence the inferences we make about others during interaction, and those inferences subsequently shape the interaction. We now turn to a review of attribution research and its influence on human communication.

Situation × Person Interaction.   Attribution theory attempts to account for the ways in which people understand and explain behavior. Considerable controversy centers upon the degree to which people attribute behavior to either personality variables (traits) or situational conditions (states). Differences in attribution have also been associated with whether or not they have been made by the actors themselves or observers (Magnusson, 1981b). Magnusson (1981a,b,c) and others argue that the best predictor of subsequent behavior is the interaction of persons and situations. This perspective has been termed the interactionist perspective (Cantor, 1981; Furnham, 1986; Giles & Hewstone, 1982; Magnusson, 1981a,b,c).

The underlying assumptions of the interactionist position are:

1. An individual's behavior influences his/her definition of the situation and situational definitions influence his/her behavior; their inter-relationships are bi-directional in nature.
2. The individual actor is purposeful;
3. Individual actors are influenced by cognitive and motivational factors; and

4. The psychological meaning of the situation is important.
(Ekehammar, 1974; Endler & Magnusson, 1976)

Generally, the interactionist view emphasizes an actor's goals in a given context.

In their analysis of how social knowledge is organized, Cantor, Mischel and Schwartz (1982) emphasize the categorical, prototypical knowledge of the person-in-situation. This prototypical knowledge reflects the typical dispositional and behavioral characteristics of a normal actor in that context. People share rich, consensual, categorical knowledge about how individuals typically behave in diverse situations. Finally, they argue that actors' goals strongly influence their perception and construal of the social world.

Actors' representations of social knowledge are also economical, ordered, and consensual. In a series of experiments, Cantor et al. found that subjects' knowledge of situations was substantial, varied, easily accessible, orderly, efficient, and provided useful guidelines for generating social behavior. They conclude by observing that concern over the routinized sequences of behavior may have undervalued the importance of situational knowledge. Situational knowledge appears to be a significant influence both in immediate social behavior and in introspection.

Cohen (1981) notes that situations provide informational inputs for people, and that their effect on behavior depends on how those situations are perceived. She also argues for the bidirectional, interactive influence of person and situation. Finally, Cohen notes that the lack of awareness of situational influences may be genuine inaccessibility or the perceiver's tendency to ignore appropriate cues.

In his overview of attribution research, Monson (1981) concludes that one's behavior will be attributed to situational factors if actions (1) are easily justified, (2) occur frequently, and (3) occur in the context of sufficient situational cues. The well-known attribution error, in which people attribute their own behavior to situational factors and others' behavior to personality factors, is also discussed. Monson (1981) points out that actors and observers base their attributions on different types of information. For example, different motives and different environmental features may be salient to actors as opposed to observers. Finally, some traits may be cross-situationally relevant (e.g., friendliness) while other traits are not (e.g., anger). It seems clear that, regardless of the causes to which one attributes behavior, a clear theory of situations is needed, especially if we are to advocate an interactionist perspective (Magnusson, 1981a,b,c).

Another significant approach views context in terms of its underlying dimensions. These approaches assume that any context can be described in terms of a set of underlying dimensions that apply to any context. In contrast to the situation × person interactionist approach, this approach focuses on universal aspects of situations, rather than their diversity and their relationship to participants' characteristics.

Dimensions of Social Situations. A number of scholars advocate a dimensional approach to situations, in which the underlying qualities of social situations are characterized (Furnham, 1986). Wish, Deutsch, and Kaplan (1976) found that the following social dimensions underlie different social events and social roles: friendly/hostile, cooperative/competitive, intense/superficial, equal/unequal, informal/formal, and task-oriented/non-task-oriented. Block and Block (1981) suggest that there are eleven underlying features that define the typical nature of situations: structure, convergence, divergence (the possibility of multiple solutions), evaluation, feedback, constraints, malleability (changeableness), impedance, galvanization (attractiveness), familiarity, and differentiation (complexity). These models attempt to capture the central features of situations and thus provide a basis for situational comparisons.

The difficulty, of course, is being certain that *all relevant features* are captured. In addition, how would such approaches deal with potential cross-cultural differences? Forgas (1983) argues that a relatively small number of connotative dimensions—self-confidence, intimacy, evaluation, and formality—implicitly serve as a basis for perceiving situations across different cultures. (It should be noted, however, that all of the cultures tested were Western). In contrast, Detweiler, Brislin, and McCormack (1983) found significant cross-cultural differences in students' descriptions of different situations. The student's culture significantly influenced the descriptor terms being used and the situations being described.

What are the implications of having different situational definitions? Forgas (1983) suggests that interaction may be more difficult when participants have different situational definitions. Argyle et al. (1981) suggest that situational definitions influence the choice of situational rules and the required social skills. In addition, Furnham (1986) notes that intergroup communication depends upon some degree of shared knowledge representations. Finally, since language itself plays a powerful role in describing and interpreting situations, participants speaking different languages may have added difficulty in defining the communicative situation. As Giles and Hewstone (1982) point out, "linguistic cues provide powerful cues for the definition of the situation, and the nature of attributions in that situation" (p. 27).

Thus far, we have looked at some cognitive and social psychological approaches that characterize participants' contextual knowledge. Cognitive approaches emphasize the knowledge structures representing the context, whereas social psychological approaches emphasize the social criteria that individuals use to understand situated action. Both approaches emphasize the importance of participants' goals: goals help organize participants' knowledge structures, and direct their actions. From the standpoint of AI research, goals are viewed as desired outcomes of a planned sequence of activity. In contrast, psychological models of goals refer to participants' motives or purposes—their reasons for their behavior. We now turn to a more specific discussion of participants' goals and their influence on interaction.

IV. ANTECEDENT CONTEXTUAL INFLUENCES: PARTICIPANTS' GOALS

Action Theory and Goals.   Action theory assumes that people plan a course of action that is consistent with fulfilling a goal (Nowakowska, 1981). Thus, action is defined as a process of goal-directed mental activity. Multiple goals may be undertaken simultaneously, and multiple actions may also be simultaneously performed (Sjoberg, 1981). Any situation establishes a participant's obligations and rights to act, and thus some constraints on actions are implied in any situational definition. Because of these constraints, actions vary in their effectiveness and force. In addition, actions are limited by the interactants' goals. Bower (1982) found that goals were most important in understanding social episodes, and the greater distance (i.e., lack of relatedness) between actions and goals, the greater the difficulty in understanding the ongoing interaction. Generally, then, any situation can usefully be described in terms of the goals that are facilitated or prohibited in that situation.

Parisi and Castelfranchi (1981) have developed a goal-centered action theory of conversation. Conversation itself requires that speakers and hearers adopt at least one goal of the other—there must be enough mutual cooperation so that a conversation can occur. Goals are viewed as social and communicative if they require a hearer knowing and adopting them. For example, my goal might be to get another participant to answer questions. Finally, they suggest that conversational cohesion is a function of the common goals among participants and is continually negotiated during the interaction. As can be seen, then, conversation offers participants an opportunity to achieve their goals, and is itself a goal-directed action requiring coordination with others.

Social Psychological Approaches to Goal-Directed Behavior.   Graham, Argyle, and Furnham (1980) suggest that participants' goals are a focal point around which other situational features are organized. Like action theorists, they argue that individuals participate in situations to accomplish their goals and frequently have multiple goals they wish to accomplish.

Participants' goals may be independent, may be compatible with one another, or may interfere with one another. According to their research, the major goals participants wished to achieve were: to be accepted, to convey information, to help another, to dominate others, to have fun, to reduce anxiety, or to seek advice. Of these goals, the three superordinate goals appear to be (1) social acceptance; (2) establishing one's own well-being; and (3) accomplishing a specific situational goal.

In both action theory and social psychological approaches, participants' goals play a key role in interpreting situations. While most scholars assume that interaction is purposive and goal-directed, many do not emphasize goals to the same degree as do the two approaches outlined above. Both of these approaches, quite rightly, emphasize the situated nature of goals—and the fact that we enter into situations to accomplish goals.

In summary, the antecedent variables thus far discussed influence participants' construal of the social situation *prior* to their actual participation in a specific social setting. As such, they "set the scene" and help interactants interpret the behavior of others as well as plan their own actions. This antecedent contextual knowledge varies in generality and abstraction, ranging from accounts of commonsense knowledge to participants' goals. Participants' contextual knowledge, however, can be modified and changed as a result of the interaction itself. Two emergent variables, the text itself and the interaction between the text and prior contextual knowledge, serve to further define the social context. We turn now to an analysis of these emergent influences.

V. EMERGENT CONTEXTUAL INFLUENCES: THE TEXT AND ITS INTERACTION WITH THE CONTEXT

Hasan (nd) discusses the relationship between the text and context by first observing that situations can be meaningfully interpreted by several distinct codes—by both verbal and/or nonverbal codes. The context may determine the text by prescribing the permitted range of message forms. During any interaction, text and context evolve concurrently and each subsequent message contributes to what is being accomplished. She suggests that changing the definition of the context requires face-to-face interaction; such changes are most likely to occur in situations where the social distance between interactants is reduced and where the context is somewhat ambiguous. Finally, Hasan notes that the interactions between text and context appear to vary as a result of the participants' social relationships and the nature of the task.

How the Text Signals the Context

The language used in a text reflects social structure as well as simultaneously creates such structure (Mead, 1934). Through interaction, new meanings emerge and influence subsequent behavior. As Brittan (1973) cogently states:

> Episodic encounters can only be structured and men's purposes laid bare by the mutuality of symbolic response. In a sense, therefore, we can argue that the grammar of sociation is really symbolic discourse; talk, conversation, dramatic confrontation, the playing of games, the attribution of motives, the definition of situation, the reifying of social constructs, are all contained in, and manifested by, the way men relate to each other by employing rhetorical and symbolic devices. . . . Talk can be construed as being representative and prototypical of all social behaviour. . . . In each episode or encounter that we engage in, we find that the situation is partially structured by past definition; it has already been defined in terms of role scripts and normative expectations. *At the same time, the episode is always open; it is subject to reinterpretation and the attendant possibility of the creation of new accounts and meanings.* (pp. 83–84; italics mine)

We shall examine two approaches that discuss how the context is reflected in the text: speech markers and Gumperz' contextualization cues.

Situational Speech Markers.   Furnham (1986), in his review of situational influences on intergroup communication, focuses on situation-specific linguistic features. First, language choice itself is determined by a range of social and situational factors. Some factors influencing language choice are (1) the social domain of activity (e.g., using one's native language in homes but a "host" or national language for formal discussions); (2) the desire to express group identity through using a specific language; (3) language tolerance; (4) the formality of the social setting; and (5) the private or public nature of the setting (see, for example, Giles & Hewstone, 1982).

Second, Furnham discusses the medium in which messages are sent (e.g., face-to-face, television, telephone, etc.). Furnham (1982) found that the choice of a medium is influenced by two important situational factors, the public/private and the open/closed nature of the interaction. People choose a medium and situation that will facilitate message comprehension. For example, some ritualized situations convey certain types of information— the business luncheon, courtroom, church, etc. Craik (1981) found that the medium used to present a situation influenced observer's perceptions and judgments of that situation.

Finally, Furnham notes that how the situation is construed affectively—whether stressful, relaxing, hostile or the like—influences the accent, expressiveness, speed, and volume of speech. It seems clear, as Giles and Hewstone (1982) point out, that language serves as a powerful cue in defining situations. Individuals have a variety of communicative strategies available to them, and their social relationships with other participants and the structure of the social situation influence their choice of a communicative strategy (Giles & Hewstone, 1982).

Brown and Fraser (1979) suggest that the communicative strategies create as well as signal situational definitions. Settings are arranged along value dimensions like public/private, serious/trivial, open/closed, and high/low cultural features. These value dimensions determine the form and content of the subsequent interaction. In addition, they argue that the participants' social relationships are constrained by the context. One's occupational role, for example, may govern language choice.

Brown and Fraser conclude that communicative strategies covary with social relationships and social situations. As such, *communication is a central, defining feature of reality*. It provides us with information about how others are construing the situation. In addition, communication can produce changes in the participants' perception of the situation, their status and their roles (Giles & Hewstone, 1982). Giles and Hewstone (1982) offer a number of propositions that reflect the interrelationship between text (speech or communicative strategies) and situation (context):

1. Speech can initially define situations when norms are ambiguous or two sets of norms could apply.
2. Situational definitions are more likely to occur and be accepted when given by a high status person.
3. Redefinitions of situations may occur when a high status person is established and at ease; when a high status person is threatened or goals are not met; when a low status person thinks that status has been unfairly distributed and desires a change, and when people are made more predictable.
4. Speech is more salient as a situation-defining cue if other constraints are obstacles to definition and redefinition.

Thus, in a myriad of ways, speech marks situational definitions and interpersonal relationships. While it is not possible to review the voluminous literature in this area, hopefully these overviews have highlighted the role of speech in construing situations.[2]

In an interpersonal context, as opposed to a group context, Giles (1979) highlights the importance of speech in impression management. Speech style differences occur as a result of age (Golinkoff, 1983; Haslett, 1985b); sex (Kramarae, 1981); social class (Bernstein, 1973, 1977); social relationships (Berger & Bradac, 1982) and a host of other variables. (These variables are discussed more completely in Chapter 8).

Gumperz' Contextualization Cues.   Another model of context-as-marked-by-text is provided by the work of John Gumperz and his associates (1981, 1982). Gumperz (1982) suggests that conversational inferences are based upon background contextual assumptions, interactants' goals, and their relationships with one another. On the basis of these inferences, interactants are able to make situated interpretations. Gumperz criticizes the research on scripts and frames as having ignored the negotiated, situated nature of interpretation. In addition, he notes that conversational analysts ignore the linguistic bases of interaction and assume shared common

---

[2]When a group interacts, individuals engage in social identification processes as well as construct their own personal view of the social situation (Tajfel, 1978). When most members of a group view the interaction primarily as an *intergroup* encounter, the more they tend to separate themselves from the perceived outgroup (Tajfel & Turner, 1979). People desire to view their group membership positively, and much of Tajfel's work has been assessing how groups differentiate themselves psychologically from other groups (Tajfel, 1978; Turner & Giles, 1981). Giles and Hewstone (1982) argue that since speech style is an important aspect of group identity, especially for age, class and ethnic categories (Giles, 1977), more research needs to be done on the correlations between speech markers and intergroup identification.

A variety of factors facilitate intergroup differences such as: the perceived status of the groups relative to each other (Tajfel, 1978); beliefs as to which groups was favored by varying socio-structural factors (Bourhis, Giles, & Rosenthal, 1981) and the extent to which the speaker perceives himself/herself as possessing high status in the group (Giles & Johnson, 1981). Giles and Hewstone (1982) also point out that construing a situation as an intergroup situation may also influence the attributions made about that situation or participants in the situation.

In addition, van Dijk and his colleagues have developed a socio-cognitive theory about the organization of ethnic representations in memory and the expression of these ethnic views in conversational interaction (van Dijk, 1983, 1984). Van Dijk (1983) suggests that prejudice is cognitively represented by negative ethnic group schemata; these schemata provide the basis for biased situational models. These biased situational models, in turn, serve as the basis for interaction. In interviews, interviewees often told stories about their experiences with ethnic groups (these narratives reflect part of their situational models for the particular ethnic groups) and typically these stories had no resolution. The lack of resolution appears to reflect frustration in dealing with other ethnic groups because resolution of different values is perceived as not being possible.

These studies reflect some of the diverse ways in which speech is used in the process of evaluating others.

background knowledge. Gumperz' model, focusing on *contextualization cues,* overcomes the deficiencies of both conversational analysis and discourse analysis (scripts, frames, etc.).

Gumperz argues that linguistic knowledge and sociocultural knowledge need to be shared for conversations to occur. Only then can participants specify the conversational inferences that enable them to make culturally and situationally specific interpretations. Gumperz (1982) defines a contextualization cue as

> any feature of linguistic form that contributes to the signalling of contextual presuppositions. Such cues may have a number of such linguistic realizations depending on the historically given linguistic repertoire of the participants. The code, dialect and style switching processes, some of the prosodic phenomena we have discussed as well as choice among lexical and syntactic options, formulaic expressions, conversational openings, closings and sequencing strategies can all have similar contextualizing functions. Although such cues carry information, meanings are conveyed as part of the interactive process. (p. 131)

Thus, contextualization cues are sets of surface features of a text that enable participants to understand the ongoing activity, to interpret semantic content, and to interrelate utterances. These cues are habitually used, but are implicit and rarely discussed. Contextualization cues, in short, enable interactants to make situated interpretations by emphasizing relevant information through the use of particular linguistic forms.

Contextualization cues are part of the emerging text (conversation) produced in an interaction. Such cues are learned through interaction with others in well-defined social settings. If interactants agree on the use of contextualization cues, the interaction proceeds smoothly and the cues are taken for granted. If, however, the contextualization cues are not mutually shared, then differing interpretations and misunderstandings may occur.

The underlying assumption of Gumperz' model is that different potential interpretations are possible in an encounter. Contextualization cues enable participants to be aware of possible interpretations that may occur, especially when interacting with others having different ethnic backgrounds. These cues, of course, exist on multiple levels and may be nonverbal as well as verbal. As Gumperz notes, different languages may have different sets of contextualization cues and the same cues may be weighted differently by different cultures.

Gumperz' model thus highlights the situated nature of conversational interpretation: contextualization cues enable participants to make the appropriate conversational inferences (i.e., those intended by the speaker). Contextualization cues thus activate relevant background knowledge needed to interpret ongoing interaction and focus on the linguistic means for signalling what the intended uptake should be. From previous interactions, we have linguistic knowledge that enables us to associate styles of speaking with contextual presuppositions. As Gumperz (1982) remarks

> All participants must be able to fit individual contributions into some overall theme roughly corresponding to a culturally identifiable activity, or a combination of these, and agree on relevant behavioral norms. They must recognize and explicitly or implicitly conform to others' expectations and show that they can participate in shifts in focus by building on others' signals in making their own contributions. . . .

> the conversational inference processes we have discussed. . . . requires first of all judgements of of expectedness and then a search for an interpretation that makes sense in terms of what we know from past experience and what we have perceived. We can never be certain of the ultimate meaning of any message, but by looking at systematic patterns in the relationship of perception of surface cues to interpretation, we can gather strong evidence for the social basis of contextualization conventions and for the signalling of communicative goals. (pp. 163, 170)

VI. CONCLUDING REMARKS

As can be seen, a very rich conceptualization of the communicative context has developed in a variety of disciplines. The communicative context, at its most general, abstract level, reflects participants' commonsense knowledge, which includes more specific, detailed areas of knowledge such as cultural knowledge, knowledge about societal institutions, knowledge about social settings, and so forth. Still more fine-grained analysis is possible if we focus on a specific social encounter. The communicative context is also defined by the text, and the goals of the interactants. Thus a multi-level, complex analysis of context is possible.

In addition to analyzing context according to macro or micro-level concerns, useful distinctions are also provided when viewing these contextual approaches as antecedent or emergent influences. Commonsense knowledge, knowledge of cultural conventions for particular social situations, situational prototypes, and goals provide significant background knowledge for participants in the interaction. Given this background contextual knowledge, participants are able to anticipate the nature of the upcoming encounter. It is against this contextual knowledge that a particular encounter is evaluated, with each encounter having a unique social setting and text.

It should be noted, however, that the antecedent and emergent variables interact with one another. The actual interaction may alter participants' contextual knowledge and their subsequent interpretations of the ongoing encounter. Thus contextual influences are *bi-directional:* the context shapes the interaction that occurs within it, yet may itself be transformed by that interaction.

Various aspects of contextual knowledge undoubtedly interact with one another, although relatively little is known about such interrelationships. Participants' characteristics, such as sex and status, are related to particular speech styles. The interactionist perspective deals with the situation × person interrelationships, with some success in predicting subsequent behavior. However, the range of mutual influences needs greater exploration. How do participants' goals influence their choice of communicative strategies? How does modifying situational prototypes alter subsequent communicative behavior, if at all? For a fuller understanding of contextual influences, it seems clear that such interrelationships need to be thoroughly explored.

Some Unresolved Problems.   Although substantial insight into the nature and influence of contextual knowledge has been developed, serious problems remain unresolved. First, more research needs to be done on naturally occuring encounters in real-life situations (Craik, 1981; Magnusson, 1981b; Sjoberg, 1981). In these situations, the consequences of one's actions have definite impact—one loses a job, gains a friend, totally misjudges a situation and is subsequently embarrassed, etc. Second, the parameters of a social situation may be extremely difficult to establish (Craik, 1981; Magnusson, 1981a,c). The boundaries of time, action, attention (i.e., what is the focus of attention and what is peripheral), and an interactant's degree of participation are complex issues to resolve. Third, the interrelationships between particular contextual features and the actual discourse produced need to be explored (Brown, 1983, 1984). Fourth, individuals vary in their awareness of situations and in their perceived control over the situation— both factors seem critical in modeling any situational influences (Cantor, 1981; Langer, 1978, 1983). Fifth, the fact that multiple goals can be simultaneously accomplished in a setting needs to be adequately accounted for. This becomes even more complex when one realizes, from a communicative perspective, that different utterances can achieve the same effect and that the same utterance, in different contexts, can have different effects.

Finally, the concept of relevance needs to be given much more attention in models of contextual influences. What aspects of actual situations are relevant to one's perceived situational construct? What aspects of common-sense knowledge become relevant in various contexts, and with what effect? Why are some aspects of the situation relevant for some participants, but not for others? These are some critical issues that need to be addressed.

Despite these complexities, our understanding of contextual influences has clearly grown. One very promising line of research appears to lie in detailed analyses of specific types of situations and the communicative encounters that occur within these settings. Research on legal settings (Atkinson & Drew, 1979), doctor/patient relationships (Labov & Fanschel, 1977) and interviews (Erickson & Shultz, 1982) have incorporated detailed situational analyses and related them to communicative behavior occurring in those contexts.

Other scholars are calling for a synthesis of research perspectives focusing on contextual influences (Brittan, 1973; Gumperz, 1982; Haslett, 1986a,b; Perinbanayagam, 1974). Discourse analysts, focusing upon frames and scripts, fail to account for participants' joint negotiation of identity and meaning in their interactions. Dramaturgical models limit actors to scripts that are supported by particular scenes and likewise ignore meanings emerging from the interplay between the text and context (Perinbanayagam, 1974). Conversational analysts utilize a very immediate, limited conceptualization of context. Participants' contextual knowledge appears to be taken-for-granted in conversational analysis, rather than being mutually established by interactants. The interactive context is provided by the rights and obligations of speakers and listeners in their encounters (Drew, personal communication). As such, the context is a universal component of conversation operating for members of a particular culture. While this may not be a critical problem when interactants are members of the same social group, it clearly is a major source of misunderstanding and mishearing in cross-cultural communication where such shared contextual knowledge cannot be assumed.

A Suggested Unit of Contextual Analysis.   In view of the complex issues discussed, a synthesis of approaches presented here appears to be the most adequate conceptualization of context. What might such a synthesis look like? I believe this synthesis should contain at least three elements. The minimal unit of contextual analysis should incorporate: (1) a cognitive representation of the perceived social situation; (2) the goals of the participants; and (3) the actual text in the encounter, including both verbal and nonverbal messages. The emphasis of this analytic unit is on participants' knowledge and their goals as they mutually interact in context. All the varied perspectives discussed in this chapter touch upon these core features, although they may emphasize one feature over another.

Several assumptions support this analytic unit. First, knowledge representation, participants' goals, and the text interact and influence one another in multiple ways. Second, alternative construals of the perceived social situation may exist, but they usually have some consensual agreement. That is, any alternative construal must be a *plausible* account of that situation when judged by other members of the same cultural group. Alternative construals must also be *relevant* to participants in the situation. Construals that are plausible but irrelevant will not be acceptable situational interpretations of that context. These construals, of course, emphasize the normative and consensual aspects of context. While individual differences obviously exist, contextual models are generally insensitive to them.

Thirdly, this model presupposes a cooperative basis for action. When participants suspect others of being deceitful, uncooperative, or in conflict, the contextual analysis outlined here will focus on participants' goals. In these circumstances, participants may change their evaluations of ongoing action in appropriate ways. In cooperative contexts, there is enormous social force to maintain face and thus to act in predictable, socially acceptable ways.

Approaches outlined in this chapter have continually referred to the idea of relevance. For example, information must be relevant to the situation, individuals judge actions according to their relevance to some goal, and so forth. Relevance appears to be a key concept in virtually every pragmatic approach, whether it is a cognitive or social psychological approach, or a structural, functional, or contextual model. In the next chapter, I outline a descriptively adequate basis for the study of verbal communication in which relevance plays a key role. In addition, the antecedent and emergent contextual influences are integrated into a process-oriented model of communication.

AN INTEGRATED
PERSPECTIVE ON
HUMAN COMMUNICATION

6 An Integrated Perspective on Human Communication

As disciplines evolve, they generally develop specialized sub-areas of inquiry; communication, as a discipline, has been no exception. While in-depth knowledge in a given discipline develops rapidly in this way, what may be sacrificed is an overall perspective. That is, what may be sacrificed is understanding communicative processes in general, and the relationships among particular areas of specialization.

The synthesis attempted here is broader in scope than most analyses of communication, and as such, it complements studies focusing on particular areas of specialization. Communication itself is the process which enables humans to cooperate, to coordinate actions, and to come into conflict with one another. Communication occurs in many diverse settings, accommodates multiple tasks, and varies as a function of individual needs and cultural style. Such complexity and richness can only be fully discerned within a broad, integrative, analytic framework.

A pragmatic approach to communication, grounded in the study of language use in context, can provide such an integrated framework. Since language itself, as a symbolic system, underlies every act of verbal communication, whether spoken or written, an approach emphasizing language use in context can provide continuity and integration over a diverse range of communicative processes. In addition, nonverbal and verbal systems of communication appear to be interrelated and complement one another (Beattie, 1981; Bull, 1983; Duncan & Fiske, 1977; Goodwin, 1981). In fact, some nonverbal scholars, like Hall (1969) and Birdwhistell (1970) have developed models of nonverbal communication that are based upon linguistic models. Thus, a pragmatic approach provides an added advantage in that it can integrate aspects of nonverbal communication with verbal communication. In sum, a pragmatic approach provides a comprehensive overarching framework for the study of human communication in general, as well as provides clarity and integration in the study of verbal communication.

Although the level of abstraction at which I am proceeding glosses over some differences among the various pragmatic views already discussed, nevertheless these views share important common underlying assumptions. These common underlying dimensions—that communication is inferential, interpretive, varies as a function of context, and the like—were set out in Chapter 1. Some views emphasize one set of underlying assumptions while others emphasize a somewhat different set; however, these shared underlying assumptions nevertheless provide a basis for the study of human communication.

Given the complexity of human communication, many scholars suggest that communication requires multi-faceted, complex, interactive theories for adequate explanation (see M.P. Atkinson, 1981 and Levinson, 1983 for excellent discussions of this point). For example, structuration (a new approach to social science theory construction developed by Giddens, 1982) would allow, in principle, for multiple perspectives within some overarching analytic framework. In addition, different explanatory models and methods of analysis may be required by different problem areas. These considerations suggest that multi-faceted, multiple theories, supported by an overarching pragmatic frame of reference and by diverse methods of analysis, could adequately describe the complexity of human verbal communication.

The synthesis being developed here, I hope, will provide an initial step toward a descriptively adequate basis for the study of verbal communication. This descriptive base must precede any theory construction. In what follows, I rely on the well-known pragmatic concepts of text, context, and language user in setting out a descriptively adequate basis for studying verbal communication. To focus on the process of communication, communication is viewed as *social action,* and I apply action theory to communicative processes. This is not a new application, since action theory frameworks are directly or indirectly implicated in many of the pragmatic approaches discussed in this book—see, for example, the work of van Dijk, Searle, and conversational analysts. For purposes of our discussion here, as elsewhere, it is assumed that speaker/hearers possess normal mastery of the language system itself, and that they are cognitively and neurologically unimpaired.

I. TOWARD A DESCRIPTIVELY ADEQUATE BASIS FOR ANALYZING COMMUNICATION

In developing a descriptively adequate model of verbal communication, I specify a set of influential communicative variables; outline the process by which these variables interact with one another during communication; and finally, develop the concept of relevance. The communicative variables are grouped in terms of whether they are pre-interactional influences, influences that emerge during ongoing interaction, and/or post-interaction influences. The communicative processes developed here emphasize the importance of participants' goals and knowledge in their interactions. Relevance, it is argued, provides an essential link among text, context, and language user; as such, it is a key feature in discourse production and comprehension.

Communicative Variables

From our preceding discussion, it should be readily apparent that human communication can be assessed on multiple levels and from diverse perspectives. Despite this complexity, communicative variables can be clustered in terms of whether they are textual, contextual, or participant variables. However, this is a relatively static view of a very dynamic, continuous process. To highlight the process of communication, I would like to cluster communicative variables in terms of whether they are pre-interaction influences, influences during interaction, and/or post-interaction influences.

Prior to any interaction, participants develop culturally-determined expectations concerning communication and how to appropriately interact with others in varied settings. These expectations as well as the interactant's goals are pre-interaction influences since they represent an interactant's pre-existing knowledge. During the interaction itself, participants' expectations, knowledge, and goals are activated and influence the on-going interaction.

Post-interaction influences affect communication in two distinct ways. First, participants may re-evaluate and re-interpret prior interactions. Interpretations are hypotheses about what is going on, and are *always subject to continual confirmation or disconfirmation*. Second, the recasting of particular encounters and their outcomes itself serves as the context for future interactions. For example, if I experience unpleasant encounters with a particular person, I may have a negative attitude toward any future interaction with that individual. (See especially Duck, 1983 and Hinde, 1981 for discussion of this point in regard to interpersonal skills and relationships.)

It should be clearly kept in mind that any analytic units (communicative variables) are heuristic devices—"idealizations" in some form—which help clarify the process of human communication. In actual communication events, however, these analytic units are fluid, dynamic, and changeable; variables interact with one another and are themselves transformed by this process. In what follows, we examine each cluster of communicative variables more closely. (For an overview of the approach being taken here, see Figures 1 and 2.)

Pre-Interaction Variables

Pre-interaction variables represent the *relevant knowledge base* and goals that participants bring to bear on the ongoing interaction. We discuss each of these in turn.

1. Relevant Knowledge Base.   The relevant knowledge base of participants reflects their general knowledge of context, text, and interaction processes. More specifically, this general knowledge includes:

A. *Commonsense knowledge* —As specified by Schutz (1964), Garfinkel (1967a, b) and others, commonsense knowledge reflects ordinary social practices in a particular society. This commonsense knowledge is grounded in the reality principle; that is, we interpret events in light of our real-world experiences (Clark & Clark, 1977).
B. *Cultural knowledge* —Cultural knowledge reflects the deep-seated cultural values of a society; accepted in varying degrees by differing subcultural groups (i.e., I refer here to belief and value structures surrounding causation, the supernatural, the relationship between humans and nature, and the like).
C. *Interactional knowledge* —Interactional knowledge reflects cultural practices and norms for interaction in different organizations, institutions, social settings, and among groups of participants. This knowledge may also be represented by scripts, frames, routines, and the like, which reflect action and interaction sequences that accomplish a particular goal, like ordering food in a restaurant.
D. *Linguistic knowledge* —Linguistic knowledge reflects knowledge of grammatical, semantic, and pragmatic principles that govern use of a given language.

From these four types of knowledge about how interactions are carried out within a given culture, participants derive a *relevant knowledge base.* Through focusing on their interactional goals, participants select, from their general knowledge of interaction, knowledge *relevant to accomplishing their conversational goals in particular settings.* Relevant knowledge thus includes (1) more detailed knowledge of the immediate social situation;

Pre-Interaction Variables	Interaction Variables	Post-Interaction Variables
Commonsense Knowledge/Tacit Knowledge Consists of: Practical reasoning Cultural norms and values (regarding organizations, institutions and individuals) Interactional knowledge Linguistic knowledge → Using the principle of relevance, determined partially by past experience and knowledge, goals in the interaction and knowledge of the other participants (if available) participants construct a *Relevant Knowledge Base.* → *Relevant Knowledge Base for Interaction (RKB)* Consists of potential frames of interpretation to be activated by the text and immediate social context of interaction: context-centered, goal-driven relevant knowledge	*IMMEDIATE SOCIAL/ PHYSICAL SETTING* *Interactant A* *TEXT** *Interactant B* RKB > Verbal ↙ RKB Goals Nonverbal Goals Interaction Interaction Skills** Skills Affect*** Affect	*Consists of the responses* interactants make to one another; goal achievement and short-term/long-term effects on their social relationship with one another

*Verbal text features would include topics, lexical items, deictic elements, presuppositions, entailment, implicature, accountability practices (like turn-taking, pre-sequences, etc.) and speech markers, like honorifics and so forth.

**Interaction skills would reflect features like communication apprehension, specially required skills such as those in interviewing, cross-examination and the like which are required in certain professions or settings, any communicative disfluencies such as stuttering, etc.

***Affect reflects the attitude (positive, negative, etc.) of an interactant toward the context and participants—for example, a participant may like the other participant but feel very negative about the context of interaction and the topics discussed.

FIGURE 2
A Process Model of Communication

Time 1

Interactant A		Interactant B
RKB		RKB
Goals		Goals
Inter. Skills		Inter. Skills
Affect		Affect

↘   ↙

TEXT*

Time 2

↙   ↘

Interactant A		Interactant B
RKB'		RKB'
Goals'		Goals'
Inter. Skills'		Inter. Skills'
Affect'		Affect'

↘   ↙

TEXT'

Time 3

(Cycle of interaction repeated, with new RKBs being produced, and potential changes occuring in interactants' goals, exercise of interactional skills and their affect)

---

*The initial text being considered here is a three-turn unit, rather than the more standard single utterance or standard utterance-response unit. Initially, the speaker makes an utterance s/he thinks is maximally relevant to his/her goal. The listener makes her/his response, on the basis of his/her projected interpretation of what the speaker meant by what was said. It is *only* upon the speaker's next utterance — the third turn — that some evaluation of the projected interpretations is rendered. That is, the speaker can confirm, reject or alter the listener's projected interpretation as *displayed* by his/her response. I would argue that this occurs even in instances in which there are only two utterances — the third evaluative turn, in those instances, is *signalled nonverbally* (e.g., head nod, silence, going on about the task at hand, etc. — no further discussion, at that moment, is required). After this initial three-turn sequence, each subsequent response adds new information to the RKB and thus influences subsequent interpretations. Thus, utterances have both a retrospective character (i.e., they reshape past interpretations) and a prospective character (i.e., certain options for future action become preferred options).

In general, then, it can be said that the *process* of communication is one of *generating hypotheses* (both speakers and hearers make inferences about what they think may occur in any interaction); *hypothesis testing* (both speakers and hearers make inferences on the basis of what is actually said and make their own remarks on that basis as well) and finally, *hypothesis confirmation* (both speakers and hearers have their respective interpretations confirmed or disconfirmed by the unfolding text produced in interaction).

120

(2) knowledge of the larger social context within which the immediate social situation is embedded; (3) knowledge of standard interpretive practices in a given social setting, including both verbal and nonverbal practices; (4) knowledge of likely goals that can be accomplished in that particular social setting; and (5) knowledge of the specific participants involved.

This relevant knowledge base is a more detailed, specific subset of general knowledge: it is goal-directed, context-centered, and applies to specific social situations and participants. Specialized knowledge about participants incorporates the influence of social relationships among participants, as well as cultural differences. For example, if both participants have an enduring social relationship with one another—such as a long-term friendship—the specialized knowledge provided by the relevant knowledge base is particularized and adapted to that relationship. However, if the interactants are members of different cultures, then specialized knowledge of the other may consist only of stereotypes of the other's culture, or each may simply react to the other as a human being (Schutz' most general level of knowledge of others). From their relevant knowledge bases, participants develop a general set of hypotheses about how they expect the interaction to proceed; these hypotheses serve as frames of interpretation for the present encounter and guide future actions.

Let me briefly demonstrate the difference between a *general* knowledge base and a *relevant* knowledge base. Suppose that you are a North American businesswoman who has been invited to a cocktail party by your superior. Your *general* knowledge base for cocktail parties reveals that polite behavior is expected (commonsense knowledge); that North American cocktail parties are used for social as well as business reasons (cultural knowledge); that a diverse range of topics can be discussed, from business to personal topics, but personal topics should not be overly serious or overly personal (interactional knowledge for the context of cocktail parties); and, finally, that formal language will be used (linguistic knowledge). From this general knowledge base, a more specific *relevant* knowledge base can be drawn. You know that your superior gives very formal cocktail parties, with formal dress required (knowledge via past experience and information from other colleagues); that primarily business topics will be discussed since your superior prefers to handle delicate negotiations in this manner (specific cultural practice in this organization, the J. B. Bubbles Company); that the specific topics likely to be discussed involve negotiations for raw materials (specific interactional knowledge regarding the topic); and that language is likely to be highly technical and legal (knowledge about the likely topic and areas of discussion). This more concrete, particularized, *relevant* knowledge base is the framework of interpretation that our North American businesswoman would use at the cocktail party, and that would enable her to formulate hypotheses about what is going on and what will be going on.

Some aspects of this relevant knowledge base will be similar for both speakers and hearers—but they need not be identical. The differing goals of the speaker and hearer, for example, will produce different relevant knowledge bases. If the speaker and hearer share the same language and culture, the commonsense knowledge serving as a basis for social order in that culture will provide the necessary intersubjective basis for interaction. However, in increasingly socially diverse encounters, the intersubjective bases for interaction may, in fact, have to be established before much interaction can take place. For example, in diplomatic discussions, a significant amount of time is spent on setting up protocol for subsequent talks.

In addition to this relevant knowledge base, participants have goals they wish to accomplish in any interaction. It is to a consideration of goals, as a pre-interactional variable, that we now turn.

2. Goals. For purposes of our discussion, I loosely define goals as what we hope to accomplish by our actions. As such, goals can be clearly separated from intentions. Intentions are motives for actions; while I can never be certain of your motives, I can infer your goals from your actions. (We do this by assuming that people are motivated to act, and that their actions are consistent with or contribute to the realization of their goals). People's acts, of course, may be misdirected in the sense that they may not facilitate goal achievement; however, this does not invalidate the general line of argument being pursued here. Action is a consequence of both knowledge and choice, and mistaken choices and mistaken knowledge frequently occur in an imperfect world.

Interactional goals may be quite difficult to analyze. First, individuals' awareness of their goals varies as a function of their monitoring skills (Berger & Bradac, 1982), their perceived control of events (Langer, 1983) and other factors. Second, goals themselves may also be quite vague (e.g., I want to be sociable) or fairly precise (e.g., I want to write a grant proposal testing solid fuel injection systems). Third, multiple goals may be pursued simultaneously (e.g., I may want to be sociable as well as write the grant proposal, etc.). Fourth, some goals, like those concerning impression-management and face, may always be present in interaction. Fifth, goals may also be closely tied to given contexts and may not be attainable outside those contexts (Argyle, 1980; Argyle et al., 1981). And finally, goals may also be weighted relative to one another, of long or short-term duration, and changeable over time. In short, goals appear to be as flexible and varied as the actions that support them.

Despite these complexities, however, people appear to act in ways that facilitate their goals. In interaction, participants make their utterances *relevant* to their conversational goals which, in turn, contribute to their personal goals (Allen & Perrault, 1980). Speakers, then, *try to be relevant* and hearers assume that speakers are trying to be relevant (see also Sperber & Wilson, 1986, who argue that speakers are trying to be as *relevant as possible*). It should be noted that speakers and listeners do not have to share goals: the only goal speakers and hearers *must* share is that of cooperating so that interaction may take place (Dascal, 1981).

The two pre-interactional variables, the relevant knowledge base and participants' goals, mutually interact and influence one another. First, a participant's goals will control what aspects of general commonsense knowledge become activated and thus constitute part of a participant's relevant knowledge base. Second, as individuals acquire new information, their goals may change. And finally, as goals change, participants will rely on different sets of information. That is, as participants' goals change, there will be corresponding changes in their relevant knowledge base.

Now that I have specified the nature of pre-interactional variables (the relevant knowledge base that participants use in an encounter, and their goals), I next discuss influential communicative variables that emerge during the interaction itself. Here I argue that the text evolving in the interaction activates the relevant knowledge base used by participants in that interaction. Through the reciprocal interplay among the unfolding text, the relevant knowledge base and participants' goals, participants produce utterances and interpret others' utterances. Interpretations of another's utterances are always tentative and projected: tentative because they are hypotheses about what is meant, and projected because speaker/ listeners base their next utterances on the hypothesized interpretation of the preceding dialogue. (Please note here that I am explicitly referring to the preceding dialogue, *not just the immediately prior utterance*.)

Interactional Variables

The actual interaction involves the immediate physical setting, the participants, and the unfolding text or dialogue. The immediate physical setting for the interaction includes the specific time, location, objects, and their arrangement. Participants are influenced by four factors: their goals, their relevant knowledge base, their emotions (i.e., feelings and values about the interactional activity, other participants, and the like), and their interactional skill. Interactional skill refers to participants' ability to appropriately adapt their communication to different participants, and to satisfy different communicative demands across a diverse set of social situations. The three communicative settings discussed in this book—the interpersonal, developmental, and educational settings—are the three major settings in which such interactional skills develop.

The text or dialogue itself consists of the sequential order of utterances made by each participant, including their interruptions, overlaps, and so forth. This text is both verbal and nonverbal. On the verbal dimension, the topics discussed, the conversational management practices used, and the lexical items used (e.g., terms of address, deictic elements such as "this," etc.) are of particular concern. These textual variables act as *relevance markers*. Out of a set of potentially relevant contexts, *the text marks the specific operative context for that interaction at that particular moment.* During the interaction, different contexts may become relevant. For example, as an amiable discussion turns into a heated argument, different goals may emerge and different aspects of the topic may be emphasized. Such changes constitute a change in what the relevant context is for that interaction.

On the nonverbal level, interactional variables include paralinguistic features (like stress and intonation) that accompany utterances, as well as nonverbal behaviors like eye gaze, touch, proximity, and so forth. These nonverbal signals help convey, albeit indirectly, what is meant (most especially, the *intensity* of what is meant). (See, for example, Denny, 1985, and Goodwin, 1981 for communication research combining both verbal and nonverbal features of interaction.)

Post-Interaction Variables

Interactional outcomes are very difficult to discuss since they are frequently unclear. If multiple goals are being pursued by participants, interactional outcomes may be further confounded. At a minimum, any response to a preceding utterance could be considered an outcome. On the other hand, we could focus upon long-term outcomes, such as how a particular encounter shapes a relationship or influences goal attainment. Some interactional outcomes, for example, may be more critical for interpersonal relationships than others. However, little is known about these critical encounters—frequently, they may not even be readily apparent to the participants themselves.

In view of the general lack of clarity in this area, and in view of some of the difficulties outlined briefly above, let us simply consider any response to a preceding utterance as an outcome. As a pattern of outcomes emerges over the interaction, participants develop a "global" sense about the encounter and how it is proceding (e.g., it is a hostile exchange; the encounter seems clear and simple; she seems nice; we are accomplishing our task, etc.). Over time, these global evaluations may influence how we approach subsequent encounters of a particular type (like interviews) or with particular individuals (e.g., over time, we may build up an adverse attitude toward someone because past encounters have frequently been painful, etc.).

In summary, these three phases of interaction—pre-interaction influences, the interaction itself, and interactional outcomes—respectively parallel developing hypotheses, testing hypotheses, and confirming hypotheses. Prior to our interactions, we develop expectations about what might occur in a forthcoming interaction. These expectations are derived from our *relevant knowledge base*. During the interaction, we test these expectations through our utterances and our interpretations of others' responses. As the interaction proceeds, our expectations are confirmed or disconfirmed; and we continually adapt our communicative behavior according to our conversational goals (i.e., interactional outcomes provide feedback about our expectations).

Although we have discussed communicative variables in terms of their influence as pre-interactional, interactional, or post-interaction influences, we must keep in mind that communication is a continuous, ongoing process. It is to the *process* of communication that we now turn. We discuss the same concepts, but emphasize their mutual interaction with one another during conversation. In particular, we shall focus upon the role of the text in highlighting relevant frames of interpretation.

II. COMMUNICATION:
STRATEGIC ACTION IN CONTEXT

In what follows, I discuss how participants achieve their goals while coordinating their communicative acts with others. In particular, I argue that the principle of relevance directs participants' utterances and interpretations. Participants' communicative practices signal an utterance's relevance; that is, they signal how speakers want their utterances to be interpreted. The view of communicative processes developed here also emphasizes the role of commonsense knowledge and the relationship of such knowledge to participants' interactional goals. Finally, the view developed here focuses on the text, and the role of the text in signalling the relevant interpretive context. It is to these issues we now turn.

Relevance: Connecting Text, Context, and Communicator

The driving force behind human communication is the goal of the speaker/ hearer: goals influence both the production of utterances and their interpretation. Goals also help determine the relevance of actions and utterances. As speakers, we utter statements we believe to be *relevant to the purposes at hand (i.e., goals); as listeners, we interpret utterances by determining their relevance to our general sense of what is going on in the interaction*. The meaning of an utterance in context is, to a large degree, a function of its perceived relevance to that context. Thus relevance, not coherence, appears to be most fundamental to communication, since relevance determines the production and interpretation of utterances in context. In addition, it is assumed that participants' conversational goals are relevant to their personal goals. Finally, it is also assumed that people act to facilitate goal achievement.

Another way of acknowledging the importance of relevance is to argue that coherence and relevance are related in the same way that semantics and pragmatics are related. Sperber and Wilson (1986) view semantics as specifying the *range* of possible senses of an utterance while pragmatics specifies the principles by which hearers assign an *actual* sense and reference to any given occasion of an utterance. In a parallel fashion, I am arguing that *coherence determines the possible range of potential, plausible interpretations of a text, while relevance, based on the speaker/hearer's goals, determines the actual interpretation of a text at a particular moment in a given interaction.* While we can never be certain what speakers intend by their utterances, nevertheless relevance establishes the accountability of the utterance. That is, an utterance's relevance determines what the speaker is *publicly committed to having his/her utterance heard as.*

For most scholars, the relevance of utterances is tacitly assumed. It is generally acknowledged that utterances are relevant with respect to some context. However—left unstated—are the principles of relevance, and the process by which interactants bring relevant aspects of the context to bear upon the interpretation of an utterance. In casual conversation, we might also hear comments like "That's more relevant to our project than to hers." Such comments indicate that relevance may be a *relative,* rather than *absolute,* matter. What is relevant at one point in time may not be relevant at another point, even within the same conversation. Relevance, as should be readily seen from these brief remarks, is not a simple matter.

Given the importance of relevance (both in terms of the views set out here and in view of the degree to which the concept is relied upon in most analyses of verbal communication), it seems essential to clarify this concept. Our loose working definition of relevance as relatedness needs to be more precisely defined. I propose, after Leech (1983), that "An utterance U is relevant to a speech situation if U can be interpreted as contributing to the conversational goal(s) of s or h" (p. 94). I am expanding this general definition of relevance to include knowledge and actions, as well as utterances. The formulation of this more inclusive concept of relevance is as follows:

> An utterance, action, or unit of knowledge is relevant to a speech situation if it can be interpreted as contributing to the conversational goal(s) of the speaker or listener.

I use the term "unit of knowledge" to include any element of general knowledge, irrespective of how such units are processed and represented in memory. Knowledge could be represented in the form of scripts, frames, propositions, communicative practices, practical reasoning, or in some other format. As can readily be seen, this more inclusive formulation is needed because general knowledge and the relevant knowledge base derived in a particular social setting significantly influence discourse production and comprehension (see especially Chapter 5).

In summary, participants try to accomplish their goals through interaction; thus utterances are generally assumed to be relevant to these goals. Speakers try to maximize the relevance of their utterances and listeners, in turn, try to infer the relevant, goal-directed interpretation of the speaker's utterances. Although speakers and listeners try to construct plausible interpretations of the ongoing interaction, what is critical is that the *relevant, operative interpretation intended by the speaker be taken up by the listener.* In interaction, then, our conversational goal is to be understood (i.e., interpreted) in a particular sense. Furthermore, this being understood in a particular sense appears to contribute—in some way, however vague or ill-defined—to our personal goals. Although one's personal goals may never be completely known to others, or even well-understood by oneself, conversational goals can be understood because the speaker *publicly commits him/herself to being held accountable by virtue of his/her communicative practices* (Garfinkel, 1962, 1967a, b; Schutz, 1962a). That is, speakers signal how an utterance is to be understood through their use of socially shared, interpretive frames of reference that govern everyday social interaction. As such, interactants empirically display, through their utterances, their orientation to the ongoing talk.

I use the general term "communicative practices" rather than "accountability practices," since my formulation of accountable practices goes beyond those outlined by Garfinkel and conversational analysts. Relevant uptake is signalled, by both speakers and listeners, through their *communicative practices* such as conversational management practices (adjacency pairs, topic initiation and so forth), speech markers, deictic elements, account-giving strategies, and paralinguistic/nonverbal behaviors relevant to text interpretation. All these communicative practices signal how the text is meant to be heard, and thus reflect ways of being held accountable for what has been said.

These communicative practices are part of our shared, culturally-determined, commonsense knowledge. In my view, communication is not possible in the absence of some shared commonsense knowledge. Earlier, we discussed commonsense knowledge in terms of a speaker/listener's general knowledge and the relevant knowledge base derived from this general knowledge. Here we discuss the type of knowledge that must be shared, and the degree to which it must be shared for communication. (see especially N.V. Smith, 1982, for an extensive discussion of this issue).

The Nature and Sharing of Commonsense Knowledge

Commonsense knowledge is complex and multi-layered: it represents different levels of abstraction, specificity, and breadth (van Dijk & Kintsch, 1983; Garfinkel, 1962, 1967b; Haslett, 1986a, b; Heritage, 1984; Smith, 1982). How is such knowledge shared? After Schutz, Heritage (1984) suggests that individuals can "know" one another in four distinct ways: as human beings, as members of the same culture, as specific persons, and as specific persons now-in-this-immediate-situation.

According to Schutz, commonsense knowledge reflects a reciprocity of perspectives that is established in two ways. First, the *interchangeability of perspectives* allows us—if we were in the same position as another individual—to experience what another had experienced for all practical purposes. (This appears to be similar to the Reality Principle, postulated by Clark and Clark, 1977, through which we acknowledge the sameness of our experiences in the physical world.) Second, Schutz suggests that participants share *congruent systems of relevances;* that is; irrespective of our unique individual experiences, "for all practical purposes" we interpret objects and events in a similar manner. Generally, for members of the same culture, one can argue this to be the case; for example, deep-seated cultural values would reflect congruency of systems of relevances. However, for many interactions, especially those in which participants are members of different cultures or in which different group identities are an issue (see, for example, Scherer & Giles, 1979), this second assumption becomes highly problematic.

Given the reciprocity of perspectives, Schutz (1967) suggests that participants appear to share knowledge reflecting typical motives, identities, actions, and evaluations of their social group. Despite the vagueness and imprecision of this knowledge, participants utilize it in planning and interpreting their interactions and behavior. In my view, this commonsense knowledge should also include (1) frames, scripts, and plans of action (as developed by Schank & Abelson, 1977); (2) models of social situations (as developed by Magnusson, 1981b); and (3) analyses of goals and situations (as developed by Argyle, 1980; Argyle et al. 1981; Harre & Secord, 1972).

Recall that commonsense knowledge reflects typical motives, typical events, typical actions, and the like (Schutz, 1967). As such, commonsense knowledge includes typical means-ends connections; that is, typical actions are connected with typical outcomes. A script, in fact, could be regarded as a typical sequence of means-ends linkages in a specified social setting. Thus, commonsense knowledge appears to be organized, in part, by links connecting *relevant actions to subsequent probable outcomes* (see Kemper, 1982). For example, suppose I want good grades (my goal) and, through experience, find that I need to study in order to get good grades (a relevant means for achieving my desired goal). My goal then becomes establishing optimum study conditions. Through experience and perhaps talking with others, I find that good studying conditions require good lighting, a quiet location, and lots of junk food (*relevant* means for achieving my goal). In brief, everyday practical reasoning, based on commonsense knowledge, appears to operate on the principle of relevance. Actions are perceived and evaluated in terms of their relevance for accomplishing some desired outcome. These means-ends linkages are not unique, but represent shared social knowledge.

Similar *relevant* linkages exist between goals and social situations; a situation may facilitate achieving some goals while prohibiting the attainment of others (Argyle, 1980). Relevant knowledge can also point out "what not to do," and we can avoid mistakes through analysis of past experience that connects certain actions to the achievement of desired goals. And people's experiences are likely to be similar with respect to their trial-and-error efforts to accomplish their goals. Thus, the commonsense knowledge used by participants in their interaction is *that knowledge which they find relevant to the matters at hand* — not a vast array of knowledge, but knowledge relevant to accomplishing one's interactional goals.

Knowledge about interaction itself is also part of our commonsense knowledge. Conversational analysts, after Garfinkel, suggest that strategies for managing conversation (like turn taking, giving accounts, preferred responses, and so on) are the basis for interpreting actions as well. That is, each strategy for managing talk is simultaneously a basis for interpreting talk. In addition to these management strategies, speech markers (like forms of address such as "Mr. President") also signal the speaker's intended meaning. Finally, conversational maxims could also be viewed as general principles used in planning and interpreting utterances. All these levels of tacit, commonsense knowledge, taken together, provide a very rich interpretive knowledge base for interaction. They are *signals of relevance through which speakers publicly signal what is meant by what is said.*

It should be noted here that, while I am emphasizing verbal communication, this in no way denies the importance of nonverbal communication in determining a speaker's intended meaning. Verbal and nonverbal communication systems, I believe, are redundant and complementary; an adequate account of what is meant cannot be established without reference to both systems. (See, for example, Atkinson & Heritage, 1984; Bull, 1983; Goodwin, 1981; Poyatos, 1983.)

In sum, the text signals the relevant aspects of commonsense knowledge that are being applied in an interaction. During interaction, the evolving text produced by the participants and their relevant commonsense knowledge interact and produce a frame of interpretation for the interaction. These relevant frames of interpretation are continually and mutually negotiated by participants in light of their individual and collective conversational goals. At any given moment, both speakers and listeners have a set of plausible alternative interpretations, say plausible interpretations "A" to "F." However, the particular interpretation actually applied in that particular setting at that specific time is signalled by the text.

Taken together, communicative practices establish the interpretive, accountable nature of conversation. The relevant knowledge base of speakers and listeners is both the interpretive *frame* as well as the *process* by which accountability is signalled. This accountability in social action is inescapable; as Heritage (1984) notes, "normative accountability is the 'grid' by reference to which *whatever* is done will become visible and assessable" (p. 117). Heritage also notes that individuals do this *routinely;* only in breaches or violations of ordinary practices are things called into question (i.e., accounts must be given). For example, if the listener mishears a speaker's utterance, then the speaker may repair that mishearing by rephrasing her utterance.

The basis of shared knowledge is richer and more complex among interactants who are friends, kin, or have an extended social relationship with one another. They are richer because we "know" one another as specific persons and as specific persons now-in-the-immediate-situation, rather than just as human beings and members of the same culture. As Miller (1978) notes, as interpersonal relationships develop, the information exchange among individuals becomes increasingly personal and idiosyncratic. Cultural expectations for specific types of relationships may become activated as well, such as "what it means" to be a friend in the U.S., or to be a family member in China, and so forth.

Although communication generally becomes more unique and specialized as interpersonal relationships develop, nevertheless general patterns of communication can be observed as a function of the type of relationship (e.g., spouse, good friend, sibling, and so forth). Cultures have institutional frameworks for enduring social relationships, like marriage; such institutional frames may have their own conversational practices (such as, for example, the use of multiple naming among intimates). In a parallel fashion, organizations and professions also develop their own conversational practices for interaction (for instance, the use of professional titles such as doctor or nurse).

Thus far, I have argued for a pragmatic, action-based approach to communication. Action theories assume that individuals try to accomplish goals and that their actions, based upon their knowledge and their ability to choose from among alternative actions, facilitate goal achievement. Actions are thus strategic—strategic because they are hypotheses about what is the most effective action that could be performed, based upon one's incomplete, fragmented knowledge. In interaction, conversational goals support both the speaker's and hearer's personal goals, which may or may not be shared.

Acts, or in the case of conversation, utterances, are thus assumed to be *relevant* to participants' goals. Using their relevant knowledge base and inferences about the probable goals of one another in the interaction, speakers and hearers coordinate their utterances and attempt to maximize the achievement of their own goals. Speakers try to be as relevant as possible and hearers assume that the speakers' utterances are as relevant as possible (Sperber & Wilson, 1986; Wilson & Sperber, 1981).

Through communicative practices used by both participants, inferences are made about what is going on in the interaction. Given the retrospective and prospective nature of action itself, these inferences are subject to continuous evaluation. But the crucial element is that of relevance— utterances are related to interactants' goals in that particular context, and are *interpreted as being so related.* In communication, signalling or accomplishing relevance is how one's activities are made sensible. *No single communicative practice signals relevance, but rather the communicative practices taken as a whole, viewed against a general sense of what is being accomplished, renders a sensible account of what is meant.*

The following example highlights some of the issues we have been discussing. This dialogue occured between a mother and her son. Relevant background knowledge consists of the fact that both parents have been annoyed at the way in which their children shout throughout the house in an attempt to locate their parents, to ask questions (usually trivial), or to request aid for some task that could be done independently by the child. The parents have been encouraging their children to look instead of shout, to complete tasks by themselves, and the like. Given this general context, the following dialogue occured during the son's lunch break from school.[1]

1. S: Mom!
2. M: Yeah.
3. S: Nothing.
   (3.0)
4. M: Rick?
5. S: Yeah.
6. M: Nothing.
   (5.0)
7. M: R::↓ick
   (5.0)
8. S: Ver:y fun↓*ny.*

---

[1]Conventions used in this transcript are based on those developed by Jefferson and found in Atkinson and Heritage, 1984.

(1.0)
9. (M laughs softly, but audibly).

Lines 1–3 are the usual scenario enacted by one of the children. The mother's query in line 4 is not untoward as she may have some request, offer or information to share. At line 6, however, the first indication of the atypical nature of this sequence appears. Parents typically request their children's attention *for some explicit reason,* and the mother explicitly states that she has requested her son's attention for *nothing.* Clearly, this is unusual, and the lengthy pause before any further utterance marks this as being unusual. Rick is uncertain as to what is going on. After the lengthy pause, mother initiates another request for attention; however, the request is marked by an atypical format, with up-down intonation and exaggerated prolonging of the name Rick. This utterance marks the way in which the mother wants her utterance to be understood; the intonation of "Rick" in line 7 marks the query for attention as being playful—or, at the least, not a legitimate query for attention. If the query is not legitimate, as would precede a request, offer, etc., Rick has to figure out how that query is relevant. Rick knows that there had been a previous query for attention that he responded to; his mother replied that the query was non-purposive. The untoward nature of that sequence, in addition to the marked stress on his name in initiating yet another potential routine, signal to Rick that another purpose, beyond the obvious solicitation of his attention, is meant. In the context of their interaction, recalling that his parents are annoyed by such non-purposive or trivial requests, Rick infers that his mother is "putting him on"—annoying him by an "empty request" (similar to those that she receives so frequently)—and, in effect, she turns-the-table on him. That Rick understands her intended meaning is signalled by the lengthy pause in front of his response, and the response itself, uttered with a marked "very" and a flat, emphatic "funny." That his mother appreciates and acknowledges his understanding is signalled by her soft laughter, indicating her enjoyment at having turned-the-table so aptly, and signalling her "playfulness" rather than hostility to Rick.

Communicative practices, such as query and response, are normal, interactional practices against which this episode is judged. Several violations of normal, standard practices occur in this episode: the response of "nothing" following a query for attention; the following of one query with another breached query, and a third query that is deliberately signalled in an atypical format (at least in that context). All these violations signal that some purpose, other than the normal range of purposes signalled by queries, is intended. The relevant interpretation is then inferred from those breaches, their sequencing, and *relevant* commonsense knowledge. Mutual understanding in the episode is acknowledged by the son's comment in line

8 and the mother's laughter. It is important to note that the communicative practices signalled in the text are a necessary, but not sufficient, condition for interpreting what is going on. Interpretations rely on: (1) relevant connections being made between text and context; (2) a specification of the a priori potentially relevant contexts; and (3) an appreciation of the conversational goals being pursued.

If there is a fundamental premise of interaction, the general principle of relevance, I submit, is it. The cooperative principle (excluding the maxim of relation) and the politeness principle (Brown & Levinson, 1978) are efficient, effective ways for achieving relevance. These three principles (relevance, cooperativeness, and politeness) are, I believe, universal principles of communication, with relevance being the most fundamental. When speakers try to be as relevant as possible, they may or may not succeed. A participant's choice of utterance will always be a *strategic, contingent choice* because participants must respond as the interaction proceeds; because their relevant knowledge bases are changing, fragmented and incomplete; and because their conversational goals are instrumentally tied to one another.

Thus far, I have tried to work out a satisfactory view of relevance as it operates in everyday interaction. Relevance is of central importance in communication because it connects actions to goals, and thus helps us interpret what is going on in an interaction. Second, as interactants, we assume, as Sperber and Wilson suggest, that speakers are trying to be as relevant as possible. Finally, as interactants, we rely on relevant knowledge bases that aid our interpretation of an interaction. As Werth (1981) notes "current accounts of conversational interaction depend crucially upon the ... notion of relevance" (p. 153).

In summary, I have suggested that communicative variables can be viewed as being pre-interactional, interactional, or post-interactional influences. In particular, the role of commonsense knowledge in interpreting ongoing interaction has been emphasized. We have also worked out a process-oriented view of communication, emphasizing relevance as the principle connecting utterances to goals and to knowledge. Given the critical importance of relevance to communication, it would also be helpful to contrast the approach being taken here to those developed by others. It is to these contrasts we now turn.

III. THE PRINCIPLE OF RELEVANCE:
SOME ALTERNATIVE VIEWS

My use of relevance, as does that of Leech (1983), connects utterances with the conversational goals of participants. However, I place much more importance on the principle of relevance than Leech; in my view, relevance is the fundamental principle underlying discourse production and comprehension. In addition, not only utterances, but knowledge structures and actions (i.e., nonverbal behaviors) as well, are connected to conversational goals through relevance. Relevance also, in my view, connects text, context, and participants, and thus permits the interpretation of communicative behavior. In what follows, I survey the major approaches to relevance in the pragmatic literature. Most scholars discussing relevance treat it as an aspect of coherence. A recent departure is the work of Sperber and Wilson (1986), who treat relevance as a cognitive universal.

1. Meaning-Based Approaches to Relevance.   Most views of relevance are meaning-based approaches; that is, the issue of relevance is the "local" issue of how utterances contribute to the topic under discussion. Schank (1977) argues that one must be topically relevant in order to be coherent. Reichman (1978) discusses "context spaces" (topics and their elaboration), and how interactants mark and shift between those context spaces. Planalp and Tracy (1980), following Reichman's distinction between issues (generalizations about a belief or feeling) and events (a specific instance), found that speakers were judged more competent when their remarks were linked immediately to the preceding discourse. A further set of investigations by Tracy and Moran (1983) found that utterances were judged to be most relevant when they responded to the key point of the preceding discourse. Such approaches emphasize coherence and the role of relevance in maintaining coherence.

   While coherence is essential for interpreting utterances, such approaches fail to provide satisfactory accounts of how we construct meanings. The missing principle, once again, is that of relevance. Interactants try to be sensible (i.e., capable of being interpreted), not *generally,* as meaning approaches would predict, but in *a particular way* (i.e., in a way contributing to their conversational goals). To be generally coherent (or sensible) provides a range of alternative meaningful interpretations; speakers go beyond (or try to go beyond) this potential range of meanings to *signal the relevant sense of the utterance.* Meaning-based approaches to relevance (such as those limiting relevance to the issue of *topical* relevance) can specify a range of plausible interpretations of what is said, but fall short of specifying what is *meant* by what is said. Conversational analysts err in another way: accountability practices are viewed as management practices in organizing conversation, and the influence of relevance, background knowledge, and other conversational practices are merely assumed rather than explicitly discussed.

Conversationalists try to make their utterances both relevant and coherent. Of the two, however, relevance is more important for interpreting ongoing interaction. This can be demonstrated in a number of ways. First, if an utterance is relevant, then it must also be coherent. That is, if the utterance is related to the general sense of the matters at hand in the conversation, then it also must be meaningful in some sense—namely, the sense in which it is relevant to the conversational matters at hand. However, an utterance may be coherent (i.e., meaningful), but not be relevant to the conversation. For example, one could retort (as many do) in an argument, "But that's not relevant to the issue." If we understand an utterance's relevance, we necessarily understand its meaning, but not vice versa. And speakers virtually *always* try to be relevant; we assume that whatever people say, *it is somehow related to the matters at hand*—otherwise, why say anything? In short, the issue is not meaning per se, but meaning for what purpose.

2. A Cognitive View of Relevance.   Sperber and Wilson (1986) emphasize the centrality of relevance in interpreting utterances, and propose a cognitive model of relevance. Underlying their model is the assumption that humans strive for the most efficient information processing possible. As a result of successful communication, the mutual cognitive environment of both interactants is enlarged. The cognitive environment is defined as a set of assumptions that an individual mentally represents and accepts as true. Given an individual's cognitive environment, Sperber and Wilson seek to explain which assumptions would be most likely to be processed; they argue that "relevance makes information worth processing for humans.

Their concept of relevance is developed in two distinct senses: a cognitive sense and a communicative sense. From a cognitive perspective, relevance occurs when a new utterance (X) combines with already known information (K) in context (C); relevant new information is derived that could not be derived from either K or C alone. Thus relevance occurs when new information is produced (by either induction or deduction) which otherwise would not have been available. In essence, relevance is equivalent to possessing new information that produces contextual effects—that is, it must alter one's cognitive environment. According to Sperber and Wilson, having contextual effects is a necessary condition for relevance; generally, the greater the contextual effects, the greater the relevance.

In their view, an individual comprehends an utterance against a context that is partially determined by previous acts of comprehension (p. 112). An utterance or assumption may lack contextual effects, and thus relevance, in three instances: (1) if the new information does not connect with any information present in the context, and thus fails to produce contextual effects; (2) if the assumption is already present and its strength is unaffected by the new information; and (3) if the assumption is inconsistent with the context, and too weak to overcome it.

> To modify and improve a context is to have some effect on that context—but not just any modification will do. As we have seen, the addition of new information which merely duplicates old information does not count as an improvement; nor does the addition of new information which is entirely unrelated to old information. The sort of effect we are interested in is a result of interaction between new and old information. (p. 109)

In addition, they assume that an individual automatically aims at maximizing relevance.

> In verbal communication, the hearer is generally led to accept an assumption as true or probably true on the basis of a guarantee given by the speaker. Part of the hearer's task is to find out which assumptions the speaker is guaranteeing as true. Our hypothesis is that the hearer is guided by the principle of relevance in carrying out this task. He expects the information the speaker intended to convey, when processed in the context the speaker expected it to be contextualised in, to be relevant; that is, to have a *substantial contextual effect, at a low processing cost.* (p. 116)

From a communicative perspective, this model of relevance leads to the presumption of optimal relevance. This presumption states that: (1) the assumptions that the speaker intends to convey to the listeners are relevant enough to make it worthwhile for the listeners to process these assumptions, and (2) the utterance of the speaker is the most relevant one the speaker could have used to convey them (p. 158). From this follows the principle of relevance:

> Every act of ostensive [inferential] communication communicates the presumption of its own optimal relevance (p. 158).

Simply put, Sperber and Wilson argue that every inferential communicative act presumes its own maximum relevance, and that both speakers and listeners act to maximize relevance. When relevance is defined as they define it (maximizing contextual effects with minimal processing effort), this claim is virtually impossible to deny. However, what I think Sperber and Wilson are discussing here is an information-processing universal that has little to do with the matter of relevance.

Sperber and Wilson's concept of relevance stresses the acquisition, through inductive and deductive reasoning, of new information (i.e., what they term contextual effects). What they ignore is the fact that humans are not *random* information-seeking machines. Humans seek information *for specific purposes—namely, information that helps them accomplish their particular goals.* Humans act on the basis of knowledge; but the knowledge gathered is *relevant* to accomplishing some goal.

I agree that humans search for information in the most efficient way—maximum information gain for minimum effort—but that is a principle of information processing and *not a unique condition of relevance.* I might add that if humans did act to maximize new information per se, their capacity to act would be impaired. Too much information would inhibit, if not prevent, any action. Sperber and Wilson could reply that information overload is not a problem since speakers act to maximize relevance and that listeners make the most accessible inference their interpretation. However, their own model seems inconsistent on this point. If speakers act to maximize relevance, they select a context that produces the *greatest* number of contextual effects. And the more contextual effects produced, the more information processed and, as a result, greater effort required. They point out that optimal relevance is the best balance of effort against effects, but how is that balance ever to be selected, since speakers and hearers may differ in their cognitive environments?

The issue of relevance, in my view, is the issue of *pertinent* information, not the issue of information which produces contextual effects. First, interactants' goals *must* be considered because those goals *direct* interactants' acquisition of knowledge. Second, we have no principled explanation of how speakers select the best context (i.e., the one in which the most contextual effects arise). Without some reference to conversational goals and principled ways of accessing the "best" context for producing contextual effects, the model seems unable to satisfy its own requirements. Third, in their view, the listener seems to be remarkably passive, generating the most readily processed interpretation and assuming its relevance. (Relevance is assumed because Sperber and Wilson's model presupposes that only the most accessible hypotheses are processed; since speakers are assumed to be maximizing relevance, the hypotheses or inferences most readily accessible to the listener are, *by definition,* the most relevant). I do agree that speakers and listeners both try to maximize relevance, but they do so in the sense of constructing utterances that facilitate, to the greatest possible extent, their own intended interactional goals.

In summary then, both the meaning-based models (such as the topically relevant models or coherence models) and the cognitive model of Sperber and Wilson, present inadequate views of relevance. First, both positions ignore the importance of goals in determining relevance. Second, while both discuss context, only Sperber and Wilson provide a principled explanation of how text and context interact in achieving relevance. However, as already pointed out, the producing of contextual effects is not a *unique* property of relevance, but seems to be a universal information-processing principle. On balance, the centrality of relevance, and its operation in communication, seem to be most adequately developed by the view being taken in this book. (Although its operation *in communication* is best accounted for by the view taken here, the alternative accounts of relevance discussed, such as that of Sperber and Wilson, may be extremely useful from other perspectives.)

Having developed in some depth the concept of relevance as I think it operates in communication, I would now like to discuss some related methodological issues. In order to provide a descriptively adequate basis for studying communicative processes, an amalgam of three paradigms appears necessary. First, from action theory, I utilize a general analysis of goals and behavior; in particular, I stress the relationships among knowledge, goals and action. Second, from ethnomethodology and conversational analysis, I utilize the analysis of commonsense knowledge, the bases of intersubjectivity, and the use of accountability practices. And finally, from cognitive psychology and, to a lesser extent, artificial intelligence research, I utilize insights concerning the structure and processing of information, and human constraints on those processes.

Every scientific approach "idealizes" the phenomena under study in some way so that it can be examined in a precise and clear manner. For example, Chomsky, in order to focus on the formal properties of languages, conceptualized an "idealized speaker/hearer." Similarly, each approach to communication discussed here has idealized some feature of communication. Conversational analysts have "idealized" the type of text analyzed (that of casual, mundane conversation) and the context (the immediate, contingent context among utterances). Both action theory and cognitive psychology have, to some extent, "idealized" views of humans as goal-seekers and information-processors respectively.

Each paradigm, taken on its own, partially illuminates the complexity of communication. Taken together, with the idealizations, assumptions, and strengths of each paradigm being complemented and "checked" by those of the others, this amalgam presents a firm descriptive base for the study of human communicative processes. These varied approaches, as a whole, constitute a system of "checks and balances" that presents a more adequate description and analysis of communicative processes than any single approach.

IV. TOWARD METHODOLOGICAL PLURALISM

Conversational Analysis

The methodological assumptions of conversational analysis deal, more directly than any alternatives, with the analysis of accountability practices (the procedures used to interpret utterances). Conversational analysts focus on the practices through which participants display their orientation to (interpretation of) the ongoing talk. These practices must be empirically manifest in the text itself. In brief, through such practices, speakers and hearers signal *how they meant to be heard*. Despite the emphasis on accountability practices, I believe that the scope and method of conversational analysis needs to be significantly altered. It should be noted that substantial diversity exists among conversational analysts, with some focusing on generic principles of conversational organization (Schegloff, 1986, personal communication) and others focusing on interaction in well-defined, institutional settings (Ten Have, 1986). In advocating these changes, those currently utilizing conversational analysis may claim that I am transforming it into a substantively different approach. Nevertheless, if conversational analysis is to be utilized in the study of communication, these modifications appear necessary. It is to these recommended modifications I now turn.

1. Expanding the Concept of Context.   Conversational analysis (hereafter referred to as *CA*) has been mistakenly criticized as not being grounded in context (Cicourel, 1980). *CA* scholars clearly do ground their analyses in context. However, their concept of context is the immediate, contingent, "local" context produced by the text itself. From this restricted view of context follows their emphasis on the sequential implicativeness of utterances and on conversational management practices. But this "local" context is embedded within larger contextual frames. What *CA* does, I think mistakenly, is *assumes* those larger contextual frames rather than incorporating them into their analyses.

Furthermore, these larger contexts are assumed to be intersubjectively shared, or at least *unproblematically* shared. Following Schutz (1962a), *CA* practicioners assume the reciprocity of perspectives. That is, they assume, "for all practical purposes," (1) the interchangeability of standpoints (if we were in the same positions, our view would be the same), and (2) the congruency of the system of relevances (despite biographical differences, we interpret and select objects in a nearly identical manner [see Heritage, 1984, pp. 53–60]). While the interchangeability of standpoints seems unproblematic, the assumed congruency of the system of relevances is problematic from a communication perspective. Let me explain.

When we are talking about social order and how it is manifest and maintained, both assumptions seem unproblematic, especially since *CA* seeks to explain how practical reasoning in a society is sustained in conversation. However, communication occurs between different cultures, between different subcultures, and between individuals who have differing social relations with one another. In these circumstances, from a communicative perspective, assuming congruency among systems of relevance is not warranted. Once again, this assumption *may* be warranted as *CA* practioners tend to invoke it—that is, in the study of casual, mundane conversations among peers in the same culture. However, a descriptively adequate basis for communication cannot fit within these narrow limits.

To counter these limitations, the concept of context needs to be expanded to include levels of context discussed in Chapter 5. Some of this is suggested in a paper by John Heritage (1980) in which he discusses the immediate, contingent context as being "nested" within larger contextual frames. Other *CA* practitioners examine institutional contexts and their influence on accountability practices (see, for example, Atkinson & Drew, 1979; Mulkay, 1981; Mulkay & Gilbert, 1982; Watson, 1981). Levinson's (1979) discussion of activity types and language use suggests some of the ways in which larger contextual frames constrain interaction possibilities. Assessing context in more detail and from a broader scope will enable scholars to more precisely specify the various contextual levels influencing communication in a particular setting.

If we are to expand context in the way I have suggested, how might this be accomplished? A 1986 conference on Talk and Social Structure, in part, addressed this issue. Conversational analysts argued that any demonstration of the relationship between conversation and social structure must satisfy two conditions. First, the social structure must be measured independently—apart from the ongoing dialogue. Second, the particular social structure being investigated must be empirically displayed in the dialogue. Conversational analysts are very critical of the use of social categories, like power and gender, that are used to explain how talk is structured, when they have not been independently measured and empirically demonstrated in the talk itself.

While these two requirements seem appropriate, conversational analysts nevertheless look at only part of the information on which participants base their interpretations of the ongoing interaction. Conversational analysis has documented, more than any other approach, *how talk is accomplished.* How talk is organized, however, is only part of the interpretive process by which we understand the ongoing talk. Simply put, the organization of talk is not equivalent to its interpretation. First, given the multifunctionality of utterances, any single utterance may have several interpretations and different utterances can have the same interpretation. Put another way, the format and sequencing of utterances can have multiple potential interpretations. Therefore, the organization of talk cannot, in principle, be a necessary and sufficient condition for interpreting talk. Second, talk itself needs to be supplemented by other sources of information so that participants can interpret what is going on. Most notably, nonverbal behaviors, an expanded perspective of context, and an awareness of what has *not* been said (but *could* have been said) provide information that helps participants interpret ongoing interaction. Finally, it appears necessary to incorporate a larger contextual frame in order to account for how participants interpret their ongoing interaction.

A useful analogy here is to compare the organization of talk and its interpretation to Chomsky's distinction between the surface structure of a sentence and its deep structure or meaning. Just as a sentence's surface structure displays its organization, conversational practices display how talk is organized. Just as a sentence's surface structure relates, in principled ways, to its deep structure; so, too, do the conversational practices that organize talk relate, in principled ways, to the interpretation of that talk. Finally, just as the surface structure and deep structure of a sentence rely upon an individual's linguistic knowledge (i.e., linguistic universals and a group's patterns of language usage); so, too, does the organization of talk and its interpretation rely upon a participant's goals and relevant knowledge base. As Mehan (1986) points out, we need to understand the larger social context in order to understand the details of talk; interactants must integrate the larger social context with the text in order to make sense of the on-going interaction. For these reasons, the interpretation of talk depends upon the larger social context and is not displayed *completely* or *solely* in the talk itself.

2. *What Communicative Acts are to be Studied?*   Following the ethnomethodological assumptions set out by Garfinkel and Sacks, *CA* scholars focus their analyses primarily on casual conversations among peers. Although there are obviously exceptions to this, this conversational setting has been the one primarily investigated. Heritage (1984) argues that this conversational setting provides a standard against which other conversations, in other settings, can be assessed. The knowledge claims following from these assumptions suggest that accountability practices are *universal, standard cultural practices* for accomplishing particular conversational aims. For example, Pomerantz' work on apologies represents the "canonical form" (i.e., the standard cultural form) for apologies, Jefferson's work on troubles represents the "canonical form" for telling troubles, and so forth. Unfortunately, within the *CA* framework, there appears to be no way to evaluate the universality of such claims. (It should be noted, however, from the *CA* scholar's viewpoint, this is not necessary or, for that matter, particularly important.)

However, from a communicative perspective, several critical concerns emerge. First, what are the criteria for determining what constitutes a casual conversation? Because these casual conversations are specified as being conducted among peers, it is assumed that participants have equivalent social status vis a vis one another and that their social relationship does not affect their interaction. That is, it is assumed that asymetrical social relationships and their influence on conversational practices are not present in such conversations. Are these assumptions valid? I would suggest that *any* communicative act is influenced by the social relationships among participants (Bateson, 1972; Watzlawick, Beavin, & Jackson, 1967). Thus any conversation, however casual, would be influenced by these social relationships. Not all scholars working in the *CA* tradition have ignored the influence of participants' social relationships. Within certain institutional frameworks, specific social relationships have been examined, such as the doctor/patient relationship (Ten Have, 1986) and the counselor/ client relationship (Watson, 1981). The accomodative work done in conversations varies as a function of the social relationships among participants; these differences should have a central role in our analysis of communication.

In view of these considerations, it seems essential to evaluate the generalizability of claims made by *CA* scholars. If we are unable to evaluate the generalizability of such claims, we have no basis for judging the variations that surround any standard communicative format. Nor is it possible to judge the potential significance, if any, of alternative variations of a format. For example, a woman may apologize one way to her children ("Hey, I'm sorry about that"), another way to a stranger ("Sorry, love") and yet another way to her boss ("I apologize for the error, I'll correct it right away"). Are there central characteristics for apologies that represent a set of necessary and sufficient conditions for apologizing? Are there significant variations across the formats in which apologies occur? If so, for what reasons and with what effect?

A partial answer to this dilemma is to examine conversations as they occur in explicitly defined social contexts; as mentioned above, some *CA* scholars are already doing this. Another option would be to explore different discourse activities and their structures; through this contrastive work, a better understanding of conversation itself, as a communicative activity, would occur. Some examples of this would be ethnographic work in educational settings (see Chapter 9); exploring different features of talk within conversations like joking (Sacks, 1974) or telling a story (Polanyi, 1979); and analyzing different genres of communication, like lectures or radio talk shows (Goffman, 1981). As Goffman notes:

> When a word is spoken, all those who happen to be in perceptual range of the event will have some sort of participation status relative to it. The codifica-

tion of these various positions and the normative specification of appropriate conduct within each provide an essential background for interaction analysis— whether (I presume) in our own society or any other. (p. 3)

3. The Primacy of Text.   The *CA* tradition is correct in its insistence on the primacy of the text (Heritage, 1984; Levinson, personal communication; Wootton, 1981). The text serves as an essential departure point for analysis because the text, as it emerges during interaction, marks the relevant context of interpretation and how utterances are meant to be understood. While we have *a priori* expectations (shaped by practical reasoning and analyses of social situations) in mind as we interact with others, these expectations set up a range of *potentially* relevant contexts of interpretation; the operative context of interpretation is invoked by the text. This is so because the text is the means by which participants *mutually convey, construct,* and *confirm* what is going on. Conversational practices are *signals of relevance* that mark how utterances are meant to be interpreted. Through the interplay of text and context, participants display their sense of what is happening in their interactions.

4. The Problem of Alternative Interpretations.   With regard to interpreting communicative acts, the concept of relevance enables scholars to identify plausible interpretations of an ongoing interaction. We can never be sure, of course, that the plausible alternative interpretations we posit are ever the *actual* interpretations that participants use in their interaction. Only the individuals themselves can "know" their own private interpretations. However, it is not necessary to know these subjective interpretations—we need only account for what participants are willing to be held publicly accountable for—namely, their communicative practices.

This position does not lead us into the morass of relativism, in which virtually any interpretation would be valid. Rather, what I am suggesting here is that alternative interpretations of interaction need to be plausible explanations for that interaction. Our everyday experience in communication amply demonstrates that interactants can produce reasonable alternative interpretations of utterances. Pearce and Cronen (1981), in fact, suggest that enduring interpersonal relationships can be maintained even when the participants have quite different interpretations of what is going on in their relationship as well as in their interaction.

What, then, is an appropriate criterion for judging whether an interpretation is plausible in a given context? I would argue that members of the particular family, group, subculture, or culture in question should judge whether or not an interpretation is plausible. *That is, participants themselves, or observers sharing the participants' relevant knowledge base, can deter-*

mine the significance of alternative accounts and their plausibility. Consensual agreement about an interpretation's plausibility thus becomes a criterion for judging an utterance's interpretation. Let me explain.

To be uninterpretable is to be judged as irrational or otherwise incompetent (Goffman, 1974). However, it is reasonable to expect that individuals may have different plausible accounts of ongoing interaction. Through the use of commonsense knowledge, an understanding of the interactants' conversational goals and knowledge of the interactants themselves, observers ought to be able to construct alternative plausible accounts, if needed, to explain what's going on. These accounts should be in the form of arguments, constructed in terms of practical reasoning, which observers could submit to others for their evaluation. What emerges as the "best" account (if such a determination is possible) may be determined on the same basis that distinguishes good theories from bad theories—namely, considerations like simplicity, elegance, parsimony, and the like. Statistical tests could, in theory, play a role in these judgments, although this is not necessary.

5. The Role of Experimental Studies.   Since adequate description of naturally occuring communication is prior to theory construction and theory verification, experimental studies become important after adequate descriptive analyses are done. We should not control and test variables *until* their significance has been demonstrated in naturally occuring discourse. Without prior determination of what are valid and significant communicative variables, we may construct models of trivial features of communication.

In addition to their essential role in rigorously testing variables and their parameters, I believe experimental studies can also make another contribution. Critics of naturalistic research can quite rightly argue that such research is inherently flawed. With naturalistic data, one is restricted to studying what actually occurs, and necessarily ignores what *might* have occured with different participants, etc. To counter this, ecologically valid experiments can be conducted to examine other communicative options. By ecologically valid experiments, I mean that such experiments must present social situations and communicative choices that have meaningful implications for the subjects. For example, instead of asking children how many different ways they would try to persuade their peers to give them some candy, researchers might present children with a carefully constructed task so that we can observe their persuasive behavior *over a range of situations relevant to them.* This calls for considerable ingenuity in designing experiments, but it seems essential to do this (see, Shotter, 1984, for an excellent discussion of this point).

6. Communicative Effectiveness.   If communicative acts are undertaken to accomplish some goal, then it seems reasonable to suggest that we need to evaluate whether or not that goal was accomplished. Although, as Searle (1969) correctly observes, factors beyond our control may determine the success of our communicative acts, I would argue that we can still determine a communicative act's effectiveness. It is in this area that contemporary communication research can benefit from rhetorical studies. Although Aristotle, Cicero, Quintilian, and other early rhetoricians focused on public speaking in political contexts, contemporary rhetoricians have extended their inquiry into other contexts (see, for example, Arnold & Bowers, 1984; D'Angelo, 1982; Hauser, 1968). Analyses of *topoi,* for example, could serve as models for situational analyses of communication. Enthymemes have long served as important models for research on argumentation and persuasion. These analytic tools, being especially suited to an evaluation of speaking effectiveness, could be extended to other contexts, purposes, and communicative acts.

In order to be effective communicators, participants must continually adapt their utterances to one another and to the context in which their interaction takes place. Interactants plan their actions on the basis of anticipated effects, and judge them in terms of effort, face, and other considerations. Being relevant, in terms of the view developed here, implies that one is being effective, or trying to be effective, as well. So communicative effectiveness appears to be an important aspect of any communicative act, and needs to be part of any analysis of communication.

One final caveat seems in order when discussing communicative effectiveness. Great caution must be taken in constructing any model of communicative competence because competence models presuppose some minimal, acceptable standard of effective communicative performance. I would argue that we, as yet, do not have an adequate descriptive basis for the study of communication. Thus it seems premature to develop conceptualizations of communicative competence. Currently, scholars use the term "competence" so loosely that it has little value. I am not saying that the search for a model of communicative competence is without merit—but I am saying it appears premature to do so now. We must first answer the question, What is communication and how does it work? and then ask, How do we communicate as effectively as possible—*and for what purpose?* The issue of effectiveness cannot be separated from the issues of a participant's goals and relevance. (For a discussion of varied approaches to communicative competence, see Spitzberg & Cupach, 1984.)

V. CONCLUDING REMARKS

In summary, I have attempted to demonstrate the centrality of relevance to any analysis of communicative processes. Essentially, communication is viewed as a goal-directed activity, in which utterances signal the appropriate context for their interpretation. In addition, analyses of communication need to be supported by theoretical and methodological pluralism. The premises of conversational analysis, when extended in the ways suggested, appear to provide a very useful approach to the study of communicative processes. In particular, the text itself and communicative practices appear to be key elements in any communicative analysis. Finally, it is suggested that the principle of relevance connects the text, context, and language user during communication.

While this perspective provides the groundwork for the study of communication, much more needs to be done in analyzing the interrelated structures and processes that comprise any communicative act. Although I have not discussed this in detail, the issue of cognitive monitoring, or awareness of communication, is a critical one. Certainly anyone who acknowledges the planned, strategic nature of communication, as I do, must be concerned with cognitive monitoring. It appears that communicative activity can be monitored, and commented upon, to differing degrees and at different levels. For example, it is highly unlikely that people are consciously aware of their physiological control over articulation, yet people can comment on events like slips of the tongue. Also related to the issue of monitoring are the issues of communicative effectiveness, and the degree to which communication can be viewed as strategic (i.e., as planned and contingent).

Another critical issue concerns the intersubjective knowledge necessary for communication. Most argue that some intersubjective knowledge is required for communication, but again, there is little agreement about what type of knowledge might provide the basis for interaction, how completely such knowledge must be shared, and so forth.

Finally, and perhaps most critically, communication scholars must integrate the verbal and nonverbal dimensions of communication in their research. To adequately describe communication, scholars need to describe the information that participants have available to them in constructing their interpretations. Clearly, this will considerably complicate the analysis of communication, but it is, at some point, necessary. Research by Goodwin (1981), Beattie (1978a,b; 1981), Bull (1983) and others have clearly demonstrated the interrelationships between verbal and nonverbal systems of communication. Our descriptions can no longer afford *not* to integrate these dimensions, even if our primary purpose is to interpret verbal communication.

The descriptive basis for the study of verbal communication set out here is intended as an initial step toward a more adequate description of communication. This perspective focuses on relevance as a key integrative principle for communicative activity. The advantages of this perspective lie in its breadth, and in its analytic and methodological pluralism. This perspective on communication provides significant advantages in that it enables us to (1) integrate the influences of text, context and language user; (2) develop both individual and transactional views of communication; and (3) describe multiple levels of context.

III COMMUNICATION IN CONTEXT

7 Communicative Development

As with any new paradigm of research, scholars advocate diverse theories and methods for studying human communication. This diversity of research approaches is nowhere more apparent than in developmental pragmatics. And there appears to be an emerging consensus among researchers that no single approach will provide an adequate account of developmental pragmatics (Bates, Bretherton, Beeghly-Smith & McNew, 1981; Dickson, 1981). In view of this, many scholars now recognize that these diverse studies need to be integrated so that more adequate theory-building and research can be done (Ochs & Schieffelin, 1979). In what follows, I attempt the first steps toward this needed integration. In addition to integrating research in developmental pragmatics, I also discuss critical research issues that have emerged.

I begin by discussing children's developing pragmatic communicative skills as they emerge over the first five years of life. The view being presented here does *not* imply that prior stages of development are causally related to subsequent stages. Although researchers are making such claims, at this time it is not at all clear that such claims are theoretically sound.[1]

In my view, early communicative skills appear to develop in four broad stages. In the first stage, *Recognizing the Interpersonal Basis of Communication,* infants recognize the fundamental role of communication in

---

[1] The relationships between antecedent and later stages is discussed in more detail in the section on continuity and discontinuity in communication. See also, Bates et al., 1981; Bruner, 1983; Sugarman, 1983.

151

establishing relationships with others. The second stage, *Creating Communicative Effects,* from approximately four months to three years of age, occurs in three sub-stages: (1) preverbal routines—in which the child acquires an understanding of the requirements of dialogue, such as role reciprocity and turn taking; (2) communicative intentionality—in which the child begins to intentionally signal his or her needs; and (3) linguistic communication—in which the child demonstrates a functional mastery of language in accomplishing social goals. The third stage of development, *Using Communicative Strategies,* begins at approximately three years of age. During this period, the child develops an increasingly diverse set of linguistic forms to accomplish a variety of communicative goals. Thus, communication becomes increasingly adapted to different participants in different communicative settings. The final stage, *Monitoring Communication,* emerges at around five years of age. Children now develop the ability to evaluate the adequacy of messages and to make repairs, when needed, in conversing with others.

Scholars have also been concerned with characterizing the relevant social knowledge about communication that enables speakers to adjust their messages appropriately in varying social situations. The second section of this chapter deals with children's developing social knowledge about communication; such knowledge develops gradually in early childhood. First, infants develop an *Awareness of Self as Distinct from Others* during the first year of life; then, *Knowledge of Others* becomes increasingly differentiated during the second and third years, and finally, *Knowledge of Communicative Contexts* begins to emerge at the third year. We now turn to a more thorough discussion of each of these developmental areas.

I. DEVELOPING COMMUNICATIVE SKILLS

Stage I: Recognizing the Interpersonal Basis of Communication

The first stage of development is concerned with developing the motivation to communicate; in infancy, babies learn early on to recognize the intrinsic value of communication itself—that it is the way in which humans establish relationships with one another. The work of Colwyn Trevarthen (1977, 1979a,b; 1980a,b; 1982) has been most prominent in this area.

Trevarthen suggests that humans possess an innate ability for intersubjectivity. He defines intersubjectivity as a natural understanding of and sensitivity to interpersonal interaction. Trevarthen's analysis focuses on how the infant's motives influence the development of infant consciousness and purposive actions. Motives are viewed as internal processes through which individuals anticipate and interpret behavioral consequences. As Trevarthen points out, motives need not take into account external circumstances (like, for example, how likely something is to happen). In addition, motives may be expressed in a variety of ways (1982, p. 79).

Intention, as defined by Trevarthen (1982), involves *regulating* one's behavior by anticipating alternatives for action. Intentional behaviors are guided by motives: how the individual behaves to satisfy his/her motives is largely a matter of individual choice (1982, p. 80).

Trevarthen hypothesizes that motives and intentions develop in two stages, *Primary Intersubjectivity* and *Secondary Intersubjectivity*. Each stage reflects the infant's growing ability to express his/her intentions to act cooperatively with others.

The first stage, *Primary Intersubjectivity,* occurs in three sub-stages. In the first sub-stage, *Primary Interpersonal Life,* from birth to approximately ten weeks, the infant moves from an initial negative period of interaction (i.e., frequent withdrawal) to a later period in which lengthy expressive exchanges occur between the adult caretaker and child (Bates, 1979; Murray, 1980; Sylvester-Bradley, 1980). In the next sub-stage, *Object Prehension and Games,* from approximately 11 to 30 weeks, infants appear motivated to interact in cycles of avoidance and approach: motives for affectionate and cooperative interaction with others alternate with motives for withdrawal and avoidance. In the final sub-stage, *Development of Co-operative Understanding and Expression of Meaning,* from 31 to 60 weeks, the infant shows strong interest in others' actions, movements, and statements. After nine months, Trevarthen believes that infant communicative signals "clearly conceive of others [as] having interests, purposes and helpful powers" (1982, p. 100). During this period, infants develop skills and motives that enable them to sustain lengthy interactions with others.

The second stage in the development of motives and intentions, *Secondary Intersubjectivity,* emerges during the second year and occurs in cycles of little growth followed by enriched growth. During this stage, infants recognize that humans possess the capability for shared intention and awareness; thus, this stage is marked by more varied and creative interactions with familiar others (Trevarthen & Hubley, 1978, p. 216).

In summary, by the end of the second year of life, infants understand the basic intersubjective function of language—its communicative use. Trevarthen highlights the importance of this development when he observes that this interpersonal motivation (i.e., primary and secondary intersubjectivity) enables humans to act collectively, to share information, and to produce distinct cultures. Thus, the infant now possesses a fundamental motivation for interpersonal communication and the functional social sensitivity necessary for such communication.

Trevarthen's work fits into both Stage I and II of the proposed developmental account of verbal communication. It seemed most appropriate to give a complete overview of his research so that a clear systematic view of his perspective could be developed. For the synthesis being offered here, however, we are most interested in the development of primary intersubjectivity, especially sub-stages I and II, since this constitutes the developing recognition of the interpersonal nature of human communication. We turn now to the research of Bates, Dore, and Halliday for the next stage of communicative development: creating communicative effects.

Stage II: Creating Communicative Effects

During this stage, children develop increasing complexity in their understanding of the communication process itself and of the effects of particular communicative acts. This understanding occurs in three sub-stages: (1) preverbal routines; (2) communicative intentionality; and (3) linguistic communication. The most significant development during this time is the child's transition from nonverbal to verbal communication. Our discussion throughout, while focusing on the *use* of language for communication, will not be concerned with the acquisition of language itself.

Preverbal Routines. From approximately two to six months of age, infants establish interactive routines with adults. Among these early routines are patterned social exchanges during bathing, bed-time, feeding, and so forth, which are subsequently embedded in games like peekaboo. Through participating in such routines, infants develop an understanding of the fundamental aspects of communication such as role reciprocity, role reversibility, turn taking, strategies for gaining and maintaining joint attention, and so forth (Bates, 1979; Bruner, 1975b; Snow, 1977a; Stern, 1977). Nelson (1981) has termed this learning "participatory imitation" since the infant's performance completes the social routine.

Bruner (1983) refers to these preverbal routines as formats. Formats are interactions characterized by four conditions: (1) each member of the dyad has a goal and the means to attain that goal; (2) each member's responses are dependent upon a previous response by the other participant; (3) each member's responses are directed toward achieving that goal; and (4) there is a termination point at which the goal has been achieved. Bruner also points out that formats themselves change as new goals and strategies develop, as goals become coordinated between participants, and as the surrounding context changes.

These preverbal routines emphasize the interactive aspects of social encounters. Infants develop expectations about how one communicates: they recognize role reciprocity, role reversibility, a sense of sequence in communication, and so forth. One important communicative skill emerging during preverbal routines is turn taking. Dialogue implies that there will be an exchange of speaking and listening roles (i.e., turn taking), and many scholars suggest this appreciation first develops during preverbal routines.

Turn taking is a mechanism used to organize conversations so that interactants smoothly exchange speaking sequences. Through turn taking, participants coordinate their conversational contributions with one another (Sacks, Schegloff, & Jefferson, 1974). Infants appear to have an early appreciation of turn taking. According to Bruner (1975b), role reciprocity (i.e., taking turns and assuming the other's role as in, for example, conversational exchanges) develops through participation in give-and-take games. These social exchanges become intentional around nine or ten months of age (Bates, 1976), and gradually become more complex and well-organized (Bruner, 1975b).

Even with young babies, interactions between infant and caretaker have a definite sequence and timing which is structured by the turn taking of vocal exchanges (Bateson, 1975; Mueller & Lucas, 1975). Turn taking appears to reflect the interactive synchrony of a wide range of human behaviors, and thus Schaffer concludes that the infant appears to be "preadapted for social exchange" (1979, p. 283). According to Halliday (1979), turn taking marks the onset of dialogue, and is a prerequisite for the later emergence of communicative roles.

Keenan (1974) found that her infant sons took turns, handled interruptions, and made audible and appropriate responses to one another. Studies by Bloom, Rocissano, and Hood (1976) and by Schaffer, Collis, and Parsons (1977) found that 12- and 24-month-old children exchanged talking turns smoothly with their mothers; overlaps were brief and caused equally by mothers and children. Through object manipulation, games, and interactive routines, Schaffer (1979) claims that the 12-month-old infant "appears to comprehend, in a practical sense, the notion of reciprocity with its attendant ideas of complementarity, synchrony and role reversal" (p. 294). However, Schaffer also notes it is difficult to assess the extent of the infant's interactive skill or the degree to which the mother maintains the dialogue. In summary, turn taking appears to develop from biological patterns of temporal sequencing and interactional synchrony; in the context of communication, sequencing and synchrony develop into role reciprocity and role complementarity.

As we have seen, many of the rudimentary skills necessary for interpersonal communication, like turn taking, sequencing, and so forth, begin during preverbal routines. The degree to which these skills come under the intentional control of the infant, however, has been a subject of much controversy. In discussing the next sub-stage of development, *communicative intentionality,* we examine the infant's emerging ability to control his/her communicative skills.

Communicative Intentionality.   Bates et al. (1979) view intentionality as behavior in which "the sender is aware a priori of the effect a signal will have on his listener, and he persists in that behavior until the effect is obtained or failure clearly indicated" (p. 36). As such, intentional behavior involves the infant (1) visually checking the adult for feedback; (2) altering his/her signal upon changes in adult behavior; and (3) the infant's signalling becoming shorter and ritualized (i.e., signals are becoming conventionalized). As these signals become conventionalized, regular and predictable communication between adult and child can occur.

A broader perspective on the emergence of intentionality is offered by the work of John Dore (1983). Dore suggests that intentionality emerges in three stages. First, there is the intent to *act,* which emerges early in sensorimotor intelligence and is primarily behavioral in nature. Second, there is the intent to *express;* the infant vocalizes while looking and handling objects—there is an apparent intent to excitedly express something to someone (although these vocalizations are not used consistently). Third, there is the intent to *convey,* which reflects the infant's usage of recognizable words. Through using words, the baby signals (1) reference to some conceptual domain; (2) her intending some function like questioning or requesting and (3) her expectation that the hearer do something about it like playing or, at a minimum, acknowledging the utterance.

Dore goes on to point out the necessary role adults play in this development; how the adult interprets the child's action is more important than the baby's own intention. That is, both the infant and adult need to focus on each other's messages; adults especially need to respond at an appropriate level to the child. Finally, Dore observes that the adult's contribution to these dialogues provides objects for the child to attend to, but also negative examples and corrective vocalizations (e.g., "Oh, no, that's not something to play with. That doll might break.").

While varying approaches have been taken to try to account for intentionality, all approaches view intentionality in terms of altering behavior. This emphasis on the infant's ability to alter his or her communicative behavior also highlights the interactive nature of communicative intentionality. Infants need the responses of others in order to gain feedback about their own behavior: they rely on others' interpretations of their behavior. The infant cannot progress from intentional communication to the use of conventional communicative signals *without* the adult's interpretation of those signals. Thus, intentionality becomes expressed by conventional communicative signals. Finally, all perspectives acknowledge children's increasing control over expressing their intentions. This matter of control reflects, in part, the child's growing awareness of his or her effect on others. While researchers place the earliest behavioral evidence of intentionality at approximately nine months, clearly infants continue to develop increasing mastery over the communicative skills by which they express their intentions.

Both preceding sub-stages, preverbal routines and communicative intentionality, are prelinguistic stages. Our final sub-stage, *linguistic communication,* develops between 12 and 18 months. During this period, the child begins to communicate using language. Two theoretical approaches have been used to account for the emergence of verbal communication; speech act theory and functional approaches. Before presenting research from either view, I will briefly highlight some differences between them.

Linguistic Communication.   Language has often been discussed in terms of linguistic form (e.g., nouns, verbs, questions, and so forth) and linguistic function (e.g., the purpose for which language is being used—to persuade, to warn, to threaten, etc.). The split between form and function reflects a basic difference in emphasis between speech act analyses and functional analyses: speech act analyses emphasize linguistic form whereas functional approaches emphasize linguistic functions. Yet speech act analysis may deal not only with linguistic form itself, but also with the intentions, presuppositions, and implicatures of a particular linguistic form. For example, in making a request, what are the different ways in which one can make a request, and what are the presuppositions inherent in making a request? In general, functional analyses deal with analyzing the purposes for which children use language. While functional analyses may seem similar to analyzing the illocutionary force of a speech act, there are several points of contrast. First, functional analyses can incorporate both perlocutionary force and illocutionary force: that is, the function of an utterance can be viewed as effect, intention, or both. Speech act theory has generally ignored perlocutionary effect altogether. This, in my opinion, has weakened speech act theory because it ignores the important linkage between intent and effect. People intend to do things in order to create a desired effect— concentrating on intent deals with only part of the communicative process. Second, speech act analyses typically focus on a single proposition whereas functional analyses may incorporate more than a single proposition. Finally, functional approaches allow for the multi-functionality of utterances whereas speech act analysis focuses on one function an utterance could perform. With these differences in mind, let us now look at developmental research from both these perspectives.

Speech Acts.   From approximately twelve to eighteen months, children develop single words that more explicitly signal their intentions. Since there is debate as to whether single words can be viewed as propositional utterances, it is not clear that single words can be viewed as speech acts (i.e., utterances that have both illocutionary and locutionary force). However, the view that single words can be treated as propositional utterances is beginning to predominate and that is the view taken here.

Bates (1976) claims that infants substitute words for those preverbal gestures used to signal their intentions. Children encode whatever they consider most important in a given context (i.e., whatever is most interesting to them); thus, an infant's utterance "presupposes that situation, treating the uncoded elements [presuppositions] as the topic for the one-word comment" (1976, p. 159). As the child's information processing capacity grows, the child begins to produce multi-word utterances, and Bates uses the comment-topic principle to explain how children organize their sentences.

Dore (1974) argues that single words are primitive speech acts; single words have illocutionary, but not locutionary force. These primitive speech acts include labelling, repeating, answering, action requests, answer requests, calling, greeting, protesting, and practicing (Carter, 1975, 1978a,b). At around 18 months, single words or primitive speech acts develop into speech acts having both an elementary illocutionary force and a propositional content. Single-word utterances become increasingly elaborate, containing both a predicating and referring expression. Each utterance performs a specific function, such as asserting, making a request, etc. At the same time, children are also mastering the linguistic forms required for producing different utterances (e.g., mastering the syntactic forms for asking questions, stating imperatives, etc.). As the child's linguistic and communicative skills become more elaborate, the child begins to produce indirect as well as direct speech acts. We now turn to an analysis of children's use of indirect speech acts, and two direct speech acts, directives and interrogatives.

1. Indirect Speech Acts. Bates (1976) found that children, aged two to four, responded to both direct and indirect speech acts used by their mothers. Shatz (1974) found that two-year-olds obeyed indirect and direct requests equally frequently. Erwin-Tripp (1976) found that children produced imperatives (i.e., a direct speech act) as well as requests (i.e., an indirect speech act). All these researchers highlight children's reliance on contextual and nonverbal features in their interpretations of on-going encounters. Generally, there is no evidence to support the view that direct speech acts are learned prior to indirect speech acts.

2. Directives. Directives are speech acts that function as requests for action; they may be direct (i.e., imperatives) or indirect (i.e., interrogatives). Garvey (1975) found that children produced both direct and indirect requests for action, and that older children produced more indirect requests than did the younger children. Erwin-Tripp (1977) found that the earliest directives used by children were accompanied by gestures, the name of the

desired object, or linguistic markers like "want." Eventually children produce a variety of indirect forms, although it appears that the desired goal or
action must be noted by preschoolers. Read and Cherry (1978) conclude
that preschoolers possess a flexible array of directive forms that may be
alternated and combined in making requests.

3. Interrogatives.   Interrogatives have been widely studied in a variety
of functions and contexts. These include their use for clarification and
information seeking (Garvey, 1975, 1977; Cosaro, 1977); their use in turn
taking allocation (Snow, 1977a); and their use as an indirect request for
action (Bates, 1976; Shatz, 1974). Erwin-Tripp and Miller (1977) found that
children understand the obligation to answer questions. Erwin-Tripp (1970)
found that the child first understands yes-no, what and where questions.
Wh-questions were understood in the following order: why, who (subject),
where from, when and who (object) (Tyack & Ingram, 1977).

In addition, Bates has examined children's talk about speech acts (i.e.,
metapragmatics). These *metapragmatic* skills develop in three stages during the preoperational period. First, children refer explicitly to hearers and
speakers, and use locatives of space and time to specifically identify the
participants and location under discussion. Second, children use conjunc-
tions that link utterances together (e.g., connectives such as "and" and "if
not"). According to Bates, the third metapragmatic stage depends upon the
cognitive capacity to coordinate three or more information units such that
the third unit is "coordinated with a relationship established between the
other two" (1976, p. 152).

Finally, children also demonstrate their understanding of speech acts
through conventions. Three speech acts, imperatives, declaratives, and
interrogatives, can be substituted for one another and can serve to "soften"
utterances (i.e., make utterances polite or more polite). For example, the
imperative "close the door!" can be softened by using the interrogative
"Could you close the door?" By 2½ years, children use polite forms to
soften requests (e.g., "please"). At three, children seem to have a general
concept of politeness, and correctly judge the degree of politeness of
various linguistic forms (Bates, 1976). Also, Bates suggests that at 2½ years
of age, speech act usage shifts from an emphasis on efficiency to an
emphasis on politeness.

During the linguistic communication stage, the child moves from
"primitive" speech acts to fully formed speech acts (i.e., multi-word utterances with a clear propositional value and illocutionary force). Children
are developing distinct types of speech acts, like directives and interrogatives,
and using communicative strategies such as politeness conventions and
indirect speech acts. Next, we assess development during the linguistic
communication sub-stage from the functional perspective. As mentioned

previously, functional approaches focus on the purposes for which children use language. Two of the most prominent functionalist researchers are M.H.K. Halliday and Joan Tough.

Communicative Functions. M.H.K. Halliday (1975) provides a developmental account of communicative functions. Halliday argues that language plays a key role in socialization and that the structure of language reflects the functions for which language is used. The functional use of language develops in three phases. Phase I develops from 10½–18 months. Each utterance, whether a sound or actual utterance, has only one function. According to Halliday, four language functions appear during this time: *Instrumental* (stating desires and demands), *Regulatory* (controlling the actions of others), *Interactional* (expressing social or affective bonds), and *Personal* (informing others about one's own actions). At 18 months, two further functions develop: the *Heuristic* (explaining actions and events) and the *Imaginative* (imagining events, actions and objects).

During the transitional Phase II period, from 18 to 24 months of age, language functions become more complex and abstract. The six functions in Phase I merge into three broad functions: the *pragmatic* function (a blend of the earlier instrumental and regulatory functions); the *mathetic* function (a blend of the earlier personal and heuristic functions); and the *interactional* function. Another function, the *informative* function (which expresses information that is not apparent to listeners from the immediate context) also appears at this time. Grammatical structure begins to develop during this time as well; according to Halliday, grammatical structures allow an utterance to perform more than one function. Much of the development during this phase occurs through the opposition of the pragmatic (action) and mathetic (reflective) functions; Halliday points out that things are both acted upon and thought about.

The final phase, Phase III, marks the onset of the adult functional system. Two basic functions, the *ideational* function (derived from the mathetic function and used to "talk about the world") and the *interpersonal* function (derived from the interactional function and used to establish and maintain social relations), emerge during Phase III. A third function, the *textual,* reflects how language can be organized to serve other functions. These three basic functions allow the speaker to accomplish an infinite variety of purposes (Halliday, 1979). Rees (1978) suggests that the ideational and interpersonal functions parallel the noncommunicative and communicative functions of language (or to use Halliday's 1978, terms, the reflective and action oriented functions or language).

Joan Tough's research (1973) provides an extension and validation of Halliday's functional analysis. Tough's theoretical perspective distinguishes four language functions, each expressing a different mode of thinking.

Each function of language can be accomplished in different ways; these alternative means are designated *uses* of language. The four major language functions are to direct action, to interpret events and situations, to imagine, and to relate to others. Tough found that disadvantaged three-year-olds used language to focus on their present experience and to monitor their own activities. Advantaged three-year-olds used language for reasoning, anticipating future events, and creating imaginary contexts more than did disadvantaged peers. Using Tough's hierarchical analysis of language functions, Haslett (1983b) found developmental differences in the communicative functions and strategies used by preschoolers in their conversations with peers.

1. The Referential Function.   One function of language, the informative or referential function, has received considerable attention because of its pervasiveness, its importance for education, and its role as a component in more complex types of communication (Asher, 1979).

One of the most consistent findings in referential communication studies is that children do not understand that speakers are obligated to send messages that uniquely identify a referent (Asher, 1979; Asher & Wigfield, 1981; Whitehurst & Sonnenschein, 1981). Also, young children do not appear to recognize inadequate instructions and are less likely to ask questions for further information than older children (Flavell, 1981a; Robinson & Robinson, 1978b,c). Other studies by the Robinsons (1976a,b; 1977a,b; 1978a,b,c) asked children to account for communicative failure or success by blaming either listeners or speakers. Young children (five) usually fall into the listener-blaming category; speaker-blamers become common around seven. Generally, referential communication skills increase with age (Glucksberg, Krauss, & Higgins; 1975).

A monograph on referential communication by Lloyd and Beveridge (1981) is of particular interest because the subjects were preschoolers; most referential communication studies have tested children five or older. Lloyd and Beveridge found that: (1) preschoolers gave messages adequately describing a referent in 45% of their messages; (2) when asked to modify their message, 70% of the preschoolers were able to do so; (3) marked individual differences were found in preschoolers' listening and speaking strategies; (4) children performed better as speakers than as listeners; (5) children's messages in a spatial task failed to describe the orientation, position, and placement of the referent; and (6) some preschoolers recognize message deficiencies. Although preschoolers can provide adequate descriptions and modify their message when asked, their comparison skills and recognition of message deficiency are generally lacking.

The functional uses of language that begin to emerge at around 12 to 18 months are well established by age three. The three basic functions of language appear to be ideational (informational), interpersonal (relational), and textual (the organization of language itself). Although other functional systems can become much more elaborate depending upon the needs of the researcher (see, for example, Tough, 1977, or Dore, 1977, for more detailed functional schemes), all of these schemes collapse into the three fundamental functions outlined by Halliday.

In retrospect, as we summarize the communicative accomplishments of the linguistic communication sub-stage, we can see the tremendous growth achieved during this period. At the beginning of this sub-stage, children had just begun to use multiword utterances designed to achieve particular social ends. Children can produce both direct and indirect speech acts, and have begun to use politeness conventions in their interactions with others by the end of this stage.

Two approaches have been used to characterize communicative development during this period—speech act analysis and functional approaches. While both these approaches detail the complexity of communicative skills children acquire during this time, each approach reflects only partial understanding of communicative development. For an adequate theory of human communication, I believe the unfortunate split between linguistic form and linguistic function must come to an end. When we communicate, form and function interact. This interplay between form and function undoubtedly emerges during early childhood, and developmental research and theory should reflect this as well. Thus, while we have an understanding of how linguistic forms and functions emerge, we have yet to develop models explaining their complex interrelationships with one another during communication. These interrelationships also need to be assessed in light of particular social relationships and given social contexts.

During the next stage of developmental pragmatics, *Using Communicative Strategies,* children experience increased interaction with other peers and unfamiliar adults (e.g., preschool teachers, etc.); as a result, children must adapt their messages to a variety of interactants in a diverse range of settings. The increased complexity of these communicative demands require children to establish communicative strategies. These strategies enable children to communicate clearly, to establish and maintain conversational topics, and to accurately interpret the remarks of others. In short, skills that emerged during the previous eighteen months become refined and expanded.

Stage III: Using Communicative Strategies

Communicative strategies, enabling children to sustain conversations with others, rapidly expand from approximately three to five years of age. Children can now initiate and maintain conversational topics (Ochs &

Schieffelin, 1979), adapt messages to others (Shatz & Gelman, 1973), link statements together to pursue a particular line of reasoning (Eisenberg & Garvey, 1981; Haslett, 1983c), creatively role play in free play with peers (Garvey, 1974; Haslett, 1983b), and so forth. Thus, children demonstrate considerable skill in interacting with others in varied settings. We shall look particularly at three communicative devices—deixis, topicalization, and use of conversational maxims—which support children's dialogues with others.

Deixis. Deixis refers to linguistic devices that clearly identify person, place, and time when communicating. Thus, deixis serves to "anchor the utterance to the communicative setting in which it occurs" (Rees, 1978, p. 210). The most basic deictic element, of course, is the "I-you" (i.e., speaker-listener) distinction in communication. Other linguistic devices, like demonstratives and adverbs, locate discourse referents in place (e.g., "here," "this," etc.) and in time (e.g., "now," "later," etc.). Rees (1978) suggests that deictic features convey a significant amount of conversational meaning. According to Bruner (1975a), an understanding of reciprocal roles in discourse is necessary for deixis.

Keenan and Schieffelin (1976) found that children at the two-word stage use pronouns to refer to objects in the present environment, but not to nonpresent objects. Charney (1979) found that children (aged 3½) understand "here" and "there" from the speaker's perspective. DeVilliers and deVilliers (1979) conclude that appropriate use of pronouns and demonstratives occurs between four or five years of age. Finally, deictic elements have also been analyzed in light of their role in cohesion and topic maintenance (deVilliers & deVilliers, 1979; Halliday & Hasan, 1976; Haslett, 1983a).

Topicalization. Topicalization refers to the speaker's ability to establish and maintain discourse topics. For coherent discourse, both speaker and listener must be able to maintain the topic. According to Keenan and Schieffelin (1976), children at the one and two-word stage can establish topics, get other's attention easily, speak clearly and intelligibly, and specify the objects being talked about. Many of these strategies for getting attention and identifying referents are nonverbal (e.g., pointing, touching, etc.).

Children also use presuppositions to maintain topic. Bates (1979) argues that the relationship between proposition (i.e., the topic) and presupposition (i.e., the comment about the topic) parallel the figure/ground relationship: children encode the new (the topic) against a background of mutually understood information (presupposition). In a cross-cultural study of communicative strategies distinguishing new from given information,

MacWhinney and Bates (1978) found that children used ellipsis, pronominalization, stress, and indefinite/definite pronouns to mark topics from comments about topics.

Once a topic is established, however, children need to maintain this topic in conversation with others. The evidence appears to suggest that children have limited success in maintaining a topic. Keenan and Schieffelin (1976) suggest that a limited attention span, misunderstanding of the preceeding utterances, and distractability may inhibit young children's ability to produce contingent, relevant responses. Bloom, Rocissano, and Hood (1976) found that, at three, less than 50% of children's utterances were contingent responses. Topic maintenance, they suggest, may not extend beyond two talking turns. However, other studies, in a variety of settings, (Garvey & Hogan 1973; Gelman & Shatz, 1977; Haslett, 1983b) found that children can sustain topics over lengthy exchanges. Further research is needed to fully explore how and why children maintain topics in some interactions, but not in others. For example, factors like the child's *interest* in the topic or *familiarity* with the social setting undoubtedly influence topic maintenance.

Conversational Maxims.   Conversational maxims refer to assumptions about the nature of human interaction (Bates, 1976, p. 27). Grice (1975) has analyzed these conversational maxims into four general rules: (1) Be cooperative (i.e., truthful); (2) Be relevant; (3) Be clear, and (4) Be efficient (i.e., avoid redundancy). Grice suggests these rules are used so that when speakers violate them, this additional information facilitates the listener's interpretation of the message.

Bates further comments that "the ability to predict whether or not the listener shares a given assumption and to plan one's utterances accordingly is one of the highest achievements in pragmatic development" (1979, p. 447). Bates' research (1976) on conversational maxims has centered upon politeness judgments. Politeness may be expressed in the linguistic form of an utterance (e.g., a request rather than an imperative) or may be signalled nonverbally (e.g., a soft rather than harsh tone). By age three to four, children are using indirect commands, the imperfect tense to soften commands, and formal modes of address as politeness strategies. Bates suggests that, by three, children have a general concept of politeness and shift from a focus on the efficiency dimension of utterances (i.e., economy and informativeness) to a focus on the politeness dimension.

During the communicative strategies stage, the complexity of communication increases substantially; language itself becomes more complex, and children are interacting with peers as well as adults in diverse settings. In order to meet these demands, children refine and extend basic skills learned previously. Joint attention and reference, developed earlier between mother and infant in their preverbal routines, now is precisely detailed through the child's use of deictic elements. Children use pronouns, demonstratives, and locatives to specify the relationships between objects, events, and individuals, and to focus attention on those relationships.

Previously, children were primarily reactive (i.e., they primarily *respond* to stimuli, rather than actively initiating their own messages—see Haslett, 1983c). However, as children develop skills for initiating and maintaining dialogues with others, they actively initiate new topics, and use presuppositions in maintaining conversations. Also aiding their ability to sustain interaction with others is children's growing understanding of conversational postulates; children have a general understanding of the communicative requirements of relevancy, informativeness, clarity, and the like.

Up to this point, the child's developing pragmatic communicative skills focus on expanding his/her competency as a speaker. In our final stage, *Monitoring Communication,* the child begins to shift his/her attention to the communicative message—its accuracy, clarity, and effectiveness. This message orientation rests on the child's ability to metacommunicate—that is, the act of communication itself must be treated as an object of evaluation and discussion. This metacommunicative ability begins to emerge at around five years of age. By middle childhood, children have a well-established set of metacommunicative strategies which they apply to messages and listeners (see, for example, Flavell, Speer, Green, & Austin, 1981; O'Keefe & Delia, 1979). We now turn to a more thorough discussion of communicative monitoring.

Stage IV: Monitoring Communication

Flavell et al. (1981) suggest that communication cannot be analyzed apart from other cognitive processes; thus, the nature and development of communicative monitoring may not be "adequately understood if examined in isolation from cognitive monitoring" in other areas (p. 37). Furthermore, Flavell's research suggests that young children may fail at communication tasks because they do not treat "messages as analyzable cognitive objects." (p. 37).

Although aspects of metacommunicative monitoring are relatively well-established at around five, earlier signs of such monitoring have been noted. For example, Bates (1979) reports metacommunicative comments (e.g., "He said no"; "She said it was red"; etc.) occurring in children's talk between 30–36 months of age. These comments, however, appear to perform a report or verification function rather than a monitoring function. Yet they reflect an important awareness among young children—namely, that talk can be treated as an object (i.e., talk can be talked about).

The use of polite forms also indicates monitoring activity. Bates (1976) found that by 30 months children were using polite or indirect forms to "soften" their utterances, and that by 36 months children had a general concept of politeness. As Bates points out, children may be polite to efficiently get what they want; this presupposes that children have previously "monitored" the relationship between politeness and goal achievement, and learned the pragmatic value of various request/politeness forms.

Disputes provide an ideal opportunity for communicative monitoring since such monitoring appears to be particularly relevant (i.e., necessary for constructing strategies and gaining one's ends). Researchers have analyzed the communicative rules and strategies children use in arguments (Benoit, 1981; O'Keefe & Benoit, 1982). With increasing age, children rely more on messages that contain more information (Eisenberg & Garvey, 1981); that reflect more flexible strategies and more adaptation to listeners (Delia, Kline, & Burleson, 1979); and that become cognitively and communicatively more complex, and more coordinated with the messages of others (Haslett, 1983c). All this suggests that children gradually become more aware of the communicative demands of disputes and more adept at trying to accomplish their goals. Such ability, again, presupposes growing differentiation in the child's metacommunicative knowledge about himself/herself, about others and relationships with others, and about task demands (Applegate & Delia, 1980; Bateson, 1976; Glick, 1978).

In summary, monitoring communication focuses the speaker's attention on the message and addressees (Flavell, 1979). Children begin to evaluate message adequacy, to adapt their messages when conflict with others' goals is recognized, to discuss the communication process explicitly, and to utilize knowledge of others in constructing their communicative strategies. These skills are beginning to emerge at five, and become well-established in middle childhood. Through monitoring communication, children become increasingly adept at sending socially appropriate messages in a variety of contexts.

Thus far, our review of developmental pragmatics has explored the child's emerging communicative skills. Early in infancy, children have a sensitivity to and understanding of communication as a means of establishing relationships and cooperating with others. This first stage of development was termed *recognizing the interpersonal nature of communication.* The next stage, *creating communicative effects,* spans from approximately four months to three years; during this stage, the child moves from preverbal routines to well-established linguistic communication. The child intentionally communicates her/his views utilizing a variety of speech acts to accomplish differing goals; language is used to express a range of functions (e.g., expressive, directive, informative, etc.). In the next stage, *utilizing communicative strategies,* children refine and extend communicative skills like turn-taking, maintaining topic, using deixis, coordinating their messages with others to accomplish differing purposes, and the like. This stage, from approximately three to five years, is also marked by increased interaction with peers; communicative strategies may expand because children are not just communicating with adults who often anticipate and fill in the missing gaps in children's messages—rather they must effectively interact with peers whose knowledge and capacities are roughly equivalent to their own. The final stage of children's pragmatic communicative skills, *monitoring communication,* develops at around five years. Here the child begins to metacommunicate, at times commenting on his/her own talk, making conversational repairs, and so forth. (For an overview of these stages and their communicative achievements, see Table 1.)

Each developmental stage reflects added cognitive and communicative complexity. The process of communication itself becomes more difficult, over time, as language is added as communicative tool, as tasks become more varied and complex, and as interactants and settings become more varied. As children mature, adults also expect more (Bruner, 1984; Dore, 1983); adults thus "up the ante" and communicative demands are correspondingly increased. The increase in peer/peer interaction, at around three years, also adds considerable complexity to interpersonal interaction. While adults typically accommodate their communication to the child's cognitive level, no such accommodation is possible by peers. Thus, children must develop communicative strategies that enable them to send socially appropriate, adapted messages. This ability, however, is not just a matter of the pragmatic skills and strategies that we have discussed: children also need to acquire social knowledge about communication that enables them to exercise these skills and strategies in appropriate settings and at appropriate times. The ability to communicate effectively involves a complex assessment of the communicative task, the interactants, and the social setting.

Before turning to a more thorough discussion of the acquisition of social knowledge about communication, a brief caution is in order. The unfortunate dichotomy between linguistic form and linguistic function is also present between communicative skills and communicative knowledge. In order to communicate effectively, one needs to possess the necessary communicative skills. However, those skills are relatively useless *without* the communicative knowledge that enables one to exercise them in an appropriate manner. *The interaction between communicative knowledge and communicative skill is a central concern of pragmatic approaches to human communication.* However, virtually all researchers focus on either pragmatic skills or pragmatic knowledge. It is not hard to understand why this is the case: tracing the development of either the communicative skills or the communicative knowledge base for interpersonal interaction is in

TABLE 1
Stages in Children's Development of Communicative Skills

Age	Developmental Stages	Communicative Accomplishments
0–60 weeks	I. *Interpersonal Basis of Communications*	
0–10 weeks	1. Primary Interpersonal Life	complex expressive exchanges
11–30 weeks	2. Object Prehension & Games	cycles of interaction and withdrawal
31–60 weeks	3. Development of co-operative understanding and expression	substantial cooperative activities and exchanges with others
4 mos.–3 yrs.	II. *Creation of Communicative Effects*	
2–12 months	1. Preverbal Routines	understanding of and participation in interactive routines; appreciate turn taking, role reciprocity and role reversal
begins at 9–10 months	2. Communicative Intentionality	purposively uses and alters messages to accomplish goals; later conventional signals emerge
begins at 12–18 months	3. Linguistic Communication	begins with single words and gradually achieves functional mastery of speech acts and communicative functions
3–5 years	III. *Communicative Strategies*	wider range of interactions demands communicative strategies that can adapt to different communicative demands; strategies include use of politeness conventions, presuppositions, deictic elements and conversational postulates; can initiate and sustain discourse topics
begins around 5 years	IV. *Monitoring Communication*	treats talk as an object to be commented upon. Beginning to check message accuracy and adequacy

itself tremendously complex.[2] But for pragmatic theories of communication to develop, such integration is necessary. Hopefully, the synthesis and views expressed here will be a first step in these efforts.

As previously discussed, when we examine the pragmatic communicative skills children develop in early childhood, we see only one aspect of the child's pragmatic competence. Communication scholars utilizing pragmatic approaches are also interested in representing the child's social knowledge that enables him/her to communicate appropriately. It is to this underlying social knowledge that we now turn.

II. DEVELOPING SOCIAL KNOWLEDGE ABOUT COMMUNICATION

Social knowledge relevant to communication appears to develop in three broad stages. The most fundamental social distinction needed for communication is the I-thou, speaker-listener distinction. This *distinction between self and others* appears to develop during the first year of life. As more interactions occur with a wider variety of interactants, a *more finely differentiated knowledge of others* is necessary for effective communication (Chandler, 1977, 1982; Flavell et al., 1981; Shantz, 1981). This increasingly differentiated knowledge of others gradually emerges during early childhood: at five, children have internalized interpersonal constructs of others (O'Keefe & Delia, 1982).

As knowledge of others increases, so too does the child's *knowledge of social situations* and their communicative requirements. Knowledge of others and of social situations appear to develop concomittantly; knowledge of others is undoubtedly facilitated by interacting with others in contexts that highlight different aspects of their personalities. Also, knowledge of the communicative demands in particular settings may be facilitated by observing how different individuals handle that situation. In sum, assessing children's developing social knowledge about communication gives us insight into how individuals begin to establish and maintain interpersonal relations with one another, and insight into the essential role communication plays in this process. Each of these aspects of social knowledge—knowledge of self as distinct from others, knowledge of others and knowledge of social situations—is discussed in turn. Although knowledge of self as distinct from others appears to be prior to and necessary for

---

[2]More research needs to be done on the interaction between communicative skills and the social knowledge underlying use of those skills. In addition, researchers have failed to assess the interrelationships among various communicative skills and among various aspects of social knowledge.

knowledge of others and of social situations, no other interactions are being advocated here.[3]

Knowledge of Self as Distinct from Others

An infant's interactions with responsive others are believed to be radically different from other exchanges because others provide the opportunity for social interactions (Bruner, 1983; Damon, 1981; Stern, 1977). By eight or nine months, infants appear to have a sense of personal agency since they use objects to obtain goals (Wolf, 1981). Wolf argues that from nine to fifteen months, infants recognize the separateness of self from others. Attachment to and fear of separation from familiar others also become evident during this time, and infants recognize that others act as independent agents (Gelman & Spelke, 1981; Harding & Golinkoff, 1979). This sense of separate identity is fundamental to the I-thou, speaker-listener distinction in dialogue.

In a longitudinal study of a single child, Wolf (1981) found that the concept of independent agency emerged in three stages: first, others were regarded as instruments; second, others were regarded as equivalent human actors, and finally, others were regarded as independent agents. These stages emerge at different times in different domains. New levels emerged first in goal-directed interaction, then in games, next in language and doll play, and finally, in addressing a co-player in dramatic play. Wolf points out that human interaction is the outcome of what a number of independent actors contribute to a situation; communicators act according to their own self-generated rules or plans (1981, p. 299).

The concept of independent agency is fundamental to the speaker/listener relationship in communication and also helps contribute to knowledge about how children form an idea of what people are like *in general* (Shantz, 1982). We have briefly sketched the development of a general concept of self as distinct from others; we now turn to an analysis of how this rudimentary knowledge of others becomes more differentiated.

---

[3]Considerable controversy exists concerning the definitions of cognition and social cognition. Researchers in social cognition point out that individuals have unique capabilities for interaction whereas objects do not; thus social cognitive processes (those processes involving individuals' understanding of themselves, others and social relationships) are viewed as quite distinct from the study of cognition (knowledge and understanding of events and objects in the world). Thus, knowledge about communication, and its influence on communicative processes, is itself problematic. Similar concerns have emerged in discussions of mutual knowledge, commonsense knowledge and their influence on communication.

Knowledge of Others

Gelman and Spelke (1981) suggest that by four, children are developing "a systematic set of beliefs about the thoughts, feelings, intentions, motives, knowledge, and capacities of other people" (p. 51). Researchers have approached the study of social knowledge of others from two general perspectives: the *person perception* perspective focuses upon various cues that others give off, which children must accommodate to; and the *role taking* perspective, which emphasizes children's ability to take another's perspective (Chandler, 1977). Chandler argues that the person perception perspective focuses on children's accommodation while the role taking perspective emphasizes the process of assimilation.

According to the person perception model, one registers cues given off by another, encodes these cues, and draws inferences from them. Children, with increasing age, move from statements describing concrete characteristics of others to describing other's feelings and thoughts (Chandler, 1977). With increasing age, children rely more on abstract dispositional constructs, and the number and abstractness of these constructs also increase. Preschool children seldom use these constructs, but they become a regular part of children's vocabulary by nine or ten years of age.

Scholars in the Wernerian tradition claim these attributions (i.e., dispositional constructs) become increasingly differentiated and hierarchically ordered over time. In studying impression formation, Scarlett, Press, and Crockett (1971) found that age was correlated with the number, variety, and differentiation of interpersonal constructs. With increasing age, children's judgments of personal characteristics were moderated by situational or temporal factors, or by the internal states of the person being judged. Bigner (1974), in a study of kindergartners through eighth graders, found that with increasing age, children's characterizations of others become more abstract and hierarchically organized. In addition, Gollin (1958) found that with increasing age, children used qualitatively different inference models in forming impressions of others; older children were more able to resolve incongruent cues. Chandler (1977) notes that children's increasing sensitivity to potential social stimuli must depend, in part, on how they integrate these stimuli with their own perspective; that is, it must depend on the child's capacity to differentiate his or her own view from another's.

Role taking.   Role taking depends on the degree to which an individual can differentiate himself or herself from others. Thus role taking has been viewed along a continuum of egocentrism (i.e., a person's view is limited to an individual, personalized perspective) to perspectivism (i.e., a person is increasingly able to distinguish between his or her view and others' views)

(Chandler, 1977, p. 10). Because of various methodological difficulties (e.g., stimulus objects being selected to give maximum contrasts for alternative perspectives, difficulty of distinguishing between role taking and stereotypic responses to situations, etc.), Shantz (1981) concludes that studies of role taking abilities have generally produced inconsistent and contradictory results. Others have suggested that contradictory findings may occur because different nonsocial and social dimensions may become salient at different ages, or depend on different levels of cognitive ability (Chandler, 1977). Shantz (1981) suggests that children may be able to take the role of another, but may not be able to encode this understanding.

Despite inconsistent findings, some trends have emerged (Chandler, 1977). Egocentrism has been found to decline and role taking skills increase with age. Children often fail to distinguish between public and private information and generally assume that others understand more than they do (i.e., children mistakenly assume that private information, known only by them, is also known by others). Greenspan, Barenboim, and Chandler (1974), in a study of first and third graders, found that older children who were sensitive to incongruent cues given by a central character were reluctant to make inferences about the character and were uncertain about their judgments. Younger children appeared to ignore the incongruent cues and expressed confidence in their judgments. Although Flavell has found rudimentary role taking among two- and three-year old children, generally the coordination of multiple items of information necessary for role taking seems to develop in middle childhood.

Higgins (1981) suggests a developmental order in role taking: first, there is situational role taking (i.e., what would I do/think in that situation). Second, there is an acknowledgment that people in the same situation may react differently; and finally, there is a comparison and contrast of one's own views with those of another. Higgins points out that controlling the intrusion of one's own view is critical in the last stage, when comparisons of viewpoints are needed. Depending upon the situation, the individuals involved and so forth, controlling the intrusion of one's view may vary in difficulty (Ross, 1981).

In summary, the infant's distinction between self and others develops gradually into a finely differentiated knowledge about others. Two approaches, person perception and role taking, have been used to characterize the infant's growing social knowledge of others. While person perception models emphasize the child's understanding of others' personal characteristics, role taking models emphasize the child's ability to take the view of another in a given situation. Thus, person perception models emphasize more enduring dispositional qualities while role taking models emphasize situationally-governed dispositional qualities. Both types of social knowledge appear necessary for effective communication, although one type of knowledge may be more important than the other in a given communicative context. For example, person perception may be most important in deciding whether or not you want to actively pursue friendship with another, while role taking may be of more value in "sizing up" people in initial encounters.

Our ability to interact effectively with others is dependent upon our recognition of them as independent actors, and our knowledge of them as individuals. The final component of social knowledge needed for effective communication is knowledge of context. Contextual knowledge may be sub-divided into two areas: knowledge of social relationships and knowledge of social situations. While we separate relational knowledge from situational knowledge here for heuristic reasons, it is important to remember that these knowledge bases do not develop in isolation, but are closely interrelated. As noted elsewhere, what has been termed "world knowledge" (Clark & Clark, 1977) or "tacit knowledge" (Bransford & McCarrell, 1974) appears to be a complex network of relevant social knowledge (of self, of others, and of context) that is activated in given social encounters and that guides our interpretation of "what is going on" in a given encounter.

III. KNOWLEDGE OF SOCIAL CONTEXT

Knowledge of Social Relationships

Damon (1981) points out that children, to become interactionally competent, must construct "their own systematically organized understanding of social relations and of the multiple types of interaction . . . that maintain these relations" (p. 160). Children, like adults, must recognize that utterances not only establish a propositional content but express a social order as well (Bateson, 1972; Watzlavick, Beavin, & Jackson, 1967). In a study that asked children to recall final key statements made in a story, Olson and Hilyard (1981) found that young children scanned utterances for their social meanings and then differentiated the propositional content of the utterance (i.e., were they being asked to *assent* to the truth value of the statement?) from its illocutionary force (i.e., were they being asked to *comply* to a request?).

A number of studies demonstrate that the form of speech acts which regulate the actions of others (e.g., directives, questions, requests, etc.) is determined by relational issues such as status and politeness. Mitchell-Kernan and Kernan (1977) found that some children give commands to other children just to establish a dominant status relationship. Erwin-Tripp (1977) found children varied their directives according to the age, familiarity, or dominance of the listener. Ackerman (1978) found that young children can recognize the intentionality in unconventional directive forms. A number of studies (Bates, 1976; Erwin-Tripp, 1977; Gelman & Shatz, 1977; Shatz, 1978) suggest that young children focus on the social meaning of the utterance rather than its propositional content.

Other researchers (Cicourel, 1972; Cook-Gumperz & Gumperz, 1976) have pointed out that role and status are continually being negotiated in conversation. In face-to-face interaction, "what looks on the surface to be a series of discrete, successive 'turns' is actually a process of continuous, simultaneously reflexive behaving and monitoring by the two players" (Erickson & Shultz, 1982, p. 246).

As we have seen, social relationships between interactants tend to guide their interpretations of the on-going interaction. The relational dimension thus plays a substantial role in communication since both the decoding and encoding of messages are governed by social relationships. However, these relationships need to be considered in light of particular social contexts. The context, for example, may govern the set of social relationships possible in that context. In like manner, social relationships may also influence the social context; they may, for example, render a business meeting less formal. While it is heuristically useful to parse out relational from contextual knowledge, both mutually influence one another in a complex variety of ways. Let us now turn to consider the influence of context, defined as the surrounding social situation, on communication.

Knowledge of Social Situations

Cook-Gumperz and Gumperz (1976) suggest an interactive interpretation of context:

> we will talk about the processes of contextualization, which build on the speaker's ability to associate certain kinds of linguistic contextualization cues, such as the first name versus full name, or choice of code, style, or pronunciation, with propositional content on the one hand and extralinguistic cues and background expectations on the other. (p. 20)

As associations build up among these cues, speakers make judgments about the communicative activity they are participating in. For example, the informal linguistic cue—use of first names—when combined with a casual conversational topic [propositional content] at a cocktail party [background expectations] lead to the conclusion that participants are engaged in small talk. Such judgments about what type of communication we are engaged in serve as frames of reference for interpreting the on-going interaction. A speaker's belief about what type of communication s/he is engaged in (for example, a lecture as opposed to a casual discussion) may be explicitly mentioned in interactions, especially if speakers need to make some conversational repairs (e.g., to correct a mistaken interpretation, to clarify previous comments, etc.). In this way, interactants make the context a shared cognitive construct and thus, interactants are *creating* context as well as *communicating in* a given social situation. Cook-Gumperz and Gumperz view context as a creative interpretation of on-going interaction; an interpretation that is created by both interactants.

Children and adults differ in their use of contextualization cues and thus misunderstandings may arise (Gumperz & Herasimchuk, 1973). While adults focus their attention on the verbal message against a background of constantly monitored nonverbal information, children appear to "regard all the available information as similarly weighted for the purpose of what is being said" (Cook-Gumperz & Gumperz, 1976, p. 19).

In a study that explored subjects' judgments of personal dispositions and situational constraints in predicting a story character's response to a situation, Ross (1981) found that young children (aged 5) gave most weight to situational constraints and least weight to the personal dispositions. Eight, eleven, and fifteen-year-old subjects gave more weight to the behavioral information about the story character which reflected his/her stable personality traits rather than the specific situation the character was in. Thus older subjects appeared to fall into the "fundamental attribution error;" a specific inferential bias that causes individuals to underestimate the power of situational constraints relative to personal predispositions in controlling behavior (Ross, 1981, p. 21).

Finally, Cook-Gumperz and Cosaro (1976) found that preschooler's interactions are guided by expectations about "what goes on" in various areas in the nursery (e.g., conventionalized role playing in the playhouse, fantasy play in the sandbox, etc.) and that different communicative strategies are used to sustain these interactions. They conclude that "specific properties of social context are part of the information children make note of and utilize in . . . interactive episodes" (1976, p. 431). Cook-Gumperz, in her study of children's persuasive talk, concludes that children rely on their "accumulated situational knowledge" as much as they rely on their linguistic knowledge in interpreting other's utterances (1981, p. 48). Mishler's analysis (1979) of children's trading talk found that speech acts needed to be interpreted in context; a subsequent remark could alter a prior interpretation of an utterance. And Schieffelin's (1981) analysis of sibling relationships in Kaluli society found that mothers carefully "school" their children in this relationship through formulaic messages that co-occur with a specific set of contextualization cues.

As previously discussed, contextual knowledge—both in terms of relational and situational knowledge—provides an important basis for interpreting on-going interactions. With the increase in pragmatic research on human communication, attention has also been directed at how humans acquire this contextual knowledge. Let us take a brief look at the research of Katherine Nelson (1981) in which she suggests that social knowledge, especially that knowledge relevant to interpersonal communication, is acquired via scripts.

Acquiring Social Knowledge

The work of Argyle (1975, 1981) and Cook-Gumperz (1981) suggest that adults interpret messages by analyzing information across various communication modalities (e.g., eye gaze, intonation, stress, posture, etc.). Cook-Gumperz and Gumperz (1976) suggest that information available in a context is interpreted against "a developed notion of what constitutes a 'normal array' of information in the background and the foreground features" (p. 18). It seems unlikely that this "normal array" of knowledge is learned piecemeal; children appear to learn the "whole routine" first and only later begin to differentiate particular dimensions or sub-routines.

Scripts, as defined by Nelson, reflect a concrete, well-specified sequence of actions, located in a spatial and temporal context, and designed to accomplish a particular goal. Young children possess general script knowledge (e.g., of everyday events like going to a restaurant, etc.) that is consistent over time and socially accurate. A study by Nelson (1978) found that preschoolers can verbalize and act out scripts; experienced preschoolers had more script knowledge than newcomers, and scripts became more skeletal in form as activities became more varied. Young children appear to be very skilled at extracting the main idea or purpose of an event, and use sequencing to connect central events in a script.

Nelson (1981) argues that children acquire scripts through experience. Adults usually arrange exchanges with infants (e.g., Bruner's formats, etc.) and infants acquire their roles through participation in the interaction. Children's roles become progressively more differentiated (Bruner, 1977) and eventually children begin acting out scripts (e.g., playing house, playing school, etc.). This social knowledge guides routine encounters, and when these encounters become well-established, individuals "run through" the sequence of actions automatically. When an individual is freed from attending to the on-going action, Nelson suggests that "cognitive space" is gained and thus attention can be focused upon problematic aspects of an encounter. She also found that children appear to be competent at dialogue organized around shared script knowledge, but are not skilled negotiators in new areas. Finally, Nelson suggests that more abstract categorical knowledge is built up from script knowledge; thus some social categories may be formed on the basis of similar roles in a number of scripts.

Thus far we have looked at the young child's developing social knowledge of self, of others, and of context. We have also explored how this knowledge may be acquired as a gestalt via scripts. In addition, we have looked at the child's developing communicative skills as well as the child's developing social knowledge about communication. These two areas of pragmatic development—communicative skills and social knowledge about communication—have been discussed separately; this, unfortunately, reflects the fact that researchers have studied one or the other, but only rarely the interrelationships between these two pragmatic components of communication. In the section that follows, I briefly discuss the research of Lubin and Forbes, and Delia and his associates, which links aspects of social knowledge with communicative strategies. In my view, such research is needed if our theories are to accurately capture the dynamic complexity of human communication.

Social Cognition and Communication

With increasing age, children develop more complex cognitive systems for regulating social behavior. This general development is influenced by many factors including motivation, the influence of peer culture, opportunities for interaction, and so forth.

Lubin and Forbes (1981) view social reasoning as the planful regulation of social behavior. As such, social reasoning relies on specific social and cognitive skills, such as making inferences and applying script knowledge to everyday encounters. They postulate three levels of social reasoning (i.e., levels of making inferences); Level 1, *Mechanistic Stereotypy,* reflects a correspondence between situational effects and individual psychological reactions—in similar situations, others would react as you would. In Level 2, *Reactive Subjectivism,* individuals *interpret* the situation in the same way (e.g., situation X is an unhappy occasion), but may *react* to the situation differently (e.g., situation X may make person A sad, while person B may not be bothered by it). On Level 3, *Constructive Subjectivism,* individuals recognize that both interpretations of and reactions to events may vary.

With increasing age, children moved from Level 1 to Level 3 social reasoning: the movement from Level 1 to Level 2 reasoning appears to move toward increasing decentration, and the shift from Level 2 to Level 3 moves from a passive view of humans to viewing others as active, intentional actors (Forbes & Lubin, 1981). Level 3 also appears similar to reciprocal role taking (Selman & Byrne, 1974) and to metacognition (Flavell, 1981a); thus these skills may develop earlier than previously thought.

Persuasive strategies were found to be significantly related to level of social reasoning. Ritualistic strategies, like appeals to rules or norms, reflected Level 1 reasoning; affect-oriented strategies reflected Level 2 social reasoning, and construal strategies, focusing upon clarification of the referent and/or intent, reflected Level 3 reasoning. Furthermore, these strategies were hierarchically stratified, with ritualistic strategies being least complex and construal strategies being the most complex. They conclude that children regulate their behavior, in part, by reasoning processes that are linguistically based.

According to Applegate and Delia (1980), research linking social-cognitive and communicative development has produced mixed results because no clear conceptual ties have been developed between aspects of social-cognitive development and aspects of communicative behavior. The work of Jesse Delia and his colleagues (Applegate & Delia, 1980; Benoit, 1981; Clark & Delia, 1976, 1977; Delia & Clark, 1977; Delia, Kline, & Burleson, 1979; Delia & O'Keefe, 1979; Delia, O'Keefe, & O'Keefe, 1982; O'Keefe & Benoit, 1982) links cognitive complexity (number of cognitive constructs) and construct abstractness with level of persuasive strategy. Persuasive strategies were classified according to the degree of sensitivity to the target's perspective. These strategies are significantly correlated with cognitive complexity and construct abstractness. Significant correlations were also found between level of persuasive strategies and independent assessments of perspective taking skills and cognitive complexity in elementary-aged children.

Over time, the growth of children's social knowledge about communication reflects increasing cognitive and communicative complexity. In the first stage of this knowledge, the infant separates the self from others. This separation depends upon the recognition of people as independent agents and as animate beings. Bruner (1983) and Damon (1981) suggest that this understanding enables the infant to recognize other people as having a unique potential for social interaction. In the next stage of developing communicative knowledge, knowledge of others becomes more finely differentiated by person perception and role taking, and knowledge of context also develops. Contextual knowledge incorporates knowledge about social relationships as well as social situations. At this point, in my view, it is not possible to clearly separate the growth of knowledge of others from the growth of knowledge about context. Both sources of knowledge are embedded within scripts that children acquire in early childhood; it appears that children begin to separate personal dispositions (i.e., knowledge of others) from situational constraints (i.e., knowledge of context) in middle childhood (Higgins, 1981; Ross, 1981). Thus, from a developmental point of view, it does not seem useful—or at this point possible—to separate them. Indeed, knowledge of social relationships may well reflect both knowledge of others and of social situations. (See Table 2 for an overview of the developmental stages of communicative knowledge.)

At this point, we have reviewed *what* pragmatic communicative skills and knowledge have been acquired. But since we are concerned with the development of pragmatic communication, it is not sufficient to discuss only what has been acquired. While this overview is of value in itself— because there has been no previous attempt to integrate the diversity of pragmatic accomplishments outlined here—nevertheless, a developmental perspective implies a concern for *how* these communicative accomplishments are achieved, not merely a concern for what those accomplishments happen to be. Now that we have charted the development of pragmatic communicative skills and knowledge, for the remainder of this chapter we explore issues in the acquisition of the pragmatic dimension of human communication.

TABLE 2
Stages in Children's Development of Communicative Knowledge

Age	*Developmental Stages*	*Communicative Knowledge*
0–12 months	I. *Self Distinguished From Others*	recognizes animacy and independence of actions of others; becomes aware of other's intentions; recognizes potential of others for social interaction
begins at 12 months	II. *Differentiated Knowledge of Others*	through the processes of person perception and role taking, gradually begins to recognize the dispositional qualities of others, the communicative and personal requisites of certain roles and situational constraints in communication
begins at 12 months, marked growth at around 36 months	III. *Knowledge of Communicative Context* 1. Relational Knowledge	initially, the child possesses relational knowledge about their interaction with familiar others; with increasing interaction with peers, relational knowledge incorporates knowledge about general social relations (like authority, friendship, etc.) and knowledge about others as unique individuals
	2. Social Situation	recognizes communicative demands of different social settings, context provides background knowledge about appropriate behavior

IV. CRITICAL ISSUES IN THE
ACQUISITION OF COMMUNICATION

This section is titled "critical issues in the acquisition of communication" rather than "acquiring communication" because there is no single theoretical account that attempts to explain how we acquire communicative abilities. As Kuhn (1970) points out, new paradigms are characterized by controversy over how the area of study ought to be defined, what appropriate methods of analysis are, and conflict over competing explanations. All of these characteristics are evident in research on the acquisition of communication. This chapter, in fact, can be viewed as an attempt to define the pragmatic dimension of communicative development.

At the present time, there appear to be two competing paradigms for explaining communicative development: those using cognitive principles as explanatory principles, and those using principles of social interaction as explanatory principles (Atkinson, 1981; Bates et al., 1981). A third paradigm, nativism, has been used to explain how language itself is acquired, but does not concern itself with the appropriate and socially adapted use of language[4] and thus is not relevant to our discussion.

The difference between the cognitive and social interaction approaches is one of degree and of emphasis, rather than of diametric opposition. Both positions acknowledge that language and communication are acquired in an interactive context (Rees, 1978). However, the cognitive theorist tends to emphasize the mental abilities of the individual and their role in communication, whereas the social interaction perspective emphasizes the dialogue and interaction that occur among interactants. Each researcher, of course, selects a perspective that highlights variables of most interest to him or her.

My own sympathies lie with the social interaction perspective, although I am not advocating any particular approach that has been developed. I believe the social interaction perspective offers a richer, more inclusive perspective from which a unified theory of pragmatics may develop. Most importantly, such a perspective focuses on the fundamental nature of human communication—its interpersonal nature; communication is a *shared* social activity, an interpersonal dialogue. Any model of pragmatics, in my view, must accommodate this fundamental fact of communication.

With the preceding discussion as a frame of reference, let us now turn to

---

[4]Nativism stresses the properties of the human mind and of language itself that permit the rapid acquisition of language by humans. Social or psychological issues do not receive much consideration in this view. However, the inclusion of increasingly broad-based concerns in semantics—such as presupposition, tacit knowledge and the like—has led many to argue that the old dichotomy between form and function is no longer useful (M. Atkinson, 1981; Pinker, 1978).

a discussion of critical issues in acquiring pragmatic communicative skills. These issues have emerged as major, current controversies among developmental researchers attempting to explain how these pragmatic abilities are acquired. Three general issues seem critical; first, the early relationship between the adult caretaker and infant—what is the nature of this relationship, and what types of relationships can be said to facilitate communicative development and why? Second, the question of intentionality—to what extent do communicators seem aware of their communicative behavior? And finally, are communicative skills continuous or discontinuous (i.e., is there continuity from preverbal behavior to verbal behavior)?

Adult Caretaker-Child Interaction

Although both the cognitive and social interaction approaches acknowledge that language is acquired in the context of dialogue (Rees, 1978), the social interaction approach places more emphasis on environmental factors (Bates et al., 1981). One such environmental factor has been the dialogue between the adult caretaker and infant. Early studies claimed that the nature of the adult language (as input) determined the subsequent quality of the child's language (Snow, 1977a; Newport, Gleitman, & Gleitman, 1977). More recently, it has been recognized that children play an active role in their dialogues with adult caretakers (Nelson, 1977). We now turn to a careful examination of the nature of the dialogue between the adult caretaker (usually the mother) and infant, and its influence upon the child's communicative development.

Within this general area, several distinct questions have emerged which concern the nature of linguistic input from the adult caretaker, the general pattern of interaction between caretaker and child, individual differences in communicative development, the directionality of effects (i.e., who is influencing whom), and the affective bond between caretaker and child.

Linguistic Input. Mothers' speech to their children is simpler, more repetitious, higher pitched, more focused on immediate events, contains more questions and imperatives, and has more exaggerated emphasis than adult to adult speech (Sachs, 1977; Snow, 1972, 1977a,b). Also, mothers' speech to their children varies as a function of the communicative demands of the situation (Snow, 1976, 1977a,b). Other researchers have correlated aspects of mothers' speech (i.e., Motherese or Baby Talk) with various measures of language production and comprehension. However, "the interpretation of correlations between relatively gross measures of language is problematic" and many researchers have turned to more specific measures of linguistic form and production (deVilliers & deVilliers, 1979, p. 141). Bates et al., (1981) reach a similar conclusion when they argue that while more language input is related to more and better language in children, specific claims, linking specific types of input to specified outcomes, need to be tested. Studies reporting efforts to use specific types of input (e.g., expansions, recasting sentences, etc.) to enhance language development have reported some success (Brown, 1976; Nelson, 1973, 1977). However, this linkage is particularly difficult to assess in spontaneous speech (deVilliers & deVilliers, 1979). Snow notes that expansions, for example, may facilitate language development because they are ways to provide "relevant, responsive and interesting input to all stages of language development" (1977b, p. 39); thus quality of conversation may be the crucial variable.

While the nature of linguistic input remains a topic of continuing research interest, evidence indicates that studies in this area must utilize more specific variables and link them to specific communicative effects (deVilliers & deVilliers, 1979). Such research should also include contextual factors (Snow, 1977b) and measures of cognitive ability of the child (Nelson, 1978). One contextual factor, patterns of interaction between adult and child, has received considerable attention. It is to this area we now turn.

Patterns of Interaction Between Adult Caretaker and Child.   Interpersonal interaction facilitates communicative development in a number of important ways. Children must participate in interactions with others in order to develop a concept of self and of one's social role (Dore, 1985; Rees, 1978; Steiner, 1969; Wolf, 1981). Sugarman (1973) points out that the twelve-month-old child already has well established communicative schemes that develop through the child's interactions with others. We have already reviewed the rich synchrony between mother and child that exists in early infancy, demonstrated by the work of Brazelton, Bruner, Dore, Schaffer, Stern, and others.

Adults tend to keep the interaction with children "going," often relying on the use of questions and turn-passing devices (e.g., "well," "but," etc.) (Bloom, Rocissano, & Hood, 1976; Ervin-Tripp, 1977; Kaye & Charney, 1981; Lieven, 1978; Mishler, 1975, 1976). Moerk (1974) found that mothers were very sensitive to their children's communicative abilities and adapted their messages to these abilities; with children's increasing age, mothers move from explicit modeling in their interactions, to using questions to cue the child's response until finally, the child spontaneously creates his/her own messages by action and talk.

Wells and his associates (1979), investigating how adult utterances are "appropriately responsive" to children's statements in their interactions (p. 341), point out that adults' interactions with their children aid the children's communication development in two distinct ways. First, adults usually adopt "Motherese" when speaking with children, thus simplifying their messages; and secondly, the communicative strategies adults use constrain the type and amount of communicative opportunities their children have (Wells, 1981, 1984; Wells, MacLure, & Montgomery, 1981; Wells et al., 1979).

Wells et al., found differences between children in their "ability to contribute new and contextually relevant matter to the conversation" (1979, p. 368). They attribute these differences, in part, to the varying ways in which mothers interpreted their children's conversational abilities and thus shaped their children's possible responses (French & Woll, 1981). Howe's (1980) analysis of videotaped mother-child conversations found that "given high motivation, the children will learn from maternal replies and will be influenced by percentages of minimal and extended replies" (p. 40). According to Howe, previous attempts to look at mother-child interaction have stressed the informational value of the exchange, whereas her findings suggest there is a motivational value as well.

Building upon Bernstein's distinction between person-centered and object-centered communication, Applegate and Delia (1980) found that person-centered maternal communication influences a child's interpersonal construct system and communicative development. In a regulative communicative context, the mother's use of person-centered communication significantly predicts her child's construct complexity, the use of listener-adapted communication in the multi-situation task, and the use of person-centered communication in interaction with others. They suggest that the influence of maternal communication style is limited by the child's own development; with increasing age, as children develop more abstract means of forming impressions of others, the impact of maternal communication style is greater (Jones, Delia, & Clark, 1979).

Social class differences in maternal communicative styles and their implications for children's development have also been assessed (Cook-Gumperz, 1973). Bernstein's studies (1970, 1971, 1973, 1977) emphasized the role of communication in his theories of socialization. Elaborated communication codes are more complex, more flexible, and permit more explicit, individualized meanings to be expressed, whereas restricted communication codes are more stereotyped, condensed, reliant on nonverbal means, and primarily reflect commonly shared social meanings. Bernstein (1977) suggests that the middle class uses both codes whereas the lower class uses mainly the restricted code.

Cook-Gumperz (1973) found that middle class mothers tend to use an elaborated, *personal* mode of communication to control their children (i.e., focused on individual motivations and needs). In contrast, lower class mothers tend to use a restricted, *positional* mode of communication (i.e., focused on the status and role the individual possessed). Turner (1973) found that middle class children tend to use positional communicative strategies (e.g., based on status obligations, etc.), while lower class children tend to use imperative strategies (e.g., commands, directives, etc.).

A series of studies by Hess and his colleagues (Hess & Shipman, 1965, 1967, 1968; Hess, Shipman, Bear, & Brophy, 1968) found that three modes of maternal communication could be linked to complementary styles of their children: (1) children whose mothers use an imperative mode tend to acknowledge and obey authority; (2) children whose mothers use a subjective mode tend to acknowledge personal considerations; and (3) children whose mothers use a cognitive-rational mode focus on task and rational principles.

Robinson and Rackstraw (1967, 1972) analyzed maternal strategies in answering questions and examined the influence of these strategies on their children's communication. Middle class mothers were more likely to answer questions, give more factual and accurate information, and use more analogies and cause/effect relationships in their responses than did lower class mothers. Lower class mothers tend to restate a question as a statement, or respond that things were "always done" in a particular way; thus, their responses appeal to authority. When answering questions, middle class children give more information; this information is more accurate and relevant than that generally given by lower class children. Lower class children reply by appealing to authority or to general behavioral rules (e.g., "You can't do that because it's naughty," etc.).

In analyzing mother-child dialogues, Robinson (1981a) found middle class mothers asked more questions of their children, regardless of the objects being discussed; their answers referred to the child's experience, and used more referential comparisons. Middle class children tended to give more appropriate responses to their mother's questions. Both lower class mothers and children used language predominantly to inform. Robinson concluded that social class differences appeared to stem from differences in the frequency of certain responses; both groups clearly used speech "mainly to seek or relay information of a proposition nature" (p. 179).

Generally, differing patterns of maternal interaction are viewed as facilitating individual differences in communicative development; however, their linkage to social class differences needs to be further explored. Many researchers (Harding, 1983; Hartmann & Haavind, 1981; Robinson, 1981b; Schiffelin, 1981; Snow, 1983) have commented on the need to explore parental attitudes toward child rearing and relate these expectations and attitudes to parental behavior. From the limited research done on cultural differences in language and communication behavior, striking differences appear to exist in maternal interaction (Schieffelin, & Ochs, 1983) that apparently reflect the cultural socializing patterns of different societies. Isbell and McKee (1980) suggest that differences in the structure of caretaker relations influence communication patterns; these communicative patterns, in turn, contribute to differences in cognitive orientation (p. 340). They argue for an interactive view of cognition which results "from the selective attention of the child to the available and salient information in her/his environment" (1980, p. 350). Differences in maternal interaction style across and within cultures focus their children's attention on different aspects of their environment and provide different opportunities for interaction.

In summary, the type and quality of interaction between adult and child shapes the child's communicative experiences. Maternal communicative strategies especially, such as general responsiveness, style of answering questions, and so forth, appear to influence the child's subsequent communicative strategies. While there is disagreement on methods used to measure these effects (Bates et al., 1981; Hartman & Haavind, 1981), most researchers agree that adult caretaker/child interaction significantly influences the child's development of communicative skills. In addition, researchers are now investigating the father's interaction with the child, and exploring potential differences between maternal and paternal patterns of interaction. Differences in interaction patterns have raised questions about individual differences in communicative development; it is to this question we now turn.

Individual Differences in Communicative Development. With the former emphasis on humans' innate predisposition for verbal communication, little attention was paid to individual differences in communicative development. As researchers analyzed the nature of linguistic input, interaction patterns between adult caretakers and infants were systematically studied. Since substantive differences were found in children's development of communication, this, in turn, raised questions about individual differences and directionality of effects.

Nelson's (1973) monograph found that individual differences in communication were related to differences in early communicative experiences. Differences were found between object-oriented (referential) children who acquired vocabulary more rapidly, and person-social oriented (expressive) children, who developed syntax more rapidly. Nelson suggested that these differences might be a function of maternal interaction styles. A subsequent study by Nelson (1976) argued that differences in children's language experiences predispose them to focus on different uses of language. Dore (1974), in a study of two children, found that one child was oriented to word-form (i.e., vocabulary) while the other child was oriented to intonation (i.e., prosodic features that reflect different language functions). Finally, Bates (1979) argues that individual differences in language acquisition may be due to differences in the use of processes underlying language acquisition; children may focus on the "whole form" of an utterance or on the constituent parts of that utterance (i.e., break down the utterances into their component parts) (p. 361).

In contrast to the earlier emphasis on children's universal (and perhaps innate) communication skills, researchers are now exploring individual differences in children's communicative development (see Romaine, 1984). Thus far, developmental differences have been linked to differences in maternal communicative styles (see Haslett, 1984a), differences in the learning strategies used by children, and contextual differences (Wells, 1985). Recent cross-cultural communication research indicates additional differences in the course of communicative development (Schieffelin & Ochs, 1983). Communicative development thus appears to proceed in different ways as a function of both cognitive and social differences (Snow & Gilbreath, 1983).

Like the issue of individual differences, the issue of directionality of effects was similarly ignored in earlier work on language acquisition. It was assumed that the adult caretaker was the teacher or role model, and the infant/child was a passive learner. However, recent research recognizes the active role of the child as a participant in a two-way dialogue with the adult caretaker.

Directionality of Communicative Effects.   As Bates et al. (1981) have pointed out, with correlational studies the direction of influence could flow from child to adult caretaker, or the reverse. As a result they have raised questions about previous research results. First, they observe that "motherese" reflects a communicative style that is used frequently when listeners fail to understand a speaker (e.g., simplification and repetition frequently occur). Thus, motherese may be a response to the child's failure to understand. Bohannon and Marquis (1977) found that when children indicated lack of understanding, adults reduced utterance length. However, Bates et al. point out that motherese could also aid comprehension: they claim "Any positive influence that motherese may have on the child is canceled out by the original negative relationship between motherese and child failure" (1981, p. 54). Carlson-Luden (1979) found a large number of negative correlations between maternal interventions and measures of children's success in completing tasks; rather than arguing that these interventions inhibit learning, Bates et al. suggest that the most reasonable conclusion seems to be "that mothers intervene to the degree their children fail to understand the task" (1981, p. 55).

Studies by McNew (1981); Belsky, Goode, and Most (1981); Nelson, Carskaddon, and Bonvillian (1973); and Nelson (1977) support the positive effects of motherese on child language development. In the Nelson studies, the maternal interventions were linked with specific aspects of language development. Bates et al. (1981) conclude that these studies support effects from parent to child although the "learning process in recast experiments is essentially child driven" (p. 59). Snyder-McLean and McLean (1978) point out that infant strategies for language learning are distinct from adult facilitation strategies; infants use interactive strategies (i.e., information-gathering strategies) as well as cognitive strategies (i.e., information-processing strategies).

The issue of directionality of effects suggests that earlier research results might need to be reinterpreted because infants are now viewed as being active, directive participants in their dialogues with adult caretakers. Studies of interaction reveal the synchrony in interaction between mother and child, and suggest that the infant may have substantial control over this process (Stern, 1977). While motherese may be a response to the child's failure to understand, it is also a typical strategy used in explanations (Haslett, 1979). It may be that some aspects of communicative development are essentially child-driven, while others are primarily directed by the adult caretaker. The notion that the child is a passive learner clearly needs to be rejected; however, more research is needed before the directionality of effects is clarified.

Analysis of caretaker-child interactions has also been confounded by the emotional attachment between the caretaker and child. For example, closer attachment probably means the caretaker and child interact more; more interaction provides more communicative opportunities and thus communicative development is undoubtedly facilitated. I shall now examine recent efforts to analyze the relationship between attachment and communicative development.

The Influence of Attachment Between Adult Caretaker and Child. Bretherton, Bates, Benigni, Camaioni, and Volterra (1979) relate the quality of the caretaker/infant relationship to cognitive and communicative development and suggest two hypothesized relationships between quality of attachment and cognitive/communicative development:

(1) Attachment-Exploration—the infant uses the mother as a secure base from which to explore the environment;
(2) Attachment-Teaching—the infant and mother establish an interactive synchrony which permits increased opportunities for the child to develop cognitive/communicative skills.

The first hypothesized relationship rests on motivational factors, while the second rests upon both motivational and learning factors. However, in their review of studies on attachment and its relationship to cognitive and communicative development, Bretherton et al. found positive relationships between quality of attachment and cognitive functioning, while the relationship between attachment and language competence was weaker (1979,

p. 236). A study by Bretherton et al. of eleven- and twelve-month-old children found a "fairly strong correlation of strange situation variables with gestural communication level" (1979, p. 257).

Recent work by John Dore (1983) extends Stern's analysis of the affective nature of the mother/child dyad. During the transitional period from babbling to words, when the baby expresses a marked affect, the mother responds by matching it (i.e., "analoguing" the same affect), by complementing it (i.e., responding with a different state), or by imitating it (Dore, 1983). Thus Dore links the affective relationship between mother and infant to the infant's intentional signalling of emotional states; these emotional states are signalled by conventional means (i.e., these symbols are socially recognized means of expressing emotion).

Those cases where the mother's response contravenes the infant's affect-state, rather than models it, are critical for their relationship. As Dore (1983) points out,

> if the infant's affect is breached by prohibition, rather than attuned to, the conflict threatens communion. Anxiety arises. Being able to express his state intentionally allows him to match positive affect and to deny negative matches. It allows him *to test the state of their relationship.* (p. 169)

Dore's work places the development of communicative intentionality and conventional communication signals in the context of the mother/child affective relationship. More importantly, Dore's work may begin to explain how the dual nature of human communication—that utterances express both propositional and relational content—is established. Finally, and in my view quite accurately, Dore emphasizes the importance of the relational element in human communication. As both Dore and Trevarthen point out, communication is, at heart, the way in which we establish relationships with others. Pragmatic models of communication are centered upon how language operates in the context of interpersonal relationships. Trevarthen's work and that of Shotter (1984) demonstrate that the human need to establish relationships with others is a fundamental motivation for acquiring communicative skills. And Dore's research recognizes that testing and expressing relational states is a fundamental aspect of the communicative process.

As we have seen, caretaker/child interaction is a multi-faceted issue; critical concerns are the nature of the linguistic input, patterns of interaction, directionality of effects, individual differences, and the influence of affective bonds between caretaker and child. Emerging themes concerning caretaker/child interaction, while still in need of further research, seem to (1) focus on children as *active* participants in their acquisition of communication; (2) acknowledge that children may utilize a variety of acquisition strategies, (3) acknowledge that different interactive contexts provide different learning experiences for the child, and thus different levels and types of communicative skills may be learned, (4) focus on the quality of interaction, especially the relational, affective quality of the caretaker/child bond, and (5) suggest that there may be complex interactive effects that operate in the acquisition of communication.

Communicative Intentionality

The degree to which communication is an intentional activity has been a subject of increasing debate (Bretherton & Bates, 1979). Langer (1978), for example, argues that much of communicative behavior is relatively "mindless." Indeed, some suggest that the routinized nature of communication, which frees interactants from the need to fully concentrate on the communicative process, enables participants to focus on problematic aspects of encounters (Nelson, 1981) or on learning other complex skills (Shatz, 1978, 1982). On the other hand, often we deliberately try to ascertain other's intentions and use this information as a basis for our interpretation of that encounter. Thus intentionality appears to be a central concern for pragmatics—and, of course, for any model of communication. While most researchers acknowledge the centrality of communicative intentionality and the necessity to deal with intentionality in modeling communicative processes, there is little agreement on how intentionality is to be conceptualized, and even less agreement about "what counts" as evidence of intentionality. For developmental pragmatics, the issue becomes even more complex because we are dealing here with the development of intentionality. In the following section, we explore some of the ways in which developmental researchers have tried to conceptualize intentionality.

Researchers in developmental pragmatics have focused on intentionality as expressed in the infant's communicative behavior. Dore's work (1983) emphasizes the mother's use of accountability procedures in helping the child achieve a desired goal. Bruner, however, focuses on the routinized nature of formats in helping the child accomplish an expected or desired goal. Ryan (1974) identifies cues adults use to interpret the child's communicative behavior. Finally, Bates' discussion of intentionality focuses on children's ability to alter their communicative behavior in response to adult feedback.

Two important points about intentional communicative behavior are reflected in these varying approaches. First, communicative intentionality is accomplished in an *interpersonal* context. Whether through formats, accountability procedures, interpreting cues, or giving feedback—the *response* of another to the message is critical. These responses by adult caretakers, in early infancy, appear to aid infants in recognizing the conventional and intentional qualities of their early communicative signals, and to correctly alter those signals when necessary.

Second, intentionality is related to the concept of *control* over one's message-sending abilities. In early infancy, control over communication may consist only in the infant's recognition of the value of communication in establishing relationships with others (i.e., Trevarthen's concept of inter-subjectivity). As infants mature, they participate in routines and develop an appreciation of what is required in order to complete these routines; particular routines take on specific meanings, and infants become "accountable" for completing these routines. Finally, infants alter their messages as a result of feedback from an adult (i.e., Bates' use of intentionality). Over time, children become increasingly adept at altering messages in response to feedback and at encoding messages in light of *anticipated* consequences. The earliest developments of intentionality, then, are experienced in interpersonal contexts and reflect increasing control over communication, both in terms of understanding and performing communicative acts.

As the child's mastery of verbal communication grows, children recognize that any utterance can convey more than one intended meaning. In addition, children realize that there are many ways of expressing the same intent (e.g., indirect versus direct requests, etc.). The recognition of message complexity is accompanied by growing complexity in the interpersonal contexts in which children communicate. Increasing interaction with others involves the child in a wide range of social relationships and social contexts; children learn they must deal with the intentions of others as well as their own.

Given this communicative complexity, speech act theory seems very limited in its views of intentionality (i.e., illocutionary force) and, in my opinion, is fundamentally inaccurate since this view does not acknowledge the interactive nature of intentionality. Damon (1981) has expressed the fundamental links between intentionality and interaction most cogently when he states:

> What, then, are the principles unique to social interaction that call for a special kind of knowing? Most significantly, there is the ability of persons *intentionally* to coordinate their actions, thoughts, and perspectives with one another. Persons do not simply react to one another, but do so consciously, purposefully, with mutual intent, reciprocal exchanges unimaginable in the inanimate world . . . Of course the character of the reciprocity changes as the social relation (as well as the participants in it) develop.
>
> But regardless of its form or its relative level of sophistication, the communication and reciprocity at the heart of all social interaction is brought about by persons intentionally coordinating their actions and thoughts with one another. (p. 109)

Whatever the particular viewpoint being advocated, researchers acknowledge the fundamental importance of intentionality in any theory of pragmatics. Much greater conceptual clarity is needed to delineate the assumptions concerning intentionality implied in a particular perspective. Careful methods for ascertaining "what counts" as evidence of intentionality also need to be clearly delimited. In particular, special attention should be given to avoiding confusion between goals and means, or motives and the realization of those motives.

Another issue that appears to be as vexing as that of intentionality is the issue of the relationship between prelinguistic and linguistic communication. In what ways, if any, does prelinguistic communication influence later communicative development? As we shall see, there are a variety of positions taken on this issue. While some theorists argue there may be a sharp break between the two (i.e., prelinguistic and linguistic communication are *discontinuous*) others suggest a gradual transition between the two (i.e., *continuity*) and still others argue that the question needs to be reformulated in a more meaningful way.

Continuity and Discontinuity in Human Communication

Sugarman (1983) distinguishes three types of relationships between earlier and later behavior: (1) *antecedents* denote behaviors that reliably precede other behaviors; (2) *precursors* denote behaviors that both precede and share some feature with other behaviors, and (3) *prerequisites* denote behaviors that are antecedent and causally necessary for other behaviors (1983, p. 5). She claims that only antecedents may be empirically justified: precursors and prerequisites are matters of theoretical interpretation. With these differences in mind, let us turn now to a closer examination of the issue of continuity/discontinuity.

Bruner (1975) presents one of the strongest claims for continuity. He discusses four major preverbal precursors to language: (1) the mother's interpretation of the child's communicative intent; (2) the shift of prespeech topic-comment organization to linguistic predication; (3) joint reference as a precursor to deixis; and (4) children's strategies in accomplishing a task with another. Bruner argues that support for continuity rests on demonstrating that a specific precursor is "an instrumental prerequisite to a more involved utterance" and on recognizing the social, meaningful nature of speech (1975, p. 260). It is this latter sense of continuity that Bruner is most concerned with; if the child knows many communicative conventions, like reciprocity of roles, then he or she is better equipped to learn language.

Bruner argues that formats frame an interaction so that children discover communicative conventions and use them to accomplish social goals. Formats limit the range of interpretation and action so that children can signal their steps in accomplishing a specific goal. Such reciprocal fine-tuning, suggests Bruner, requires an interplay between pragmatic and linguistic factors. This interplay also reflects the social cognitive knowledge of self, others, and relations with others that was discussed earlier (Damon, 1981).

In contrast, Bates (1979) emphasizes cognitive prerequisites for communication; she claims that homologous relationships exist between language and proto-dialogues (like postural synchrony, patterns of turn-taking, etc.) because of their shared cognitive base (pp. 15–36). A correlational study of 25 American and Italian children by Bates, Benigni, Bretherton, Camaioni, and Volterra (1979) found that symbolic play, imitation, tool use, and combinatorial play appeared to have a homologous relationship with language. Also, the same cognitive capacities that relate to language development were also related to some preverbal communicative behaviors that correlate with language (p. 316). Other studies have related aspects of cognitive development to various communicative skills (Harding & Golinkoff, 1979; Nicholich, 1975; Sugarman, 1977). Bates et al. (1981) conclude that a "neo-Piagetian approach, emphasizing specific language-cognition relationships, has received support" (p. 15).

Thus far we have analyzed the arguments showing continuity (or alleged continuity) between preverbal communication and verbal communication. Bruner's work emphasizes social interaction factors in providing continuity, whereas Bates' research emphasizes cognitive bases in providing continuity. A third position—claiming that *both* continuities and discontinuities exist— has recently emerged. This view, I believe, most adequately reflects the complex interrelationships between prelinguistic and linguistic communication. Research on communicative development demonstrates that there are a variety of acquisition strategies children use—it seems reasonable to assume that some strategies will emphasize social interaction variables, others will emphasize cognitive factors, and that some aspects of communicative development will be continuous and others relatively discontinuous.

Sugarman (1983) states that communication, as it moves from prelinguistic to linguistic communication, is both continuous and discontinuous; the communication is the continuity, but the means are different (discontinuous). She argues we must look for the points of continuity and discontinuity in communication, and specify the units of analysis (i.e., dimensions) being assessed. If one focuses on language as a communicative system, one sees more continuity than if one focuses on language as a formal, symbolic rule system.

Snow and Gilbreath (1983) also point out that both cognitive factors and social interaction influence communicative development. They claim that "any hypothesis about the social environment implies a hypothesis about the cognitive mechanisms the child uses in language acquisition" (p. 18).

For example, if certain types of social information are most beneficial, then so are the cognitive mechanisms needed to process that information. They go on to discuss several claims about the role of social interaction in communicative development and analyze the underlying cognitive assumptions of these claims.

Finally, the analysis of social interaction has documented the divergent interactive processes found across cultures. Different social variables appear to be relevant in some cultures, but not in others (Brazelton, 1977; LeVine, 1977; Schieffelin & Ochs, 1983). In fact, Snow and Gilbreath conclude that communicative development is "highly buffered." A variety of cognitive and interactive abilities are available to the child in developing communicative skills—if some abilities are not present, others may be used. This feature of communicative development—its emergence in a wide variety of diverse contexts and at differing cognitive levels—may explain both continuity and discontinuity in communicative development, as well as individual differences in such development. Bates (1979) reaches a somewhat similar conclusion when she argues that social interaction may affect language development by providing some minimal "threshold level" which can be achieved in a number of different ways.

Thus far, our discussion of continuity and discontinuity points to the following tentative conclusions. First, some achievements that were viewed in the past as representing new developments (i.e., transitions) now appear to be the result of more gradual shifts in development. Second, while there generally appears to be a sharp distinction between cognitive and social interactive explanations of development, theorists are now beginning to acknowledge their interactive effects (Bates, 1979; Bruner, 1983; Nelson, 1977; Snow & Gilbreath, 1983). Third, variables must be more carefully specified and linked to specific outcomes. In particular, it appears that there are multiple pathways to achieving communicative competence, and that cultural and individual differences influence this process. One final consideration of the continuity/discontinuity issue needs to be noted; if language is innate, how does this influence the continuity-discontinuity issue and, more broadly, does this rule out the possibility of important social interaction influences on language development?

Most theorists claim that the innateness hypothesis is a separate issue (Bates, 1979; Bruner, 1975; Snow, 1979; Sugarman, 1983). Chomsky (1965) himself did not rule out the possibility of considerable environmental "finetuning" for communicative development. As Sugarman (1983) states, "that we are somehow constrained to develop the language that we do does not say *how* we do it" (p. 4).

Catherine Snow (1979), in reviewing the studies concerning the cognitive and social inputs to language and communicative development, offers the following conclusions:

First, information about the nature of communicative systems and the structure of language is available, not only from the linguistic input to young children, but also from many aspects of the caretaking and play routines used by parents. The belief that babies are able to communicate supports a style of interaction with them through which they can learn to communicate. Second, if one assumes that language is learned by exposure to meaningful input, then the syntactic notions that must be mastered in order to achieve adult competence are considerably less abstract than generally thought. Third, the complex syntactic system of the adult language may not be fully acquired for 10 or more years after language acquisition starts. Quite complex utterances of younger children can be explained as the product of semantic and pragmatic rules, involving only partial syntactic analysis. Fourth, a critical period during which brain plasticity allows language acquisition to occur quickly and easily, in the absence of large amounts of simplified and relevant linguistic input, seems not to exist. Fifth, the presumption that all native speakers of a language have achieved an equivalent level of competence needs to be further researched, but appears unlikely on the basis of the available evidence. (p. 100)

In sum, it appears that pragmatic researchers offer arguments either countering nativist claims or pointing out their irrelevance.

As our knowledge of human and animal communication grows, our research on the discontinuities and continuities between prelinguistic and linguistic communication will change with respect to the research questions we ask, and the evidence required to support different perspectives. It seems to me to be most helpful not to set aside the innateness hypothesis, but to reframe the issue in terms of continuities and discontinuities across a range of human communicative behaviors, including that of handicapped individuals such as the deaf and blind, and in terms of how human communicative behaviors compare with communicative behaviors of primates.

In summary, the discussion of critical issues has highlighted some of the conceptual and methodological difficulties in constructing a developmental theory of communication. Significant differences exist in how problems are conceptualized, in what explanatory principles are invoked, and in the methods of research used. I believe future research must not only increasingly specify the linkages between variables and their effects (Bates et al., 1981; Robinson, 1981b), but also deal with the complex interrelationships among linguistic, cognitive and social interaction factors in communicative development. Complex interactions must be assessed *within* particular problem domains (e.g., within the domain of adult caretaker/child interaction, patterns of interaction between them need to be viewed in light of the affective bonds between caretaker and child, etc.) as well as *across* previously separated problem domains (e.g., communicative knowledge must be related to communicative skill).

Different developmental theories may be needed to account for different aspects of communicative development. Undoubtedly, different cultural and individual acquisition strategies will emphasize different aspects of communication. Thus, it comes as no surprise that no single theoretical account, at this point, offers an adequate account of communicative development. However, when the child interacts with others, all these skills and knowledge converge to produce appropriate messages. So, at some level, our explanations need to focus on this convergence.

V. CONCLUDING REMARKS

As we have seen, the child's first five years of life reflect substantial communicative accomplishments. I have attempted to integrate this vast array of skill and knowledge in an effort to provide some coherence to this area and some insights for further research. It is glaringly apparent, however, how limited any synthesis must be; while we can confidently say that communication, over time, becomes more complex in a variety of ways, as yet we have only a limited understanding of this complexity, whether it be relational, linguistic, or cognitive in nature. The discussion of continuity and/or discontinuity in communication reveals the difficulty in relating various stages or aspects of communicative development with one another. While many researchers are calling for more *detailed* analysis (linking specific variables to specific effects) I hope this overview of developmental pragmatics has shown the importance of *broadening* our analysis as well. In my view, research must integrate form and function, skill and knowledge; and this integrated research perspective must be grounded in the interpersonal context in which human communication occurs. The promise of the pragmatic approach is that it does offer such a perspective.

As can readily be seen, the view of communicative development taken here rests on the *same* underlying assumptions that provide the foundation for a pragmatic perspective on human communication. That is, developmental communicative processes have been demonstrated to be intentional, inferential, conventional, systematic, and dependent upon contextual knowledge. In fact, these features of communication are among the earliest to be acquired by infants. As skill and experience in interaction grow, children become aware of individual differences in communicative style and the influence of participants' social relationships upon their communication. Children, early on in their communicative development, begin to integrate text, context, and participant's characteristics.

8 Pragmatic Approaches to Interpersonal Communication

The importance of interpersonal relationships has been widely recognized, and its qualities studied from many diverse perspectives. Establishing close relationships with others is essential for well-being and happiness (Berscheid & Peplau, 1983; Bochner, 1984; Duck, 1976, 1983). Through our interpersonal relationships, we establish our personal identity; express our thoughts and feelings; engage in colloborative activities with others, and satisfy our needs for affiliation with others. Regardless of the particular research perspective taken, all scholars acknowledge the fundamental role of communication in making possible human relationships.

Developing interpersonal relationships and communicating interpersonally both imply an interaction between at least two individuals. Becker (1964) suggests that interaction presupposes that participants are reciprocally responsive to one another. This reciprocal responsiveness is possible through the use of symbols, and participants actively monitor their own activities as well as those of others. Gouldner (1960) suggests that reciprocity is implicit in social order itself. However, as Brittan (1973) observes, while reciprocity provides a basis for interpersonal relationships, this reciprocity among individuals may not necessarily be equivalent.

Communication plays a central role in developing and maintaining interpersonal relationships because social activity is not possible without communication. According to Bochner (1984), communication helps organize relationships, constructs and validates shared world views, expresses feelings and thoughts, protects vulnerabilities, and fosters positive impressions. As such, communication provides the context in which we create and maintain relationships (Cronen, Pearce, & Harris, 1982; Pearce & Cronen, 1981).

Communicative processes and social relationships mutually influence one another. As Hymes (1972) points out, any social relationship has a set of communicative processes appropriate to it. These communicative processes, in turn, shape the nature and outcome of the social relationship. As the social relationship changes, so too will the communicative processes that maintain the social relationship. Each social relationship, as Hymes points out, will have communicative means appropriate to it and thus communication varies across different social relationships. (For a general overview of discourse and social relationships, see van Dijk, 1985a, volume 4 and van Dijk, 1985b).

This chapter focuses on the communicative processes involving the development, maintenance, and dissolution of relationships. Although it is assumed that all messages have both a content and relational dimension (Bateson, 1972), our emphasis will be upon *how verbal communication is used to establish, maintain, and change relationships among interactants.* We shall explore communicative processes within the family and among friends. The development of communicative skills and social relationships has been discussed previously (see Chapter 7). However, in this chapter, I go beyond preschoolers' social and communicative development to incorporate the development of relationships among adolescents and adults.

In order to discuss the role of verbal communication in relationships, an adequate conceptualization of interpersonal relationships, especially close relationships, is necessary. Different relational contexts, such as casual friendship or marriage, necessitate different communicative strategies. In this chapter, the nature of interpersonal relationships is discussed. Although the research on interpersonal relationships is vast, and a detailed review well beyond the scope of this chapter, the discussion here focuses on core concepts used to analyze interpersonal relationships.

Next, we examine the role of verbal communication in interpersonal relationships, analyzing various approaches according to their relative emphasis on the text (messages), context (viewed here as the participants' social relationship, whether one of friendship, marriage, etc.) or participants (viewed here as individual characteristics such as age, gender, and social class). In addition, based upon a survey of empirical research in this area, some general conclusions about interpersonal communication processes are proposed. Finally, we examine some thematic issues, like self-disclosure, attraction, and power, that cut across different types of relationships and discuss some critical research problems in this area.

Again, as we explore the role of communication in interpersonal relationships, a variety of approaches and methods are surveyed. Many of the underlying pragmatic assumptions developed throughout this book emerge in the analysis of interpersonal communicative processes as well.

The assumptions about the interpretive, inferential, jointly negotiated character of communication appear particularly important in interpersonal communication.

I. THE NATURE OF INTERPERSONAL RELATIONSHIPS

In their book *Close Relationships,* Kelley et al. (1983) discuss the diversity of concepts, theories, and methods used to investigate interpersonal relationships. Despite this diversity, however, some core concepts and issues can be discerned. In addition, many scholars attempt to integrate the diverse research on interpersonal relationships in their own work (Bochner, 1984; Hinde, 1981; Kelley et al., 1983).

Hinde (1981) argues that adequate descriptions of relationships must be provided before we can have a science of interpersonal relationships. He suggests the following eight areas must be assessed in order to adequately describe relationships:

1. content of interactions—what do participants do together;
2. diversity of interactions—relationships may be *multiplex* (involving many types of encounters, such as in friendship) or *uniplex* (limited to few types of encounters, such as limited encounters at work);
3. qualities of interaction—its intensity, valence and style;
4. relative frequency and patterning of interaction;
5. reciprocity or complementarity of interaction;
6. intimacy of interaction;
7. perception of the interaction by participants, and
8. relational commitment.

In addition, these factors must be looked at in terms of their dynamic, evolutionary interaction with one another in the relationship.

Since friendship is probably the most common interpersonal relationship that most people experience, it serves as a general model for the study of relationships. We now turn to a review of friendship, and the communicative processes used in establishing and maintaining friendship.

Establishing and Maintaining Friendships

The underlying dimensions of friendship reveal the basis on which friends are selected and judged. Wish, Deutsch, and Kaplan (1976) suggest that people perceive interpersonal relationships along the dimensions of being cooperative/uncooperative; equal/unequal; intense/superficial, and socioemotional (informal)/task-oriented (formal). With the exception of the intensity factor, Triandis and his colleagues (Triandis, 1972) uncovered similar factors of association/disassociation, superordinate/subordinate, and intimacy.

LaGaipa (1981a) points out that relationships fulfill certain goals and needs. In general, relationships serve to fulfill needs for identity, affection, understanding and emotional support, companionship, and instrumental aid (such as material goods). Different relationships may fulfill different needs and offer different resources. In addition, as a relationship develops, different needs may be fulfilled.

Interpersonal relationships also vary in terms of duration and intensity. Acquaintanceship usually refers to infrequent or relatively superficial relationships whereas personal relationships, such as close friendship or family relationships, are of long duration and strong mutual influence. Berscheid and Peplau (1983) define a close relationship as "one of strong, frequent and diverse interdependence that lasts over a considerable period of time" (p. 38). Examples of close relationships include friendships, love affairs, marriage, or parent-child relationships. Wish, Deutsch, and Kaplan (1976) characterize close friends as having relationships of high mutual influence, frequent and diverse interactions, and reciprocity.

How do relationships change from acquaintanceship to close relationships? Miller (1976) suggests that relationships become more personal as psychological information is increasingly exchanged. Thus, close relationships are characterized by increasing differentiation and more idiosyncratic rules. As close relationships develop, participants' knowledge about each other, mutual attraction, and interdependence increase (Morton & Douglas, 1981).

Relationships also vary over one's lifespan. Conceptualizations of friendship change substantially from childhood to adulthood (Dickens & Perlman, 1981; Duck, 1983). With increasing age, children's friendships become less egocentric, and more reciprocal and complex (Selman & Selman, 1979). Bigelow and LaGaipa (1975) found that young children's expectations of friends were based on propinquity (providing an opportunity for interaction) and common activities. Older children had normative expectations for friends (i.e., that they are loyal, supportive, etc.) and judged their friends on personal traits such as genuineness, truthfulness, etc. Adolescent friendships are important for the "chum" skills they provide (Fine, 1981) and the intimacy/confiding that can develop (Kon & Losenkov, 1978). Both aspects of adolescent friendship develop social skills needed in adult friendship (Dickens & Perlman, 1981). Adult friendships appear to vary as a function of marriage, social class, gender, and age (Dickens & Perlman, 1981).

As this brief overview has shown, relationships are very complex and not easily defined. Relationships are continually changing and thus difficult to measure. There is no consistent agreement on the nature of close relationships although most approaches agree that they strongly influence both participants, are highly interdependent and reciprocal, last over a long period of time, become increasingly intimate, involve diverse activities and evolve through different stages (Bochner, 1984).

Alternative Approaches to Interpersonal Relationships

Different models have been proposed to account for the development and maintenance of relationships. Information-processing theories emphasize the role of person-perception and knowledge about the other in relationships (see, for example, Berger & Bradac's uncertainty reduction, or Altman & Taylor's social penetration theory). Approaches emphasizing an individual's personal characteristics and their influences on relationships may be psychoanalytic, behavioral, existential, or cognitive in orientation (LaGaipa, 1981a). Exchange models stress the exchange of resources, like money, goods, or services, as a basis for relationships. Sociological approaches have taken a structural functionalist approach, a social exchange approach, a symbolic interactionist approach, or a conflict approach (Berscheid & Peplau, 1983).

The dramaturgical models (such as Goffman, Harre, or Burke) emphasize the social actions performed by participants as they try to manage the impressions others have of them. In contrast, rules approaches (see, for example, Cushman & Sanders, 1981) focus on the communicative rules people use in maintaining and developing relationships. Process models (such as Knapp, 1978 or Duck, 1973) focus on the evolution of a close relationship from its initial stages of acquaintanceship to its dissolution. Bateson and his colleagues (Bateson, 1972; Watzlavick, Beavin, & Jackson, 1967) focus on repeated patterns of interaction in families and marriages. Structural models (such as Argyle, 1980) emphasize the form of social relationships and the social interaction skills that facilitate relationships.

The range of views and models presented here is intended to highlight the parameters of interpersonal relationships. Despite this diversity, common themes and assumptions emerge. First, close relationships are generally viewed as long-term, enduring relationships with highly interdependent, reciprocal influences exerted between participants. Second, relationships vary in intensity, intimacy, duration, and type. Third, relationships evolve over time. Finally, the inferential, interpretive, negotiated character of relationships is generally recognized. With this brief overview of the nature of interpersonal relationships and some alternative models of relationships, we now turn to an analysis of interpersonal communicative processes in establishing and maintaining interpersonal relationships.

II. APPROACHES TO INTERPERSONAL COMMUNICATION

Communication skills are highly important in the process of friendship formation (Argyle, 1980, 1983; Duck, 1984b; Hart & Burks, 1972). Different approaches emphasize different communication skills and processes. Argyle emphasizes analyzing social situations and training individuals in the interactional skills required for specific situations. Duck (1983) suggests that friendship relies on good interaction skills. Individuals must make accurate assessments of the social setting so that opportunities for friendship encounters are well-timed and well-placed. In addition, individuals must enact the appropriate communicative style, both verbally and nonverbally, build up mutual trust and commitment, adapt their behavior to others, and appropriately pace the friendship.

The process of friendship, as we have seen, is a complex, multifaceted activity. Strong individual differences also exist in drives for friendship (Duck, 1973), and across factors like age, sex, self-esteem, culture, and stage of life. Because friendship provides many important social, personal, and health benefits (Duck, 1984a, b), and because communication plays a key role in the development and maintainance of relationships, it seems of critical importance to more closely examine communicative processes in interpersonal relationships. It is to this issue that we now turn.

Models Emphasizing the Text, Context, or Communicator

The perspective developed in this book rests on the assumption that all three subsystems of the human communication system—text, context, and communicator—must be accounted for in any adequate analysis of communicative processes. While a program of research may focus on just one component, or the interaction of two components, an adequate account of interpersonal communication requires all three aspects. Various programs of relational research can be characterized in terms of their emphasis on text, context, or communicator. These programs are presented in Table 1.

As can readily be seen, most relational communication research emphasizes the interaction of text and communicator. However, much of this research analyzes the actual utterances spoken by participants. Such analyses reflect the surface structure of the text, but not necessarily the text's meaning. For example, Rogers and her colleagues use the grammatical form of a text's utterances in their analyses. Those analyses based only on the text ignore the communicator and the context: such analyses have limited value since texts may have differing significance for different communicators in particular contexts. Text-based analyses, such as "speech markers" reflecting social class or ethnic differences in communication, are

TABLE 1
Research Focus of Current Relational Communication Studies

Focus	Research Program
(1) *Text*	
Form	Speech Markers; Giles and colleagues
	Conversational Moves (interruptions, turn-taking, etc.)
Content	Self-Disclosure research
	Language Intensity; Bowers, Bradac, Mehrabian
(2) *Communicator*	Individual characteristics and relational development; Argyle, Duck & Gilmour, Hinde, Kelley and other social psychological approaches
(3) *Context*	Simplistic generalization
(4) *Text & Communicator*	Explores the relationship between individual characteristics/ relational states and communication;
	Altman & Taylor—relational longevity and communication patterns;
	Bradac—individual characteristics and language use;
	Cushman, et. al.—self-concept and communication styles;
	Fitzpatrick—marital types and communication patterns;
	Knapp—relational development and communication patterns;
	Mehrabian—relational states and language intensity;
	Norton—communicator and communication style;
	Pearce & Cronen—relational definition and communication patterns;
(5) *Text & Context*	Explores the relationship between the relational context and the text;
	Berger et al.—initial impressions and uncertainty reduction;
	Goffman—context and forms of talk;
	Searle—utterances and their social force;
	Tacit knowledge, scripts, etc.—provided plans for interaction in specified settings
	Rogers et al.—relational state (power/dominance) and communication patterns
(6) *Context & Communicator*	Explores the relationship between communicator characteristics and context;
	McCroskey et al.—communicator apprehension in particular contexts
(7) *Text & Communicator & Context*	Explores interrelationship among the text, communicator and context;
	Delia et al.—communicator characteristics (constructs) & message strategies & persuasive settings;
	Haslett—communicator characteristics (age, sex) & communicative strategies & play with peers (context)

202

also of limited value. The value and significance of these cues for participants in particular contexts is not specified. For example, in what contexts are such text-based differences emphasized, ignored, or irrelevant? And for what types of communicators? Clearly these judgments are critical for communicators who need to coordinate their behaviors with those of others.

A somewhat different approach to text-based analyses suggests that a certain communicative feature always conveys a given interpretation. For example, the use of tag questions always signals a hesitant, female communicator. However, tag questions help minimize the risk of presenting potentially face-threatening messages since they soften the forcefulness of a message (e.g., "Our report is not very good, is it?"). It seems unlikely that any communicative feature always conveys a specific meaning; rather, meaning is a function of the interaction of text, context, and communicator.

In contrast, communicator-based models focus on the communicator's social/psychological characteristics and their influence upon developing relationships. However, such approaches frequently ignore communicative processes in developing relationships. Much research has been done on relational contexts, both in terms of examining the nature of particular relationships (like friendship or marriage), and the communicative patterns characterizing those relationships. More research needs to be done, however, on exploring communicator characteristics and their impact on relational contexts and interpersonal communication. Research focusing on only one subsystem needs to incorporate the other pragmatic subsystems so that the full complexity and richness of interpersonal communication processes can be understood.

Interactive Models.   Research programs incorporating the interaction of two or more pragmatic subsystems are more valid and adequate than approaches including only a single subsystem. A text-communicator approach explores the relationships between participants' characteristics or their relational states and the messages they construct. For example, Fitzpatrick's research looks at spousal relationships and communication style; Rogers and her colleagues look at relational states (power/dominance) and communicative behavior; Cushman explores the relationship between communicator self-concept and their utterances, while Pearce and Cronen examine how participants view their relationship with one another and their communicative behavior. And numerous studies have analyzed marital communication and its influence on marital satisfaction.

However, interactive models stressing text/communicator interrelationships ignore the influence of the relational context. Yet the relational context is always important because it helps determine relevance and coherence. It should be noted that the influence of context varies across different texts and different communicators. For example, Rogers and her colleagues seem to assume that relational control is at issue in every interaction. However, a cursory look at everyday communication reveals many encounters across varied relationships in which relational control is not at issue. Even if we assume that relational control is always being disputed, we need to ask *in what relational contexts* relational control issues are of critical importance—as, for example, in marital conflict or child-rearing practices. Cushman's analysis of communicator self-concept and its influence on communicative style also needs to account for the influence of relational context. It would seem reasonable to assume that different relational contexts present different "risks" for interactants. Thus, an interactant's self-concept may be most salient in relational contexts that are important to his or her self-identity. Simply put, relational context appears to be an important communicative variable in a number of different ways.

Other interactive approaches, such as those integrating text and context, are found in the work of Goffmann, and in the work of Berger and his associates. Berger and his colleagues analyze the communicative strategies participants use to reduce uncertainty about one another in their initial interactions. Here again, however, questions remain. In what areas and to what extent do interactants reduce uncertainty? Are there marked individual preferences in the need to reduce uncertainty? The general difficulty in text/context interactive approaches is that they ignore the potential effects of individual differences. And individuals appear to vary in their ability to diagnose situations as well as in their ability to use necessary social/communicative skills (see, for example, Argyle, 1980).

Few studies have investigated the interaction of text, context, and participants. A recent example of such research would be van Dijk's (1984) work on the expression of ethnic prejudice (a text variable) in everyday encounters (a context variable) among family and friends (reflecting both context and participant variables).

All of these research programs clearly contribute to our understanding of relational communication. It would be of even greater value, however, if researchers examine the significance of relevant, but previously unexplored areas. For example, not all researchers have to incorporate communicator characteristics in their analyses, but, at a minimum, researchers need to acknowledge, in principle, what their potential effects and influences might be. This is not to suggest a paradigm shift, but merely to suggest we sharpen our own conceptual analyses.

In summary, in order to adequately understand human communicative processes, one must look at the interrelationships of text, context, and communicator characteristics. Each element gives us part of the picture, but adequate description and theory rest upon a consideration of the systematic interaction among all three. Interactive models—for example, those linking communicator characteristics with the text—are likewise incomplete and fragmented. Any focus upon a particular subsystem, such as the text, must be done in light of potential influences from the other subsystems of context and communicator characteristics.

This brief reframing of current approaches to interpersonal communication highlights the primary focus of each approach. By this characterization, however, I am *not* suggesting that any particular approaches need to be modified; but merely suggesting that significant variables influencing particular models be noted and that research conclusions be appropriately qualified. For example, although Berger and his associates focus on initial impressions (the context) and uncertainty reduction (the text), their findings will be strengthened when qualified by an acknowledgment that individuals may vary in their tolerance of uncertainty.

Despite the diversity of models and methods of analysis, some important general conclusions about interpersonal communication processes have emerged. We discuss these general findings in each subsystem of communication; the text, context, and communicator characteristics. Taken together, these general findings provide considerable insight into interpersonal communication. It is to these general findings we now turn.

III. PRINCIPLES OF
INTERPERSONAL COMMUNICATION

Interpersonal Texts

Text-based approaches to interpersonal communication focus on message style and content. In what follows, we examine message characteristics that are instrumental in developing and maintaining interpersonal relationships. Two general influences, the amount of self-disclosure and the developmental stages in the relationship, influence the text produced by the interactants.

Self-Disclosure.   Self-disclosure refers to the disclosure of personal information by one interactant to another. This information could not be inferred by other means and is intentionally conveyed to others (Morton & Douglas, 1981). Altman and Taylor (1973) found that as relationships develop, the breadth and depth of disclosures increase. Self-disclosures are initially superficial, but become more intimate as the relationship develops. Jourard (1971) found that interactants reciprocate self-disclosures.

Bochner (1984) suggests the following generalizations about research on self-disclosure. First, people believe in high self-disclosure to others they like. Second, people tend to overestimate their self-disclosures. Third, self-disclosure does not cause liking. Finally, liking inhibits self-disclosure; more discriminating self-disclosers were more liked. In addition, Bochner notes that it is difficult to define when messages are self-disclosing and when the self-disclosure is genuine. Self-disclosures may also represent potential threats to a relationship because of the need to protect one's own vulnerability and to not threaten another's.

Stages in a Relationship.   Texts also vary as a function of the stage in a relationship. In the initial, opening stages of acquaintanceship, Berger and Bradac (1982) suggest that messages are designed to reduce uncertainty and thus make the other interactants more predictable. Knapp (1978) points out that communication varies as relationships evolve. Miller (1978) argues that as interpersonal relationships develop, more psychological information is exchanged. In brief, as interactants' relationships change, so does their communication with one another.

Contextual Influences on Interpersonal Communication

As we have seen, communicative patterns vary as a function of the participants' social relationship. Contextual influences, as defined in this chapter, refer to the different types of social relationships that people develop. Social relationships among interactants form their immediate interactional context. In particular, we are concerned with those social relationships that perform important socialization functions such as friendships, marriage, and family relationships. Within each of these contexts, we examine the general research findings about interpersonal communication.

Friendship

In contrasting family relationships with friendship, LaGaipa (1981a) observes that an individual's friends are less closely monitored than his or her family. Friends usually have equal status while status varies among family members. For example, status in the family may vary as a function of one's age or sex. Furthermore, friends are usually selected by free choice, and friends are not usually members in intense social networks as are family members. Friendships may also be maintained for distinct purposes (e.g., business friendships, etc.). Finally, style of friendship varies as a function of sex (Gouldner, 1984), social class (Allan, 1977), stage of life (Dickens & Perlman, 1981; LaGaipa, 1981b), and marriage (Blau, 1973). Friendships also vary in communication satisfaction (Hecht, 1984a, b); and communicative style (Knapp, 1978; Ellis, 1979).

Models of Friendship Development.   In what follows, we look at a number of alternative models of friendship. Each model discusses developmental stages in friendship, although the developmental processes vary in each model.

A. *Duck's Personal Construct Model of Friendship.*   Duck (1973), utilizing Kelly's personal construct theory (1955, 1970), has modelled the friendship process. Constructs are categories that people use to interpret ongoing activity. They may be verbalized or unverbalized, and allow people to simultaneously group sets of similar objects and exclude others. Thus constructs are salient features of objects and events that people use to predict and interpret ongoing activity.

Duck suggests that friendship proceeds through several distinct phases: acquaintance, attraction, friendship, and intimacy (potential marital choices). These phases are not separable stages, but may overlap and fluctuate greatly. Indeed, friends may not be in the same developmental stage at the same time.

Friendship occurs when we disclose information revealing our psychological similarity to another and do not present negative information about ourselves. When people have similar interpretive processes, communication is facilitated and thus friendship results. As we reveal that our constructs are similar to another's, we confirm that individual's sense of social reality and thus are more attractive to that person. In this manner, Duck utilizes Kelly's personal construct theory to integrate the influences of similarity and attraction, two significant influences on developing friendships.

B. *A Filtering Model.*   Cushman, Valentinsen, and Dietrich (1981) argue that friendship formation occurs three stages: at each stage, a different set of cues act to filter out certain individuals. In initial encounters, participants have a "field of availables" (potential friends) identified. After a positive initial interaction, participants select—or are left with—"a field of approachables." Participants continue to interact with others they perceive as similar and supportive. From this field of approachables, a "field of reciprocals" emerge and comprise our friends. Cushman et al. suggest that friendship develops when each partner confirmed and supported the other's view of him- or herself.

Different filters are used to evaluate others as potential friends. These filters vary as a function of the stage of the friendship (e.g., in the acquaintanceship stage as opposed to the attraction stage, etc.), age, sex, and social group context. Generally, initial filters rely on situational norms and simple evaluations of another. At later stages, participants gather information about another's psychological characteristics, such as perceived similarity in attitudes, in order to select their friends. Friendship, therefore, is a process of selectively filtering out individuals for potential friendship.

C. *Knapp's Relational Stages.* Knapp (1978) models the relationship process by specifying stages in the bonding and dissolving of relationships. Bonding includes: *initiating* (initiating encounters); *experimenting* (eliciting information); *intensifying* (reflects close friendship in which self-disclosure of private information occurs, individuals adapt to one another, and conversational convergence occurs); *integrating* (the individual partners seem to coalesce) and *bonding* (the relationship is expressed by formal, public commitment, like a wedding or engagement). The stages for dissolving relationships include *differentiating* (individual differences between partners become increasingly emphasized); *circumscribing* (communication becomes restricted in depth and breadth); *stagnating* (the relationship maintains its current status); *avoiding* (partners begin to actively withdraw from the relationship) and *terminating* (distancing and disassociating from one another). Knapp also offers an analysis of the communicative patterns characteristic of each stage, emphasizing the subtlety of both verbal and nonverbal messages. Like Duck, Knapp suggests that people may move within and across stages at different rates and that there are significant individual, cultural, and social constraints on this process.

Family Communication

Families perform an important socializing function since they act out and interpret the surrounding sociocultural milieu (LaGaipa, 1981a). Other social networks such as kinship networks, religious networks, educational institutions, and government agencies support the family. Families represent very complex communicative systems because of the dynamic, multiple relationships of parent/child, husband/wife, and sibling/sibling which may be present. Finally, families generally present family members with extended obligations and constraints. In what follows, we briefly review some of the most well-known research on family interaction.

The Palo Alto Group. The seminal work of Gregory Bateson and his colleagues on family interaction has contributed significantly to understanding human communication. Several important generalizations about family interaction have developed from this perspective. First, communication can be analyzed on a number of different levels of meaning, of logical type, and of learning. Second, family members act to maintain a balance or equilibrium in their relationships with each other; as family members change, other family members react to those changes, attempting to modify or diminish those changes. Third, the unit of interactional analysis is triadic as well as dyadic. Researchers may examine husband/wife interaction (a dyadic unit), but also may examine grandfather/father/son interaction (a triadic interaction). Fourth, family members' relationships may be symmetrical (reciprocal) or complementary. Symmetrical relationships exist when participants' behavior mirror one another; in complementary relationships, one participant's behavior provides a counterpart for the other. For example, in a symmetrical relationship, anger is met by anger; in contrast, in a complementary relationships, anger could be met by an apology. Fifth, enmeshment—the degree of involvement and interlocking in a relationship—varies across families. Some families may be intensely involved with one another, while other families are not. Sixth, feedback can be given on many levels, and may be positive or negative. And finally, several disruptive communicative patterns, such as double binds, disqualifying, and irresistible runs, have been identified. (For an excellent discussion of this work, see Hoffman, 1981.)

While a comprehensive review of this work is not possible, some insight into this approach can be gleaned by focusing on analyses of distressed families by its proponents. In distressed families, most relationships are coalition relationships (for example, father and son aligned against the mother) (Hoffman, 1981). Family relationships are very tightly interconnected, and coalitions may occur across generational lines. Minuchin (1974) points out that in psychosomatic families, children often obscure or deflect parental conflicts. Parents frequently enlist children in a coalition against the other parent. Generally, distressed families have more aversive interaction, accentuate the negative aspects of situations, are inconsistent in their standards, and show less emotional support for one another than non-distressed families (Burgess, 1981; Gottman, 1979).

Marriage

The final relational context we shall examine is that of marriage. Marriage is considered the most intimate relational bond individuals form with one another. Burgess (1981) defines marriage as a socially sanctioned, enduring, highly interdependent relationship that includes sexual bonding between partners. Wood (1982) suggests that intimates form their own relational cultures—privately transacted systems of understandings that partners use to coordinate their actions and interactions.

Bochner (1984) suggests that interpersonal bonding occurs when individuals respond *selectively* and *specifically* to one another. Thus, marriage is an example of interpersonal bonding. Interpersonal bonding implies that people interact in highly organized ways. This relational organization determines what actions take place, and how these actions are expressed. These relationships are not necessarily positive relationships, and are subject to tensions between autonomy as opposed to interdependence, openness as opposed to closeness, and vulnerability as opposed to protecting oneself, and the like.

Several basic assumptions underlie the interpersonal bonding that occurs in marriage:

1. Comprehensive bonding, such as that occurring in marriage, presupposes that people have more knowledge about one another; spend more time together; gain and/or lose psychologically in the relationship, and have a long-term, enduring relationship.
2. Communication in interpersonal bonding is symbolic and dynamic; its chief consequences are the meanings participants construct in their relationship.
3. What people say and how they act express the relationship, and
4. Relationships evolve and change over time. (Bochner, 1984).

Pressures and Expectations about Marriage. According to Burgess (1981), images of marriage typically include a husband, wife, and children living in a single home. The husband is the major provider, and the wife cares for the family. The family collaborates on problem solving; and this family unit is expected to be an enduring one. However, given the rapid rate of economic, social, and cultural change, this model of marriage reflects an increasingly small segment of the population. Nevertheless, despite these changes, marriage is still expected to be the most intimate, significant, enduring relationship individuals establish (Slater, 1968).

Among the many pressures affecting families are (1) expectations of affection and intimacy; (2) the conflict between dependence and independence; (3) sexual freedom; (4) conflicting expectations about men, women, and their social roles; and (5) the organization of the family (Orford & O'Reilly, 1981). Men appear to be more satisfied in marriage than women; Bernard (1972) suggests that women make more significant accomodations in marriage and thus are less satisfied. In addition, the presence of children results in a decline in marital satisfaction (Campbell, 1975). Dual-career couples experience both high strain and high satisfaction in their marriages (Rappoport & Rappoport, 1971). Burgess (1981) concludes that marital satisfaction seems to be most predicted by the couple's temperamental compatibility and social adaptability.

Peplau (1983) discusses three "ideal types" of marriages:

1. *Traditional marriages*—males dominate; strong, traditional sex-role specialization in which men are the breadwinners and women take care of the children and the household; major decisions tend to be jointly made.
2. *Modern marriages*—male dominance is muted; less sex-role specialization; man's career is more important; women have to handle home responsibilities as well as work.
3. *Egalitarian marriages*—based on power equity; equally shared work responsibilities; dual career families come closest to this model.

Marital satisfaction does not vary significantly across marital types; however, most satisfaction occurs where there is a balance in decision-making and most conflict appears where there is disagreement concerning marital roles (Peplau, 1983).

Marital Dissolution and Repair.   Given the substantial emotional and social expectations and pressures in marriages and in the family, current divorce rates are perhaps not surprising. Clearly, the dissolution of the marital or family bond is a very painful, emotionally wrenching experience. Adjusting to divorce or separation appears to be similar to grief experienced at the death of a loved one; individuals go through stages of numbness, denial, bargaining, anger, depression and finally acceptance (Juhasz, 1979).

Duck (1984b) suggests that repairing relationships is done differently at different stages. One repair strategy involves the resolution of personal doubts by changing one's own attributions. For example, instead of believing one's spouse is irresponsible, one could acknowledge relevant situational problems like overwork. Marriage counselors could work with the couple as a dyad; or third-party interventions, from in-laws or other relatives, could take place. In addition, spouses can reframe the relationship. Like Duck, Baxter (1984) found that different relationships are terminated in different ways.

Marital breakdowns are influenced by many factors. Hicks and Platt (1970) found that unhappy marriages are also unstable, and both factors are believed to contribute to divorce. Newcomb and Bentler (1981) argue that many factors can contribute to marital breakdown: age, ethnicity, personality, and interactional factors (e.g., dissimilarity, conflict, etc.) have been correlated with marital breakdown.

Marital Communication.   Communication in intimate relationships significantly influences those relationships (Bochner, 1984; Gottman, 1979: Hoffman, 1981: Watzlawick, Beavin, & Jackson, 1967). Gottman (1979) found that marital success was positively related to the couple's ability to resolve disputes. Burgess (1981) also suggests that the quality of intimate relationships depends upon the amount of interaction and reciprocity of interaction.

Patterns of marital interaction have been explored from a variety of perspectives. The Palo Alto group (Bateson, 1972; Watzlawick, Beavin, & Jackson, 1967) focuses on repititive exchanges in families. In particular, their research examines symmetrical, complementary, and transitive patterns of interaction and their effects in distressed families (i.e., those needing clinical counseling). Utilizing the perspective of the Batesonian group, communication scholars have examined patterns of control found in intimate relationships (Ellis, 1979; Millar, Rogers, & Bavelas, 1984;

Rogers-Millar & Millar, 1979). Fitzpatrick and her associates (Fitzpatrick, 1977; Fitzpatrick & Indvik, 1982) analyzed patterns of interaction as a function of spousal perceptions and type of marital relationship.

Many communicative studies contrast distressed marital interaction with normal (presumably happy or satisfied) marital interaction. Baxter and Wilmot (1983) found that marital breakdowns did not uniformly influence the different dimensions of marital communication. Narvan (1967) found that satisfied spouses talk more to one another, convey mutual understanding to one another, talk about a wide range of topics, maintain open channels of communication, are sensitive to their partner's feelings, and utilize both verbal and nonverbal channels of communication. Burgess (1981), reviewing studies of distressed marriages, concludes that distressed families use more rigid, ritualized patterns of interaction; show fewer positive responses (like support or approval); display more negative interaction and reciprocate negative or coercive behaviors.

Conflict resolution appears to be an important communication skill. Gottman (1979) found that marital success was positively related to the couple's ability to resolve conflict. Hicks and Platt (1970) found that open communication was correlated with both marital success and conflict resolution. Bochner, Krueger, and Chmielewski (1982) found that spousal perceptions (e.g., what she thinks he thinks of her performance of instrumental and companionship roles) are related to marital satisfaction. Mettetal and Gottman (n.d.) found that, although both distressed and nondistressed couples reciprocated positive affect, the distressed couples were more likely to give negative affect to one another. In nondistressed couples, wives do not appear to reciprocate negative affect past their initial negative response. This pattern was found regardless of age, years married, degree of marital satisfaction, type of task, and setting.

Thus far, we have surveyed research focusing on text characteristics and the social context of relationships (i.e., marriage, family, and friendship). We next turn to examine participant characteristics, such as age and sex, and their influence on interpersonal relationships and interpersonal communication.

Participant Characteristics:
Their Influence on Interpersonal Relationships and
Interpersonal Communication

All societies and cultures use social characteristics to organize and maintain their way of life. However, every society uses a unique configuration of social characteristics to organize its cultural life. Although vast diversity exists, three social variables—age, gender, and social group membership—strongly influence human behavior, especially human communication, across many cultures. Age, for example, influences an interactant's speaking rights and obligations, conversational style, and linguistic complexity. Gender differences in communication have been documented with regard to interruptions, talking time, language choice, and a number of other variables. Finally, social class membership has been found to influence communication style, responses to questions, and general approaches to language use.

Personal characteristics also influence an individual's conceptualization of different types of social relationships. For example, children's concepts of friendship vary as a function of age (LaGaipa, 1981b). In what follows, we examine how communication differs as a result of age, gender, and social group membership. In addition, we discuss how age, gender, and social group membership influence one's conceptualization of social relationships. Both factors need to be examined because, as has been amply documented, individuals' expectations and knowledge about interaction influence their communication.

Our discussion of these influences is selective, focusing on the most general, pervasive findings, because a more comprehensive review is beyond the scope of this chapter. It should also be noted that cultural differences provide an additional, deep-seated layer of complexity to the influence of age, gender, and social group membership on communication. Such influences are *expressed differently and with differing significance* by different cultures. However, relatively little is known about these cultural differences.

Communicator Age

Age and Its Influence on Interpersonal Communication.   There are three distinct ways in which age influences communication. Age, as a *maturational* constraint, influences the linguistic skills and abilities of interactants. In general, the younger the participant, the more limited their language and communication skills. (The development of communication has been throroughly discussed in Chapter 7.)

Secondly, age may be viewed as an *interactional* constraint. Generally, the speaking rights and obligations are most restrictive for young interactants. There are four areas of importance to assess in reviewing the effect of age on participant's interactional skills: (1) speaking rights and obligations; (2) topicalization; (3) coherence; and (4) communicative functions. Depending upon cultural practices, children's speaking rights and obligations vary substantially. However, children discover strategies to engage others in conversation, even when their "right" to do so is restricted. For example, French and Woll (1981) found that children use questions to initiate a conversation or change topics in adult/child conversations. Children apparently use the strong cultural pressure to answer questions as a technique for engaging others in talk. (For a more detailed discussion of these and other communicative strategies children use, see Chapter 7.)

Finally, age may be viewed as a *cultural* constraint. There is considerable cultural variation in how age is viewed and in the constraints this may impose on communication. Most societies limit, to some degree, children's speaking rights and obligations. Some societies, like the Kaluli, do not recognize children as competent communicators until late childhood and thus children's speaking opportunities are restricted in important ways (Schieffelin, 1981). Other societies, like most Western, technologically-developed societies, emphasize parent/child and child/child interaction in early childhood as an important developmental process. Still other cultures use state-run nurseries in order to provide significant early interactional experiences. As Wells and his colleagues (Wells et al., 1981; Wells, 1985) have demonstrated, different contexts provide different interactional opportunities and as a result, children develop different communication skills.

Some societies have very diffuse kinship networks while others have fairly tight kinship networks. Depending upon the network structure and the age limitations associated with it, people will have different interactional opportunities. Age thus plays an important role in determining what types of relationships can be developed, and their degree of autonomy and responsibility.

Age and Its Influence on the Conceptualization of Interpersonal Relationships. As previously noted, a communicator's age not only influences his or her communication skills, but also influences how he or she conceptualizes interpersonal relationships. Talk serves different purposes for children, depending upon how they view their social relationships with others and their abilities to interact competently with others.

As we have seen, with increasing age, children's concepts of friendship become less egocentric, more reciprocal, and more psychological in nature. That is, older children begin to make attributions about desirable qualities in friends, like loyalty, and judge friends according to those criteria (Bigelow & LaGaipa, 1975; Hartup, 1978; Rubin, 1980). Mannarino (1980) concludes

> With increasing chronological age, children develop a progressively more differentiated and hierarchically organized conceptual system with which to think and talk about their interpersonal relationships. . . . there appears to be a developmental progression in children's conceptions of friendship with joint activities and propinquity serving as common denominators of preschool friendships, conformity and cooperation marking the friendships of middle childhood, and loyalty, mutuality, and self-disclosure characterizing preadolescent friendships. (p. 59)

Children's play provides the most important opportunity for learning about interaction and friendship (Hartup, 1978; Haslett, 1983b, c; 1986d).

Early interaction with peers is a strong influence upon subsequent relationships (Duck, 1984a; Hinde, 1979). Hartup (1978) suggests that children's friendships provide them with opportunities to learn a variety of social and cognitive skills. Duck, Miell, and Gaebler (1980) note that girls seem to have intensive friendships (focused on one person) while males seem to form extensive friendships (with a group of other children). In addition, they note that friendship is fairly unstable (up to about eleven years) with the child's subjective experiences of each encounter influencing friendship choice (e.g., someone shared a toy or candy with them, etc.).

In adolescence, friends provide important social support and a training ground for developing adult coping strategies (Fine, 1981; Kon & Losenkov, 1978). Hinde (1979, 1981) suggests that early relationships are particularly important since they influence all subsequent relationships. With increasing age, then, the complexity of relationships and communication both increase. As such, generally the older the child, the more communicative strategies they can use to establish and maintain relationships.

Gender

Gender Influences on Interpersonal Communication.   Like age, gender effects vary as a function of one's cultural and social group. Most scholars suggest that gender differences in behavior begin early in life.[1] For example, Etaugh (1983) argues that gender-specific behaviors begin in very early childhood: significant gender differences have been found in toy preferences (Goldberg & Lewis, 1969), fantasy play (Connolly, Doyle, & Creschin, 1983), feedback on children's play activities (Faggot & Leinbach, 1983), and play group interactions among preschoolers (Haslett, 1983b, Haslett & Bowen, 1986; Liss, 1983).

Gender differences in communication also exist among adults. Aries (1976) found that conversational topics shifted as a result of the sex composition of the group. Men used a more personal style in mixed sex groups. Shimanoff (1983) found that men talked more about their emotions if their listeners were female rather than male. Females appear to engage in more casual, non-task-oriented talk than do men (Baxter & Wilmot,

---

[1] There is, of course, considerable controversy over whether gender differences are innate or learned, or perhaps a combination of the two. Space does not permit a lengthy discussion of this issue, however, readers should be aware of this debate. Some aspects of early communicative development may be innate. Some scholars, such as Hinde (personal communication), have been pursuing linkages between the behavior of humans and other primates, and have found striking parallels in behavior. Differences have also been found with respect to gender; for example, the male of a species seems more agressive than the female. Much more research will be needed to clarify these influences and their potential interaction. I agree with Bates' (1979) argument that both innate and environmental factors interact in unique ways to produce social behavior.

1983). Ogilvie and Haslett (1985), using Norton's communicator style inventory (1983), found significant gender differences in communication in a small, task-oriented group. Men and women appear to use different influence tactics: females create and maintain close relationships, whereas males try to attract attention and to assert dominance (Maltz & Borker, 1982). Falbo and Peplau (1980) found that men use direct, logical strategies to persuade whereas women rely on indirect strategies, like withdrawal.

Several studies (Baird & Bradley, 1979; Hall & Braunwald, 1981; Lakoff, 1975) found communicative style differences between men and women. Women are viewed as attentive, supportive, and friendly whereas men are described as aggressive, direct, and dominant. Key (1975) suggests that women rely on tag questions, modifiers, intensifiers, modal constructions, and imperatives in their communication. Johnson (1983) found differences between men and women in their use of expletives and in evaluative judgments about use of expletives. Haas (1979), in her review of gender differences in spoken language, found that men were more loquacious and direct, used more nonstandard forms and talked about more different topics than did women. In contract, women appear to be more supportive, expressive, polite, and deferential.

Men tend to initiate and receive more interaction than women (Aries, 1976), while women tend to react more to other's remarks (Shaw & Sadler, 1965). McMillan, Clifton, McGrath, and Gale (1977) found that both sexes interrupted women more frequently than men. Zimmerman and West (1975) found that men interrupted and overlapped in mixed-sex conversations significantly more than did women.

In their review of cross-sex conversations, Maltz and Borker (1982) note that women ask more questions; women do more work maintaining conversations; women use more positive minimal responses; women use more inclusive pronouns; and after interruptions, women are usually silent. Men, however, interrupt more; dispute others' statements more; ignore others' comments more; use more control mechanisms; and talk more generally. Explanations for these differences tend to rely on the social power advantage men have over women in most contexts. Maltz and Borker conclude that misunderstandings are likely to occur in cross-sex conversations over the interpretation of questions, topic maintenance, displays of verbal agressiveness and topic shift.[2]

---

[2]A thorough review of the extensive research on sex differences in communication is beyond the scope of our discussion here. However, for an overview of gender and communication see Eakins & Eakins, 1978; Kramarae & Treichler, 1986; West & Zimmerman, 1985; and Pearson, 1985; for a discussion of language, power and gender, see Kramarae, Schulz, & O'Barr, 1984.

Gender Differences in the Conceptualization of Interpersonal Relationships. Gender not only influences communicative style but also the way in which relationships are perceived, established, and maintained. Women tend to have intensive relationships with others, while men have activity-oriented relationships that extend over a wider range of individuals (Booth, 1972). Generally, Dickens and Perlman (1981) conclude that men and women have similar size networks of friends. However, women appear to form qualitatively richer relationships: women share emotionally whereas men share activities. Such differences appear among adolescents as well (Waldrop & Halvorson, 1975). Same-gender friends assume greater intensity and importance around 8–12 years of age, particularly as children change from childhood to adolescence (Dickens & Perlman, 1981).

Gender, Marriage and Friendship. When married, women tend to have more cross-sex friends than single women. For men, their closest friend is their wife while for women it is often another woman (Blau, 1973). Marriage, for both sexes, limits contact with the opposite sex and the intimacy of relationships that develop.

In her review of gender and marital relationships, Peplau (1983) suggests that sex-role expectations—how we expect men and women to behave—exert a significant influence on marital interaction. Sex-roles expectations vary as a function of the cultural environment, personal characteristics and attitudes, the requirements of various social systems (like marriage), the relative power of men and women, and the surrounding social network. Men and women both desire enduring relationships, companionship, and affection. However, women value self-disclosure more than men and establish more dependence on their friends than do men (Cochran & Peplau, 1983).

Social Group Membership

Social Group Membership: Its Influence on Interpersonal Communication. Behavior that varies as a function of age and gender also differs as a function of social group membership. The most seminal work in this area is that of Basil Bernstein and his associates (1973, 1977). In particular, his theoretical model provides a very useful approach for integrating social class and communication. Social class, for our purposes, is assessed by economic wealth, education, and occupation. While many societies may not utilize social class as a social criteria, most societies accord power on the basis of these three criteria, either as a single factor or in combination with one another. While the discussion thus relies on data in Western countries, these concepts are believed applicable to social systems generally.

Bernstein's Theory of Class, Codes and Control. Bernstein argues that communication transmits the "genes" of social class from generation to generation. Through a network of complex social relationships, including work, community and family relationships, communicative practices or codes are shaped. These communicative practices, in turn, influence future social interactions and relationships. Each social group, through a unique set of social relationships and a particular communication code, transmits its dominant values to future generations.

According to Bernstein, social role behavior is learned via the family, peer group, school, and work. He broadly distinguishes two role systems. Individuals raised in families with open roles have personal, individualized meanings, an ability to cope with social ambiguity, and a motivation to explore the environment. In contrast, individuals raised in families with a closed role system have communal, collective meanings, and a strict definition of social context with little social ambiguity. In brief, open role systems encourage individual development whereas closed role systems encourage individuals to fulfill socially prescribed roles.

Within the family, these roles become more explicitly developed and reinforced by the use of elaborated and restricted communication codes. Elaborated codes facilitate open roles, while restricted codes support closed role systems. Families use either personal or positional appeals to reinforce their role systems. Positional appeals reinforce communal group values while personal appeals rely more on individual motivation and intent. Table 2 summarizes these distinctions.

Social Group Membership and Language Differentiation.   Another significant research tradition concerning social group differences in communication is that of Tajfel, Scherer, Giles, and their colleagues. Collectively, their work suggests that, in any interaction, participants can either emphasize their in-group status (by the use of jargon, special terms of address, etc.) or emphasize their differentiation from another (e.g., using a formal mode of address, using a different language or dialect, etc.).

Such speech markers indicate social group identity in two ways (Giles, Scherer, & Taylor, 1979); first, by identifying the roles and hierarchical positions of group members and second, by communicating important attitudes as well as the emotional states of others. For example, we can choose to emphasize our ethnicity, or volunteer comments about our psychological state. However, Brown and Levinson (1979) suggest that these speech markers are not simple social signals. Rather, they interact in complex ways to define the ongoing interaction and its context. Whatever intervening factors may be at force, clearly participants use language to help interpret their ongoing interactions.

In summary, different approaches to interpersonal communication may emphasize either text, context, or communicator variables. Texts vary as a

TABLE 2
Bernstein's Theory of Class, Codes and Control

Family

Open Role System	*Closed Role System*
1. individualistic meanings	1. communal, collective meanings
2. motivation to explore	2. well-defined social situations
3. ability to cope with social ambiguity	3. little ambiguity in social roles
4. decisions are a function of the psychological qualities of the individual	4. decision making is invested in the member's formal status
5. roles not clearly defined	5. clear separation of roles
6. children's peer group associations subject to family discussion	6. children's peer group associations subject to legislation by adults
7. *achieved* status	7. *ascribed* status important
8. role discretion (range of alternatives) wide	8. few role alternatives
9. verbal elaboration of individual differences	9. verbal elaboration of judgment (its consequences)

Communication Means

Elaborated Code	*Restricted Code*
1. relies on verbal "explicitness"	1. relies on gesture, intonation, and metaphor
2. has wide range of syntactic alternatives	2. has a narrow range of syntactic alternatives
3. flexibly organized	3. rigidly organized
4. complex planning involved	4. little planning involved
5. doesn't rely on shared object, events or meanings	5. relies on shared identifications and common assumptions
6. verbal communication is important	6. extra-verbal means important (non-verbal dimension stressed)
7. intent of other person is not taken for granted	7. intent is taken for granted
8. oriented toward individual persons	8. oriented toward common group or status membership
9. verbally "elaborate"	

(Supported by)
Appeals for Social Control

Personal Appeals	*Positional Appeals*
1. learning social relationships	1. process of learning rules
2. deals with motivation and individual attention	2. child reminded of what he shares with others
3. explanation given, e.g., "I know you want to but she will feel bad if you do"	3. required to follow norm defined by status e.g., "Little girls don't do that."
4. rule *achieved* by individuals	4. learns role obligation and differentiation

function of the type of social relationship, and its developmental stage. In addition, participant characteristics, such as gender, age, and social group membership, influence texts. With regard to contextual influences, viewed here as the *relational context,* substantial communicative differences exist across different types of relationships (i.e., friendship, marriage, or family context) and across different participants. Both the communicative processes themselves as well as the conceptualizations of relationships vary as a function of communicator characteristics. Finally, communicator characteristics— gender, age, and social group membership—influence how relationships are defined, how social settings are defined, and what communicative styles are appropriate. Taken together, these interpersonal communication variables and processes offer a very rich, complex picture of human communication.

Given this complexity, it is not surprising that many critical issues remain in need of further study. It is to these critical issues we now turn: These issues cut across text, context and communicator influences and the varied approaches taken to modeling these influences.

IV.   CRITICAL ISSUES IN INTERPERSONAL COMMUNICATION RESEARCH

Although the use of an integrated approach to interpersonal communica- tion will enhance research efforts, problematic issues still remain. The first critical issue concerns the interplay between the text and the participants' social relationship. In other words, what do texts tell us about participants' relationships and how do these relationships influence text production and comprehension? Second, when is a relationship an interpersonal relationship? And finally, what are appropriate research methods for studying interper- sonal communication?

The Text and The Relationship: A Problematic Connection

The heart of this issue is the connection between relating and the relation- ship or, in other terms, the text and the relationship. The nature of a relationship and its expression appear to reflect two distinct phenomena. However, many scholars have differing views on this matter. Duck, Lock, McCall, Fitzpatrick, and Coyne (1984) explicitly discuss these positions when they state:

> interaction is significantly affected by the relationship between the com-
> municators, and vice versa. Theories here can be classified on a continuum
> that is bounded, on one end, by assumed isomorphism between communica-
> tions and relationships and, on the other, by symbolic theories in which

isomorphism is denied. The isomorphic theorists. . . . view communication as a reciprocal negotiating process defining the relationship between communicators. Individuals relate to one another by talking and their interaction *is* the relationship. Conceptually, every unit of communication equals a unit of their relationship. Conversely, the symbolic theorists make a clearer differentiation between communication and relationships. . . . In this perspective, the assumptions granted to relationships are different from those granted to communication. Messages are assumed to have different meaning for each participant. A major focus here is the individual's perceptions of communication relative to perceptions of the relationship. For workers in the symbolic tradition, the relational significance of messages is essentially based on the personal relevance of messages. . . . There is a difference, yet a mutual dependence, between communication and relationships: qualitative shifts in relationships are marked by qualitative changes in communicative behaviors. (p. 3)

The view that relationships and texts are isomorphic has several serious weaknesses. First, as we have seen, texts are multifunctional. There is no one-to-one correspondence between form and function; each form may have a different meaning to different participants. Second, identical texts may take on different meanings in somewhat different contexts. Third, different aspects of the text will be relevant as a function of individual and/or contextual considerations. As the text's relevance changes, so too will its meaning. Finally, any text is necessarily incomplete. Some aspects of a relationship, for example, may never be expressed in any text. And, of course, not everything that is spoken will be relevant for the participants' relationship. For these reasons, it appears more accurate to say that a text *expresses* a relationship, rather than being the relationship. The text symbolically expresses the relationship in a significant way since, as previously noted in Chapter 6, the text publicly signals what participants are willing to be held accountable for.

In the perspective being taken here, the text itself and the interactants' social relationship mutually influence one another. As Hymes (1972) observes, each social relationship (SR) has a particular set of communicative practices (CP) associated with it, which make up the text of the interaction. The text, in turn, determines the outcome of the interaction and indirectly influences future interactions as well. For example, two individuals, Jack and Jill, are friends having a casual conversation. If Jack says something to Jill that is offensive (an inappropriate communicative practice since they are friends), Jill may become angry and refuse to talk further with him. Her anger may cause her to avoid future encounters with Jack and thus their friendship is affected. The interaction of text and the participant's social relationship appears to be bi-directional, and cyclical. This interactive process can be diagrammed as follows:

$$SR \rightarrow CP \rightarrow \text{Interactional Outcomes} \rightarrow SR^1 \rightarrow CP^1 \rightarrow \text{New Outcomes}$$

What Relationships are Interpersonal Relationships?

Any field of inquiry must, of course, define its parameters. The study of interpersonal relationships suffers from definitional disputes as do many other areas. Part of the lack of order, synthesis, and conceptual clarity found in the study of enduring relationships is due to these definitional disputes (Fitzpatrick, 1977).

When we contrast current approaches to interpersonal communication, different emphases and definitions become apparent. For example, Cushman, and Pearce and Cronen, focus on participants' ability to coordinate their activities with one another. In contrast, Bochner focuses on interpersonal bonds of a particular quality; namely, long-term, enduring relationships in which interpersonal bonding occurs. Both Knapp and Duck have focused on the different stages and processes in developing interpersonal relationships.

Because each approach conceptualizes the development of interpersonal relationships in distinct ways, the role of communication in such relationships varies. For Cushman, interpersonal communication is governed by standardized rules that operate in situations requiring coordination among interactants. Pearce and Cronen emphasize the interpretation of messages by each interactant. Each participant's interpretive rules construct his or her meanings for any given episode; these meanings, in turn, provide the basis for the participant's action in the episode. Miller and Steinberg (1975) look at the content of the message—its psychological information—and attempt to assess the influence of such messages on the relationship. Bochner outlines several functions that communication serves in interpersonal relationships that are intimate and enduring. In his view, interactants maintain a balance between opposing needs, such as the need to be open with others, yet maintain some privacy.

Significant differences exist among approaches to interpersonal relationships in terms of how they are defined and what relational features are emphasized. Given these differences, communication also appears to serve different roles in each approach. Furthermore, each approach regards different aspects of interpersonal communication as most important. In view of such differences, a necessary first step is to clarify these differences, so that various approaches and their research can be fully understood (Bochner, 1984; Fitzpatrick, 1977).

Methodological Issues

The third area of concern focuses on methodological issues. These concerns focus upon (1) the ecological validity of interpersonal communication research; and (2) the nature of the basic unit of analysis in interpersonal communication.

The Ecological Validity of Interpersonal Communication Research. What I am suggesting here is that scholars analyze interpersonal relationships and social situations that are relevant to individuals and that have consequences for those individuals. For example, if scholars focus upon control in relationships, then researchers should analyze those situations in which control is a salient factor. While such research may be more time-consuming, naturalistic, context-grounded research is needed to complement existing experimental studies.

What is the Basic Unit of Analysis for Interpersonal Communication? Considerable debate revolves around whether the individual or the dyad should serve as the focal point for analyzing interpersonal communication. In some instances, the individual may be the appropriate focus for analysis; in other instances, the dyad may be the focal point. However, in yet other instances, both perspectives may be necessary. For example, control of an interpersonal relationship may reflect a tension between individual needs as opposed to both participants' needs in the relationship.

It seems reasonable to assume that analytic units change as a function of a researcher's purposes, the particular relationship in question and the participants in the relationship. Rather than looking for a single unit of analysis, scholars need to evaluate what type of analysis is best suited for a particular research investigation.

V. CONCLUDING REMARKS

As we have seen, satisfying interpersonal relationships are essential for an individual's well-being, and interpersonal communication plays a critical role in the development and maintenance of such relationships. Interpersonal relationships can be characterized as being reciprocal, existing on multiple levels, complex, diverse, and enduring. Similarly, the interpersonal communicative processes which support these relationships are also multilevel, complex, and diverse. Many of the underlying pragmatic assumptions developed in this book, such as the intentional, inferential, and interpretive nature of communication, have been underlying premises found in interpersonal communicative processes. Interpersonal communication, as we have seen, varies as a function of relational context (marital, friendship, etc.) and participant characteristics (age, gender, and social group membership, etc.).

Although many disputed issues characterize research on interpersonal relationships and interpersonal communication, major concerns focus on the relationship between interpersonal communication processes and interpersonal relationships, appropriate units of analysis, and the ecological validity of interpersonal communication research. A more thorough analysis of the debates on these issues is beyond the scope of this chapter.

In the midst of this rich diversity of method, theory and conceptualization, many scholars (Ayres, 1984; Kelly et al., 1983; Montgomery, 1984) recognize the need for integrating research findings. One model, I believe, offers great potential for integrating research on interpersonal communication. Conversational analysis focuses on the interpretive procedures people use in making sense of conversational activity. Within each conversation, interactants negotiate their ongoing encounter, interpreting others' utterances and being held accountable for their own. With respect to interpersonal relationships, conversations reveal how the participants interpret their relationship, what contextual factors they consider relevant and again, most importantly, they signal the accountability of their actions. Thus, conversational analysis can be said to simultaneously reveal both intra- and inter-individual influences.

9 Educational Communication: A Pragmatic Perspective

Education plays a vital role in any society; it socializes members into a society, trains future workers, and creates a literate, educated society. Given their importance, educational practices have been extensively studied from a number of diverse perspectives. Major concerns have been teaching and teaching effectiveness, the planning and implementation of curriculum, the evaluation of pupil knowledge, measurement of children's academic abilities, literacy, and a host of other problem areas.

The role of communication in transmitting knowledge has received increasing attention from educational researchers. Communication is a critical component in both teaching and learning because of its intrinsic value, its role in gaining and displaying knowledge, and its role in social interaction in the classroom (Eder, 1982). As Mehan (1979) notes, students

> not only must know the content of academic subjects, they must learn the appropriate form in which to cast their academic knowledge. That is, competent membership in the classroom community involves employing interactional skills and abilities in the display of academic knowledge. They must know with whom, when, and where they can speak and act, and they must provide the speech and behavior that are appropriate for a given classroom situation. Students must also be able to relate behavior, both academic and social, to varying classroom situations by interpreting implicit classroom rules. (p. 133)

Many scholars analyzing communicative processes in education follow research traditions developed in the ethnography of speaking, sociolinguistics, and ethnomethodology. One particular approach, termed "teaching as

225

linguistic process," is concerned with how people learn through language, including their learning about language itself and the use of language in educational settings. In brief, this approach emphasizes how people learn from and use language to participate in face-to-face interaction in educational settings, and how this learning supports and/or constrains other learning (see, for example, Green & Wallat, 1981a).

This perspective is a pragmatic one since it deals with language usage in context; the context of concern, of course, being that of education. Many of their underlying assumptions parallel those developed in this book. In this view, classroom communication processes are viewed as being inferential, goal directed (i.e., intentional), conventional, and jointly negotiated by teachers and students. Communication varies across different teachers, different students, and different classroom settings (e.g., small group work, work involving the entire class, teacher/student conversation, etc.). Communication in the classroom also relies on commonsense knowledge and occurs sequentially, within specified time and space limitations. Finally, communication processes vary as a function of the social relationship between teacher and student (Green & Wallat, 1981b).

Green (1983), in her review of teaching-as-a-linguistic-process, identifies six assumptions underlying this pragmatic view of educational processes:

1. Face-to-face interaction among teachers and students is rule-governed. Teachers and students use language to achieve educational goals, to evaluate learning and to develop and maintain social relationships that facilitate learning. These processes are rule-governed and serve as constraints on appropriate classroom behavior.
2. Educational contexts are constructed by participants in face-to-face interaction. Participants must signal and recognize ongoing activities by contextualization cues and/or recognizing participation structures.
3. Meaning is context-dependent. As such, the multifunctionality of utterances is explicitly acknowledged. The same utterance can also have different meanings in different contexts (Wallat & Green, 1979).
4. Comprehension is an inferential process. Inferences are derived from the frames of reference of teachers (e.g., pedagogical beliefs, etc.) and of students (e.g., values concerning education and its importance, etc.), as well as from the actual interaction occurring in the classroom.
5. Classrooms are viewed as communicative environments. Considerable communicative skill is required to participate in classroom activities, both socially and academically (Mehan, 1979; Wilkinson, 1982b).
6. Teachers play a critical, directive role in classrooms. Teachers use communicative, pedagogical strategies to achieve instructional goals, and to create an environment for learning. Teachers also shape the social interaction that occurs in classrooms.

In this view, teachers and students have specified roles, with the teacher primarily directing classroom activities. Classroom activities are also shaped by the curriculum being taught and communicative processes reflect the asymmetrical roles of teachers and students. Generally, the teaching/learning process is a dynamic, social, evolutionary process that is negotiated by both teachers and students (Griffin & Mehan, 1981).

With this overview in mind—which emphasizes teaching and learning as communicative processes—we shall look more closely at educational practices. First, we consider the classroom as a cultural and institutional context; and then examine classrooms as self-contained educational settings. Second, we consider classrooms in light of their communicative processes, looking especially at various models of classroom communication. And finally, we focus more specifically on the communicative skills of both teachers and students.

I. THE EDUCATIONAL CONTEXT

Classrooms are surrounded by the existing values of a culture. Classrooms reflect a culture's general beliefs and values about education, such as how much education is valued, what is appropriate knowledge to transmit, how this knowledge is to be transmitted, and so forth. The larger social context in which education occurs has been termed the "hidden curriculum" (Cook-Gumperz & Gumperz, 1982). This hidden curriculum exerts a powerful indirect influence on the transmission and evaluation of knowledge.

The Cultural Context of Education

Bourdieu and his associates (Bourdieu, 1973; Bourdieu & Passeron, 1977) suggest that both the transmission of knowledge and access to it is determined by a society's values. Bourdieau (1973) refers to the knowledge passed on during schooling as cultural capital. Schools legitimize both the knowledge they transmit as well as the culture itself. Face-to-face interaction in classrooms occurs in the broader context of a school's educational practices, and is shaped by those practices (Cook-Gumperz & Gumperz, 1982). In turn, the school itself is part of a larger institutionalized system of educational policies, practices and ideologies. Thus classrooms reflect the hidden curriculum represented by educational practices governing the transmission of knowledge. All societies exercise some control over the transmission of knowledge, whether it be by legal procedures like the Scopes trial or banning books at the local library. According to Bourdieu, this hidden curriculum is encoded within language itself.

The British sociologist, Basil Bernstein (1971, 1973, 1977) has developed one of the most comprehensive theories concerning the social transmission of knowledge. Bernstein (1971) argues that there are three major message systems involved in the transmission of knowledge: (1) the curriculum which determines what knowledge is valid; (2) the pedagogy which determines the appropriate means for transmitting knowledge; and (3) the evaluation system which determines what counts as a valid realization of knowledge. Through schooling—the legitimized cultural transmission of knowledge—children acquire ways of organizing experience and realizing meaning. One of the major sources of acquiring knowledge, according to Bernstein, is in instructional settings (see also, for example, Edwards, 1981, and Bernier, 1981).

In the United States, the work of Hymes and his colleagues has explored the connections between educational practices and the local community. Ogbu (1974, 1978) has detailed the importance of the subculture and family in terms of their support for education, and the ability of education to provide upward mobility (see also Heath, 1982a, 1983). Gilmore and Glatthorn (1982) focused on community and school ties, especially as they are reflected in the practices of school administrations.

With this larger cultural context in mind, we next examine the classroom itself. Classrooms may be considered social microcosms whose organization reflects cultural values and beliefs.

The Classroom as Context

Although classrooms vary along many dimensions, such as size, content, and participants, some dimensions appear to be universal. In general, instructional settings are characterized by the asymetrical roles of teachers and students, with teachers directing classroom activities (Green & Harker, 1982). Teachers dominate communication in instructional settings, talking about 70% of the time in classrooms (Barnes, 1976).

Instructional activities involve social dimensions as well as academic dimensions (Erickson, 1982; Wilkinson, 1982a,b). Erickson (1982) suggests that *academic task structures* organize academic content. These structures reflect the logic of the subject matter, the sequencing of content, the strategies for completing tasks, and the use of physical materials. In contrast, *social participation structures* organize interaction in classrooms by establishing speaker's rights and obligations, coordinating activities, and providing opportunities for participation. As Mehan (1979) observes, students need to master both academic content and social participation rules.

With this brief overview of the larger social environment surrounding instructional settings and a brief consideration of the classroom itself as a context, we next turn to a detailed examination of classroom communication. Here we shall examine the organization of classroom communication, the participants in the interaction (teachers and students) and their relative contributions.

II. COMMUNICATION IN THE CLASSROOM

The Organization of Classroom Communication

Models of Classroom Communication

Most models of classroom interaction measure the amount and type of talk as well as who is speaking. Flanders (1963) found that classroom talk comprises about 70% of the activity in classrooms; teachers talk about 70% of that time. Some scholars, like Barnes (1976), argue that the communicative dominance by teachers is even higher than Flanders' estimates. Although these global measures provide some insight into classroom communication, more detailed analyses are needed. A substantial number of studies have been done concerning both quantity and type of talk, and various models of classroom communication have been proposed. It is to these models we now turn.

1. Flanders' Interaction Analysis. One of the earliest comprehensive models of classroom communication was Flanders' categorization of teacher/student talk. These categories are general, but nevertheless capture the flow of communication in the classroom. Flanders' (1970) system involved the following categories:

Teacher talk:
    Responses: accepts feelings
                praises or encourages
                accepts or uses ideas of pupils
    Questions:
    Initiations: lectures
                gives directions
                criticizes or justifies authority
  Student talk: response
                initiation
  Silence
      (p. 34)

Although these categories give a rough profile of communicative behavior in the classroom, this system is very limited in its analysis. Mehan (1979) notes that Flanders' interaction analysis has several major flaws. First, it largely ignores students' contributions to classroom interaction. Second, these categories ignore the interrelationship between verbal and nonverbal cues. Third, the context-bound nature of classroom behavior is ignored. And finally, it does not reflect the multiple functions that utterances can perform.

Other models, like those of Bellack and Davitz (1972), Barnes (1976), Sinclair and Coulthard (1975), Wells and Montgomery (1981) and Tough (1977), base their models of classroom communication on the teacher's instructional goals and how communication facilitates those goals. As such, these models offer more detailed analyses of classroom communication, incorporating pedagogical concerns and linguistic analyses in their models.

2. Bellack and Davitz.   Bellack and Davitz (1972) use Wittgenstein's notion of language games as a basis for their model of classroom communication. According to Bellack and Davitz, there are three major uses of language in the classroom—pedagogical usage, content usage, and affect usage. *Pedagogical moves* involve structuring, soliciting, responding, and reacting on the part of teachers. *Content moves* refer to the presentation of the subject matter in the classroom. *Affect moves* reflect the emotional dimension in the classroom.

Their analyses demonstrate that teachers move through cycles of initiating and responding behavior. Teachers dominate classroom talk; with thirty percent of their talk soliciting comments from students; thirty percent being evaluative comments, and only six percent being structuring moves. Students respond more than initiate, and fifty percent of their responses are factual in nature. While this model is also general, it has more detailed analyses of pedagogical moves and adds a new dimension, that of affect.

3. Sinclair and Coulthard.   Sinclair and Coulthard (1975) model classroom communication by using a very explicit analysis of language use in the classroom. In addition, their model incorporates nonlinguistic features of classroom communication.

Their analysis of classroom communication incorporates three levels of analysis: (1) *nonlinguistic organizational factors* (the course, time period and topic); (2) *discourse factors* (the lesson, transactions, exchanges, moves and acts); and (3) *grammatical factors* (sentences, clauses, words and morphemes). Their analysis centers on the discourse level, its hierarchical organization, and grammatical structure.

The discourse level reveals how classroom communication is organized. Acts are considered minimal communicative units that perform a single communicative function. Acts can *nominate* (e.g., you, Tom, etc.); *ack-*

nowledge (e.g., yes, alright, ok, etc.); *comment* (e.g., that's pretty, etc.); or *evaluate* (e.g., that's correct, etc.). These acts combine to form moves. Moves perform the communicative functions of opening, answering, following-up, framing, or focusing classroom talk. For example, an *opening move* in a teaching exchange may include the acts of *nomination* and *comment* (e.g., John, it was a nice trip to the zoo, wasn't it?).

A sequence of moves builds into exchanges, and these exchanges build into transactions. Boundary exchanges serve to frame classroom activities and to focus those activities. In contrast, teaching exchanges form the basic triadic unit of classroom communication: teacher initiation, student response, and subsequent teacher feedback. Finally, these exchanges combine to form transactions; transactions serve to provide information, direct activities or elicit responses. As is readily apparent, transactions are usually performed by teachers.

Their model can be diagrammed as follows:

Acts	→	*Moves*	→	*Exchanges*	→	*Transactions*	→	*Lessons*
nomination		opening		teaching		informing		
acknowledge		answering		boundary		directing		
comment		follow-up				eliciting		
evaluate		framing						
		focusing						

In addition, Sinclair and Coulthard have broken down teaching exchanges into more specific sub-types. Teaching exchanges can inform, direct, elicit, re-initiate (after a student has given an initial incorrect response), list, reinforce, and repeat. Student exchanges can inform, elicit, and check (i.e., seek confirmation of a response).

Although this model is much more detailed in its analysis of teaching exchanges and in its linguistic analysis, it fails to adequately address the multifunctional nature of communicative behavior. While it includes reference to broader concerns, like courses and topics, these connections need to be more fully developed.

4. Wells and Montgomery.   Wells and Montgomery (1981) focus on the relationships between language as used in the home and in school. Generally, they suggest that children's use of language in the home may interfere with or facilitate their subsequent learning in school. Wells and Montgomery (1981) assume

firstly, that the knowledge and values a child comes to draw upon in his dealings with the social and physical world are learned largely through his interactions with other members of his culture, particularly his parents and teachers; and secondly, that such interactions are achieved to a very considerable extent through linguistic communication. (p. 210)

Their work attempts to identify styles of interaction as they develop at home and at school, and to examine the different opportunities they provide for developing communicative skills.

Like Halliday, they view the exchange as a basic unit of interaction. Exchanges involve two major systems: *commodities* which refer to what is being exchanged (e.g., goods, services, information, etc.) and *discourse roles* which characterized a participant's role in the exchange process (e.g., requestee, buyer, etc.). Combinations of commodities and discourse roles define basic communicative acts. For example, the communicative act of demanding requires that someone request (a discourse role) a service or goods (the commodity). Answering requires that someone give information (a commodity) upon request (the discourse role). As verbal skills develop, the child develops a more diverse set of communicative responses and learns to manage status and power as well (Wells, Montgomery, & MacLure, 1979).

Several modifications to this basic system have been made, incorporating distinctions between nonlinguistic information and discourse information (i.e., information contained in the text). Another modification concerns a measure of the thematic coherence in discourse. Effective communication reflects thematic continuity in which participants respond to topics introduced by one another.

In their model, discourse roles include initiating remarks, continuing the conversation/topic, or responding to another's comments. Discourse commodities include either goods/services or information. They point out that giving information may be contingent on the text, and can specify, reiterate, or confirm that text. Finally, some utterances can be incorporated by either teacher or student in their ongoing conversation.

Wells and Montgomery (1981) conclude that models for classroom communication must capture the social features of interaction. In their contrast of two teaching styles, they point out that

In encouraging her to relate the familiar experiences of her life at home to the less familiar content and activity of reading, the teacher is providing a bridge which may enable Rosie [the student] to move into the realm of more 'disembedded' problem solving which is associated with "curricular" knowledge, without experiencing the defeating bewilderment which the more straightforwardly didactic approach of the first teacher seems to engender.

Just as at home, both "supporting" and "leading" parental strategies of interaction provide different, but in some ways complementary, opportunities for learning to use language, so in the classroom, too, different strategies are likely to be appropriate in promoting different educationally valued ends and perhaps also with different children at differing stages in their school careers. (p. 237)

From the models of classroom communication reviewed thus far, we can see significant differences in their emphases. Models vary in terms of whether they are teacher-centered or student-centered: Flanders, Bellack and Davitz, and Sinclair and Coulthard center on teacher-talk and teacher control of the classroom. In contrast, Wells and Montgomery focus on skills students bring to the instructional setting as well as the impact of teaching style on students' opportunities to learn. Models also vary in terms of their use of interactional categories (like Flanders, and Wells & Montgomery) or linguistic categories (like Sinclair & Coulthard). Another difference is their inclusion of pedagogical concerns (Sinclair & Coulthard) or their relative lack of concern for pedagogy (Bellack & Davis).

All these models, despite their contributions to our understanding of classroom communicative processes, are limited in two significant ways. First, these models rely on coding categories which ignore the multifunctionality of utterances. Second, these models tend to focus on either teacher talk or students' skills, but not on *classroom interaction as jointly negotiated by teachers and students in instructional settings*. While the model developed by Wells and Montgomery comes closest to an interactive model, nevertheless, they still focus primarily on the impact of teaching style on the student. For learning to occur, students and teachers must jointly participate in that process.

Research identifying context-dependent interpretations of classroom behavior and recognizing the multifunctional nature of communicative behavior needs to complement existing models of classroom communication. Edwards (1981) suggests that sociolinguistic approaches to classroom communication address some of these concerns. It is to these approaches we now turn.

Sociolinguistic Analyses of Classroom Interaction

Hymes (1972, 1977) and Gumperz (Gumperz & Herasmuchuk, 1973; Cook-Gumperz & Gumperz, 1982) have been instrumental in developing sociolinguistic approaches to education. Sociolinguistic researchers use theoretically-grounded, naturalistic observations in their analyses of classroom behavior. Green (1983) notes that these observations are made over different types of classrooms, different activities, different age groups, and over long periods of time. Frequently, researchers interview both teachers and students about their interpretations of ongoing classroom activity. Mehan (1979) refers to these approaches as "constitutive ethnography" in which both the structure and management of classroom activities are given equal attention. We shall now examine how classroom communication is characterized by sociolinguistic approaches.

1. Communicative Cues Used to Interpret Classroom Activities.   Green and Wallat (1981b) claim that communicative rules help define a classroom context. Both teachers and students need to be aware of the following sets of cues which indicate "what's going on" at any given time. Participants should:

1. Monitor classroom activity by observing participants' physical orientation and proximity.
2. Pay attention to differences in social meanings.
3. Understand and follow speaking rights and obligations.
4. Be cooperative (follow Grice's cooperative maxim).
5. Be available for classroom activities, and
6. Be aware of different patterns of interaction.

Paying attention to these sets of cues help participants understand ongoing classroom activity.

Teachers and students appear to differ on how they use these potential cues (Mehan, Lazden, Coles, Fisher, & Maroules, 1976). Teachers and students formulate academic tasks in different ways, with teachers verbally specifying their views and students relying more on the context for their understanding of academic tasks. For classroom interactions to occur, participants need to attract the attention of the other interactants and to involve them in the interaction. This is accomplished in different ways by students and teachers. If learning itself depends on interaction, then it is crucial for students to understand and use communicative strategies that enable them to participate in classroom activities. Wilkinson (1982b) suggests that students must be competent in understanding both linguistic structure and function; and that individuals differ in these abilities. Mehan (1979) found that teachers direct activities and elicit information, while students give and receive information.

In general, sociolinguistic research focuses on the practices governing classroom interaction. Social interaction in classrooms is complex, multifaceted, and largely controlled by teachers (Green & Wallat, 1981a; Wilkinson, 1982a, b). As Merritt (1982) points out, classroom participants are required to simultaneously process information and participate in classroom activities. Participants must assess their own activities as well as those of others, and respond to demands of academic tasks as well as to the requirements for social participation. Merritt suggests that both teachers and students must focus their attention on shared activities; this focused attention is signalled both verbally and nonverbally.

Classroom discourse varies along several dimensions. Some communicative strategies are spontaneous improvisations on basic patterns of interaction (Griffin & Mehan, 1981). Communicative patterns also vary as a function of type of lesson (Green, 1983; Merritt & Humphrey, 1979) and cultural background (Cooper, Marquis, & Ayers-Lopez, 1982; Philips, 1972, 1974, 1976). Finally, Brown (1983) points out that the nature of face-to-face interaction requires complex processing skills because immediate feedback is required. For students acquiring second languages, specific training may be required so that communicative signals can be recognized.

In summary, sociolinguistic research characterizes the classroom as a complex interactional setting, involving both academic tasks and social participation demands. Thus, interactional skills are required for learning as well as for social involvement with others. Generally, teachers direct classroom activities and students respond to those activities. Finally, communication varies as a function of task, participants' skills, and their cultural background.

2. Defining the Classroom Context.   Contexts can be inferred and interpreted at many different levels (Erickson & Shultz, 1977; Gumperz, 1981; Merritt & Humphrey, 1979). Green (1983) characterizes context on four distinct levels: (1) *local context* refers to the immediate, current activity; (2) *event context* signals the general type of event (e.g., reading, group lesson, class news, etc.); (3) *setting context* refers to the surrounding physical environment; and (4) *mutual biographical context* refers to the interactional history of the student and teacher. The classroom context, as defined by the participants, influences communication in that context (Genishi, 1979; Gumperz & Herasimuchuk, 1973; Hymes, 1972). Both teachers and students can modify the classroom context to meet their own goals or needs (Cole, Griffin, & Newman, 1979; Hrybyk & Farnham-Diggory, 1981).

III. TEACHER COMMUNICATION IN THE CLASSROOM

Our purpose here is to examine teachers' patterns of communication in instructional settings. First, we explore the structure of teachers' communication in the classroom generally. Next, we examine the use of questions in the classroom and teachers' evaluative comments. Finally, we discuss some features of teachers' communicative styles.

The Structure of Teacher Communication

The basic unit of instructional communication in the classroom is a three turn unit: the teacher makes an utterance that requires a response, a student responds, and the teacher comments on the student response. This tripart unit has been documented for several decades, over various types of classrooms, teachers, students, and tasks (Bellack & Davitz, 1972; Green & Wallat, 1981a; Mehan, 1979; Sinclair & Coulthard, 1975; Stubbs & Hilliard, 1983; Wells, 1981, Wilkinson, 1982a). Although this sequence constitutes a basic unit of instructional communication, Mehan (1979) points out that teachers often improvise when unanticipated disruptions occur. When disruptions occur, teachers can do nothing, "get through," accept the disruption, or open up the discussion (pp. 107–110). Griffin and Mehan (1981) also point out that both teachers and students jointly construct classroom conventions, and that some flexibility is built into these conventions.

Teachers' communication relies primarily on three language functions: (1) *directing others* (serves to define classroom procedures and practices); (2) *informing others* (serves to share knowledge, usually academic task information); and (3) *eliciting responses* from others (serves to solicit student responses) (Mehan, 1979). When soliciting responses from students, teachers frequently control this process by nominating the student who is to reply (Mehan, 1979). For example, "John, could you tell us when Washington crossed the Delaware River?"

Teachers select communicative strategies that enable them to accomplish their instructional goals and that create a climate for learning (Wilkinson, 1982b). Academic content needs to be presented by the teacher, who simultaneously manages classroom activities as well as disciplines students (Merritt & Humphrey, 1979). To accomplish these simultaneously occurring demands, teachers must continuously evaluate classroom activities as well as direct them (Merritt, 1982). Teachers must focus on what is relevant instructionally, monitor student activities, correct or repair misunderstandings, and maintain the flow of classroom activity.

Teachers organize instructional activities in a variety of ways, using both verbal and nonverbal means (Stubbs & Hillier, 1983). Teachers' communication varies in terms of their opening moves (Morine-Dershimer & Tenneberg, 1981); their use of directives (DeStefano & Pepinsky, 1981); their monitoring of students (Stubbs & Hillier, 1983), and their instructional tasks (Merritt & Humphrey, 1981). Teachers also develop routines for important messages (Florio & Shultz, 1979) and for shifting from one task to another (Erickson, 1982; Merritt & Humphrey, 1981).

Teachers, like adults, enjoy an asymmetrical power and status relationship to children/students. Like adults, teachers can evade questions, insist on student attention, unilaterally terminate encounters, allocate turns, and scrutinize responses to answers. In addition, teachers can interrupt at any time or add additional information. Even if students respond, teachers evaluate the appropriateness of their response!

Despite the varied communicative and instructional activities teachers engage in, two processes stand out in terms of their critical role in instructional activities—teachers' use of questions and their evaluations of student responses. Soliciting information from students is, of course, accomplished primarily through the use of questions. While evaluation of responses can be accomplished in a variety of ways (e.g., praise, criticism, correction, etc.), its importance lies in the feedback provided for students. Without such feedback, students have no evaluation of their learning. We shall look at both of these communicative strategies in more detail.

1. Teachers' Use of Questions.   A question and answer sequence is one of the most basic instructional exchanges. Questions are asked for a variety of purposes, however, and frequently students must carefully evaluate what type of question is being asked (Morine-Dershimer & Tenenberg, 1981). Questions may be based on an assignment; they may be psuedo questions (in which the teacher is checking student knowledge); or they may be real questions (in which the teacher is soliciting unknown information).

Answering teachers' questions requires considerable student skill. French and MacLure (1983) note that students must make an on-the-spot assessment of what sort of question is being asked. Students rely on their knowledge of the teacher, the explicitness of the question, and the context to determine their responses. Teachers frequently ask predetermined questions (Morine-Dershimer & Tenenberg, 1981) and may want the answer given in a specified format (Stubbs, 1975). Even though teachers may "foreshadow" a student's answer by highlighting relevant information for students to focus on, nevertheless a student may still have to select one of several alternatives (Mehan, 1974).

2. Teachers' Use of Evaluative Comments.   Teachers' evaluations provide the student with feedback concerning his or her learning and performance. Nash (1973) notes that teachers evaluate students both academically and socially. He found that teachers' rankings of students' abilities matched that of students' own ratings of their ability. Furthermore, teachers' ratings correlated with measures of student abilities. Teachers also evaluate students' friendships and students appear to be aware of those judgments. Nash points out that subtle cues—such as the amount of attention a student receives, mention by name, and minor reinforcement—convey the teacher's judgment of a particular student. He concludes by observing that schools teach children to measure themselves against one another; and that children early on know their relative status in school, both academically and socially.

Rosenthal and Jacobsen (1968) suggest that teachers form expectations about students' abilities and interact with students on the basis of these expectations. Through their differential interactions, teachers indirectly influence students' subsequent performance. Research by Brophy and Good (1974) and Nash (1973) support this model. Wilkinson (1982a) notes that teachers are inconsistent in their expectations, and that their expectations vary as a function of the task being performed. Teachers' expectations also influence their evaluations of students.

Evaluation plays an important role in educational processes. These evaluations may be formal, as done by yearly testing and examinations, or informal, as done by teachers on a daily basis in the classroom. Evaluations may also be fairly direct, such as immediate feedback on the accuracy of an answer, or quite subtle, as revealed in patterns of attention and response to individual students. Teachers also use praise as a strategy to evaluate students. Teachers give more praise to academically talented students (Morine-Dershimer & Tenenberg, 1981) and use similar praise techniques for both individual and group work (Merritt & Humphrey, 1981). Teachers can sanction inappropriate behavior in a number of different ways: through loss of privileges (Hrybyk & Farnham-Diggory, 1981), through redirecting activity (Merritt & Humphrey, 1981), and through verbal reprimand (Merritt & Humphrey, 1981).

Teachers' communication can also be characterized in terms of general teaching style. Teaching style focuses upon a teacher's manner of presentation, attitude toward students, general enthusiasm, and pedagogical strategies. It is to this issue we now turn, looking particularly at studies focusing upon overall judgments of teacher style and effectiveness.

Teacher Style. Solomon, Bezdek, and Rosenberg (1963), observing twenty-four different classrooms with two teams of observers, assessed teaching style and subsequent student performance. Measures from a variety of previous studies were incorporated into their rating instrument (which included 169 items referring to teacher behavior). Factor analysis revealed eight factors underlying teaching style: (1) permissiveness vs. control; (2) lethargy vs. energy; (3) aggressiveness vs. protectiveness; (4) obscurity vs. clarity; (5) encouragement of content-related student participation vs. non-encouragement of participation; (6) dryness vs. flamboyance; (7) lecturing vs. encouraging student participation; and (8) warmth vs. coldness. A teacher's clarity was positively associated with the transmission of factual material. Student ability to deal abstractly with the curricular material was correlated with moderate positions on permissiveness-control, energy, aggressiveness, and flamboyance.

Their study concluded that student-centered classrooms (classes which are participative, integrative, and rate highly on instructor warmth and acceptance) are superior with regard to student acquisition of complex cognitive skills. Although these factors vary in importance depending on class size, type of course, student characteristics, and class level, nevertheless they highlight important characteristics of teacher behavior. Communication skill, noted by such factors as "verbal fluency," "communication behavior," or "clarity," have been important dimensions of teacher behavior in a variety of studies and settings.

In summary, teachers use a complex set of communicative skills in their teaching. Teachers must direct, monitor, and evaluate student activity in instructional settings. In order to accomplish those goals, teachers must clearly communicate the task itself, any changes in the task, and classroom rules for social interaction. In short, teachers "frame" instructional activities and convey these frames using a variety of communicative strategies. We have reviewed some of these communicative strategies, focusing particularly on questions and evaluations, and on general teaching style. Clearly, teachers must be sophisticated communicators in the classroom. However, equal skill is required of students and we now turn to an examination of students' communicative skills and obligations in instructional settings.

IV. STUDENT COMMUNICATION IN INSTRUCTIONAL SETTINGS

As Mehan (1979) and others point out, students must not only master curriculum content *but must also present their understanding of that material in appropriate ways.* Considerable academic knowledge and effective interactional skills are required for competent classroom behavior. Additional complexity arises when we acknowledge students' differing abilities and skills, their asymetrical status with respect to teachers, the variety of academic materials and in classroom activities, and the obligation to interact with their peers.

Five important aspects of student communication and participation in classrooms emerge from educational studies. We examine each aspect more closely. First, students rely on inferences and interpretive rules to account for "what's happening" in the classroom. Second, a number of studies focus on the social participation structure in the classroom and the communicative demands that students face. Thirdly, the issue of individual differences across students needs to be explored, especially as it involves differing cultures. Fourth, the continuities and/or discontinuities between "home language" and "school language" are explored and their implications for subsequent student learning are discussed. Finally, we examine the opportunities for peer/peer interaction, both for social interaction and instructional purposes, that classrooms offer.

Interpretive Rules and Inferences.   In order to interpret ongoing classroom activities, students must recognize discourse rules (e.g., when one can talk, to whom, etc.); understand correct forms of address; identify important classroom events; respond to questions appropriately and integrate classroom materials with ongoing activities (Green, 1983). As Gumperz (1981a) points out, every classroom activity

> involves different modes of cooperation and learning, as well as rules for the evaluation of behavior and for the interpretation of what goes on. Children must learn what these structures are; they must know how transitions between structures are signalled and what behavioral strategies are required to gain the teacher's attention or to obtain entry into a place of study and secure cooperation of the peer group. *Knowledge of strategies appropriate to these structures is a precondition for obtaining access to learning.* (Italics mine). (p. 7)

Mehan et al. (1976), in a year-long study of an ethnically mixed classroom, note that teachers and students use different interpretive strategies. Teachers rely on lexical specificity for their interpretations, whereas children rely on the context. Social participation structures are created by communicative conventions, although these conventions may be signalled in different ways by students and teachers.

Gumperz (1981) argues that learning and participating in instructional settings requires the use of conversational inferences. To involve people in conversations, initially their attention must be attracted and their active participation gained. Interactants must share an understanding of how the interaction is proceeding, and share conventions for signalling these understandings. Interactants must also be able to shift the focus of their activities and to "fit individual contributions into some broader theme" (p. 13). Individuals use the text, the context, background understandings of events and people, past interactional experiences, and the task as a basis for interpreting ongoing activities. As Gumperz notes, conversational inferences help us identify the meaning and significance of ongoing activities. When such inferential processes differ, as they do in ethnically mixed classrooms, these differences create misunderstandings about what is going on. Gumperz' study demonstrates some of these miscues. One pattern, for example, was the statement by young black children "I can't do this:" rather than signalling an inability to perform the task, black children were asking for company in doing the task.

Fredriksen (1981) notes that inferences are based upon cognitive knowledge as well as interactive processes. Teachers, according to Merritt (1982), must signal their involvement, attention, and shifts in activity; their stu-

dents must accurately interpret these cues in order to effectively participate in the classroom.

We now turn to a consideration of students' participation in the classroom,
both in academic and social terms. As we shall see, students' participation
is dependent upon their ability to interpret ongoing activities and to utilize
communicative strategies to secure their own participation.

Student Participation in the Classroom.   Erickson's (1982) model of
social participation structures in classrooms examines the ways in which
interactions are patterned, roles are defined and rights/obligations are
distributed. Examining the structure of classroom participation is important because it influences how students learn.

Participation structures may be signalled in a variety of ways. In addition,
children appear to follow different strategies in order to secure their
participation. Wootton (1981), for example, notes that children exaggerate
their questions in order to gain a teacher's attention and response. A desire
to participate may also be signalled by nonverbal changes in distance
(Erickson, 1982); contextualization cues like syntax, prosody, gaze, body
movement, posture, speech rhythm, and word choice (Cook-Gumperz &
Gumperz, 1976; Gumperz, 1982); the discourse itself (Frederikson, 1981);
and the topic and accessibility of the conversation (Merritt & Humphrey,
1979, 1981).

Griffin and Mehan (1981) note that teachers and students jointly determine the particular communicative conventions used in a classroom.
Although speaking and listening roles alternate between students and
teachers, students typically respond to teachers' queries and must learn
how and when to interject their comments. When making their own
queries, students maintain a delicate balance between directness and
rudeness; indirect requests are more polite, yet more unclear (Wilkinson,
Calculator, & Dollaghan, 1982). Children may understand the communicative rules, but not utilize them; or, conversely, they may use rules in a
routine way, but fail to apply them in other appropriate settings. Rules
for participation also may change when the task changes (Erickson,
1982). In short, classroom participation appears to be a complex process
that requires the student to interpret a diverse set of cues for effective
participation.

In addition, students vary in their success at participating in classroom
activities. Gaining access to classroom participation depends, in part, on
the student's background knowledge, willingness to tolerate disagreement,
and avoidance of premature closure of the discussion (Barnes, 1976).
Green (1983) notes that the most successful students are those who respond
to teachers' questions. That is, successful students have secured some

participation in the classroom. Requests are strategies which provide an opportunity to participate, and they are most effective when a variety of request forms are used (Wilkinson, Calculator, & Dollaghan, 1982). Wilkinson and Calculator (1982) found that effective requests were on-task, direct, sincere, and directed to a designated listener.

As we have seen, students use a variety of communicative strategies that enable them to participate in instructional settings. In particular, students need to secure the teacher's attention and thus requests are important. However, as previously noted, students vary in these skills and in their ability to use conversational inferences. These differences may limit the student's participation in the learning process. It is to these differences we now turn.

Individual Differences in Communicative Skills.   Different cultures have different sociolinguistic rules and assumptions underlying their communicative behavior. Florio and Shultz (1979) suggest that children adopt participation structures from their home environments. Furthermore, they point out that different cultural groups, such as American Indians, Hawaiians, and Alaskan Indians, have differing communicative strategies from those used in the mainstream educational system. These differences may constrain the amount and quality of learning available to these students.

Students also differ in their ability to meet the demands of classroom learning and participation. Since these demands vary across time, classrooms, and lessons (Cooper, Ayers-Lopez, & Marquis, 1981; Erickson, 1982; Green & Harker, 1982), accessing the learning environment becomes even more complex. Philips (1972) found that communicative patterns among young American Indian children minimize the obligation of children to perform publicly. For them, the instructional demands for public answers and talk contradict the communicative practices in their culture and thus the learning process is more difficult.

Rubin (1982) notes that cultural mismatches in learning may occur in four distinct areas: (1) norms for loquacity may vary; (2) norms for language structure and sequencing may vary; (3) norms for classroom participation may vary with some cultures viewing the classroom as inappropriate for speech; and (4) members of different cultures may differ in their construal of questions (Heath, 1982b, c). The Scollons' (Scollon & Scollon, 1981) impressive study of interethnic communication, for example, discusses the differences in discourse style between Alaskan natives and their teachers' standard English.

Students who are neglected or ignored in the classroom also have difficulty participating in classroom activities. Garnica (1981) referred to such children as "omega children" and studied their classroom interaction. Children who are lowly rated (either socially, academically, or both) tend to be ignored by both teachers and peers. Omega children have fewer conversations, fewer turns during conversation, fewer invitations to talk, less use of their name, shorter interactions, and use more private talk. When omega children make indirect bids for attention, they are usually ignored or rejected. When direct requests were made, they receive insults or taunts. Such experiences obviously limit the omega child's participation in and access to learning, especially from peer/peer interaction.

Many scholars suggest that individual differences in communicative skills develop in the home. Wells and his colleagues (Wells, 1981) found that the nature of mother/child interaction presents children with different types of interactional experiences. As a result, children learn different strategies and skills (Wells & Montgomery, 1981). With respect to educational achievement, it has been suggested that some home environments develop communicative strategies that limit or interfere with learning in the school. It is to this issue—the relationship of home language to school language—that we now turn.

Home Language vs. School Language.   Florio and Shultz (1979) point out that children learn "ways of making sense of the world" in the home. In cases where there are differences between language usage in the home and in the school, children may find it difficult to interact effectively in the classroom. As a result, their learning and participation is limited. As Gumperz (1981) remarks, more research is needed to understand how knowledge is acquired, the influence of home/ethnic background on this knowledge, and how this acquisition process relates to educational progress and student motivation to learn.

Hall and Guthrie (1980) detail the ways in which a student's home language may not facilitate her performance at school. First, teachers' judgments of a student's language may be negative, and thus the student may be evaluated negatively in a social sense. Second, a particular interaction style will give access to a certain set of ideas, and develop certain communication skills, while ignoring others. That is, different interaction styles offer different opportunities for cognitive growth. These cognitive skills, fostered by the language used at home, may not facilitate learning or participation at school. Finally, a student's home language may not prepare her adequately for reading; for understanding instructional discourse; for interpreting conversational inference; for answering questions and so forth— all important skills for effective classroom participation. They also conclude that important language differences exist as a function of social class differences, ethnic differences, different settings and different interactional patterns.

While many scholars argue that interactional differences between the home and school have important consequences for learning, Wells and

Montgomery (1981) suggest that the nature of the information exchanged is the more critical problem. Teachers need to help students recognize and cope with knowledge that is removed from their practical, everyday experience. However, given the importance of interactional skills in gaining access to information, it seems impossible to separate the knowledge itself from its transmission since one must *process the knowledge via communication* (the process of transmission).

Another important method of learning is through peer/peer interaction. In the classroom, both the social interaction with peers and the learning from peers provide opportunities for student growth.

Peer/Peer Interaction in Instructional Settings.   Children themselves, from preschool age onward, are involved in networks of social relationships reflecting *affiliative networks* (liking); *dominance networks* (control and power relations); and *competence networks* (skill in valued tasks) (Damon, 1981). Within instructional settings, therefore, students interact within a classroom context (reflecting the larger social systems of the school and culture), with a particular teacher (reflecting a power, dyadic relationship), and with other students (reflecting social group relations). Given the simultaneously occurring networks in the classroom, students use a complex set of communicative skills in order to coordinate their actions with others and to participate in learning.

Chapter 7, on communicative development, outlines the communicative skills children develop during the preschool years. By five, children display considerable social cognitive knowledge about others and about social contexts. They can readily interpret ongoing activities, identify communicative rules, and, if they have attended preschools, they possess some concepts about learning and instructional settings. They also manage cooperative actions with others; handle disputes with one another, and establish friendships with selected others.

Children's interactions control their play activities, but also form an important part of instructional activities. Recently, educators have explored the potential for peers to teach one another. For example, Steinberg and Cazden (1979) set up *instructional chains* in which teachers instruct a student and that student subsequently teaches other students. Children can teach one another effectively, although the knowledge is transmitted by using different communicative skills than those a teacher would use. Cooper, Marquis, and Ayers-Lopez (1982) examined peer learning from kindergarten through second grade. Instructional strategies used by peers varied as a function of (1) children's ability to reflect on their behavior and (2) their knowledge of others. Peers also change communicative styles depending upon what peer they are talking to, or whether they are talking with the teacher. Younger children teach segment by segment, whereas older children give an initial general orientation and then more detailed information. Another study by Cooper, Ayers-Lopez, and Marquis (1981) found that peers use informative messages in peer/peer learning. Peers also rely on nonverbal cues to focus attention and give information (see also Josephson & DeStefano, 1979). Cooper, Ayers-Lopez, and Marquis (1981) report that, when teaching one another, peers use conversation to orient their partner, control and direct behavior, solicit responses and evaluate actions. Peers infrequently praise or criticize their partners in instructional tasks. The more relevant and specific peers' comments were, the more successful the teaching episode. Finally, students also learn by observing other students (Morine-Dershimer & Tenenberg, 1981; Wilkinson, 1982a).

Peer/peer interaction also provides additional opportunities for cognitive growth. Children learn from their peers since they cooperate with them, need to justify different actions to them and need to reach consensus on actions (Bearison, 1982; Damon, 1981). According to Perret-Clermont (1980), working with peers who possess different perspectives *forces* a child to restructure his/her own cognitive framework. Doise and his colleagues (Doise & Mugny, 1981) report a series of studies investigating children's work on solving different cognitive problems (e.g., conservation of length, number, or weight, etc.) with a peer. The most effective learning in peer dyads occurred when peers were both at intermediate levels of knowledge and worked on problem-solving together (Mugney, Perret-Clermont, & Doise, 1981).

A series of studies by Murray and his colleagues (Botvin & Murray, 1975; Murray, Ames, & Botvin, 1977) found that peer interaction influenced the interactants' cognitive development and change. Bearison (1982) concludes that dialectic exchanges (where peers confirm and disconfirm each other's actions) lead to cognitive growth. These dialectic exchanges must be understood in context, and may occur both verbally and nonverbally.

As we have seen, although teachers direct instructional activities, these activities require the cooperation and participation of students. Students exercise considerable sophistication in interpreting ongoing activities, gaining access to learning and interacting with peers. Through their interactions with peers, students have additional opportunities for learning and growth. Finally, some students may face difficulty in school if their home language does not provide them with the communicative skills needed to suceed in school.

V. CONCLUDING REMARKS

The perspective on educational communication developed here integrates the three fundamental aspects of pragmatics: the text, context, and participants. Language use and interpretation in instructional settings presupposes many of the underlying communicative dimensions suggested in Chapter 1. Common underlying themes reflect the inferential, intentional and conventional nature of classroom communication. Classroom communication is also jointly managed by student and teacher, and varies as a function of task, goals, context, and participants.

The contextual frame for educational activities incorporates (1) cultural values related to education and knowledge; (2) the social organization of educational institutions like schools; and (3) pedagogical practices concerning the validation, presentation and evaluation of knowledge. The immediate social context—a particular classroom—reflects school procedures, the particular teacher's teaching style, and students' characteristics. Finally, different patterns of interaction appear to develop as a function of particular educational tasks, such as reading or math.

Communication in the classroom is characterized by teachers' domination of talk. The basic unit of classroom communication is teacher initiation, student response, and teacher evaluation. Teachers use questions to solicit student responses and use informative statements to share knowledge. Questions may test student knowledge or request new information. Teachers rely on both verbal and nonverbal signals to organize classroom activities and they need to simultaneously monitor many different classroom settings in order to maintain classroom control. Finally, teaching style varies as a function of the academic task being done and the teacher's personal characteristics.

In contrast, students respond to teacher questions and try to gain access to participation and learning. Considerable communicative skill is needed to interpret ongoing activity, to gain access to conversations, to respond appropriately to a teacher's questions, and to interact effectively with peers. Students also learn directly from one another. Important individual differences in communicative skill may exist because of home/school discontinuities, cultural differences, and general social/academic competence.

While this perspective offers a rich view of communication in instructional settings, some features of classroom interaction need further exploration. Although a full treatment of second language acquisition and its educational implications is beyond the scope of this chapter, clearly it is a vitally important concern in today's multicultural classrooms. The work of Tough (1983) suggests that teachers can be trained to become more sensitive to cultural differences. DiPietro (1981) argues that acquiring a second language needs to be done in appropriate cultural contexts. He stresses the use of structured dialogues to integrate the use of language with its appropriate situated context. The work of Gumperz and his colleagues (Gumperz, 1982; Tannen, 1985) also contributes significantly to an understanding of cross cultural communication and of potential sources of miscommunication.

While this chapter focuses on face-to-face interaction, more research is needed to explore the relationship between different modes of communication. In particular, we need to further explore the links between oral and written communication since both skills are heavily used in educational settings (Brazil, 1983; Brown, 1983; Florio & Clark, 1982; Haslett, 1983a; Heath, 1981; Mosenthal & Na, 1981; Tannen, 1982). Nonverbal and verbal cues must also be analyzed in terms of their interaction with one another (Erickson, 1982; Gumperz, 1982) because both teachers and students rely on them to interpret and signal meanings. The significance of either type of cue can only be evaluated by reference to the other.

Finally, the interaction of teacher and student behaviors needs to be assessed. More detailed, microanalytic studies of ongoing classroom activities must be done so the delicate interplay between teaching and learning can be more adequately understood. While these studies are clearly limited in terms of their generalizability, nevertheless generalities across instructional settings can be noted.

References

Abrahams, R. (1970). *Positively black*. Englewood Cliffs: Prentice-Hall.

Ackerman, B. (1978). Children's understanding of speech acts in unconventional directive frames. *Child Development, 49,* 311–318.

Allan, G. (1977). Sibling solidarity. *Journal of Marriage and the Family, 35,* 177–184.

Allen, J., & Perrault, C. (1980). Analyzing intention in utterances. *Artificial Intelligence, 15,* 143–178.

Altman, I., & Taylor, D. (1973). Social penetration: The development of interpersonal relationships. New York: Holt.

Applegate, J., & Delia, J. (1980). Person-centered speech, psychological development, and the contexts of language usage. In R. St. Clair & H. Giles (Eds.), *The social and psychological contexts of language.* Hillsdale, N.J.: Lawrence Erlbaum Associates.

Argyle, M. (1973). *Social interaction.* London: Tavistock Publications Ltd.

Argyle, M. (1975). *Bodily communication.* London: Methuen.

Argyle, M. (1980). Interaction skills and social competence. In M. Brenner (Ed.), *The structure of action.* Oxford: Blackwell.

Argyle, M. (1981). The experimental study of the basic features of situations. In D. Magnusson (Ed.), *Toward a psychology of situations.* Hillsdale, N.J.: Lawrence Erlbaum Associates.

Argyle, M., Furnham, A., & Graham, J. (1981). *Social situations.* Cambridge: Cambridge University Press.

Aries, E. (1976). Interaction patterns and themes of male, females, and mixed groups. *Small Group Behavior, 7,* 7–18.

Arnold, C., & Bowers, J. (1984). *Handbook of rhetorical and communication theory.* Newton, MA: Allyn & Bacon.

Asher, S. (1979). Referential communication. In G. Whitehurst & B. Zimmerman (Eds.), *The functions of language and cognition.* New York: Academic Press.

Asher, S., & Wigfield, A. (1981). Training referential communication skills. In W. Dickson (Ed.), *Children's oral communication skills.* New York: Academic Press.

Atkinson, J. M., & Drew, P. (1979). *Order in court.* London: Macmillan.

Atkinson, J., & Heritage, J. (1984). *The structure of social action.* Cambridge: Cambridge University Press.

Atkinson, M.P. (1981). *Explanations in the study of child language development.* Cambridge: Cambridge University Press.

Austin, J.L. (1962). *How to do things with words.* Oxford: Clarendon Press.

Ayres, J. (1984). Four approaches to interpersonal communication: Review, observation, prognosis. *Western Journal of Speech Communication, 48,* 408–441.

Bach, K., & Harnish, R. (1979). *Linguistic communication and speech acts.* Cambridge: MIT Press.

Baird, J., & Bradley, P. (1979). Styles of management and communication: A comparative study of men and women. *Communication Monographs, 46,* 101–111.

Barnes, D. (1976). *From communication to curriculum.* London: Penguin.

Baron, R. (1981). Social knowing from an ecological event perspective: A consideration of the relative domains of power for cognitive and perceptual modes of knowing. In J. Harvey (Ed.), *Cognition, social behavior, and the environment.* Hillsdale, N.J.: Lawrence Erlbaum Associates.

Bartlett, F. C. (1932). *Remembering.* Cambridge: The University Press.

Bates, E. (1976). *Language and context: The acquisition of pragmatics.* New York: Academic Press.

Bates, E. (1979). *The emergence of symbols.* New York: Academic Press.

Bates, E., Benigni, L., Bretherton, I., Camaioni, L., & Volterra, V. (1979). Cognition and communication from nine to thirteen months: Correlation findings. In E. Bates (Ed.), *The emergence of symbols.* New York: Academic Press.

Bates, E., Bretherton, I., Beeghly-Smith, M. & McNew, S. (1981). Social basis of language development: A reassessment. In H. Reese & L. Lipsitt (Eds.), *Advances in child development and behavior.* New York: Academic Press.

Bates, E., Bretherton, I., Carlson, V., Carpen, K., & Rosser, M. (1979). Next steps: A follow-up study and some pilot research. In E. Bates (Ed.), *The emergence of symbols: Cognition and communication in infancy.* New York: Academic Press.

Bateson, G. (1972). *Steps to an ecology of mind.* New York: Ballantine.

Bateson, G. (1976). A theory of play and fantasy. In J. Bruner, A. Jolly, & K. Sylva (Eds.), *Play: Its role in evolution and development.* London: Penguin.

Bateson, M. C. (1975). Mother-infant exchanges: The epigenesis of conversation interaction. *Annals of New York Academy of Science, 263,* 101–113.

Baxter, L. (1984). Trajectories of relationship disengagement. *Journal of Social and Personal Relationships, 1,* 29–48.

Baxter, L., & Wilmot, W. (1983). Communication characteristics of relationships with differential growth rates. *Communication Monographs, 50,* 264–272.

Beach, W., & Dunning, D. (1982). Pre-indexing and conversational organization. *Quarterly Journal of Speech, 68,* 170–185.

Beach, W., & Japp, P. (1983). Storifying as time traveling: The knowledgeable use of temporally structured discourse. In R. Bostrom (Ed.), *Communication Yearbook 7.* New Brunswick, NJ: Transaction.

Bearison, D. (1982). New directions in studies of social interaction and cognitive growth. In F. Serafica (Ed.), *Social cognitive development in context.* New York: The Guilford Press.

Beattie, G. (1978a). Floor apportionment and gaze in conversational dyads. *British Journal of Social and Clinical Psychology, 17,* 7–16.

Beattie, G. (1978b). Sequential temporal patterns of speech and gaze in dialogue. *Semiotica, 23,* 29–52.

Beattie, G. (1981). Language and nonverbal communication — the essential synthesis. *Linguistics, 19,* 1165–1183.

Beattie, G. (1983). *Talk.* Milton Keynes: Open University Press.

Beattie, G., & Stephens, J. (1986). *Projecting ahead in conversation to take the turn or avoid saying anything: How turn-taking proceeds or doesn't.* Paper, Talk and Social Structure Conference, Santa Barbara, California.

deBeaugrande, R., & Colby, B. (1979). Narrative models of action and interaction. *Cognitive Science, 3,* 43–66.

Becker, H. (1964). *Social interaction: A dictionary.* London: Tavistock.

Bell, R., Zahn, C., & Hopper, R. (1984). Disclaiming: A test of two competing views. *Communication Quarterly, 32,* 28–36.

Bellack, A., & Davitz, J. (1972). The language of the classroom. In A. Morrison & D. McIntyre (Eds.), *The social psychology of teaching.* London: Penguin.

Bellack, A., Kleiman, H., & Smith. (1966). *The language of the classroom.* New York: Teachers College Press.

Belsky, J., Goode, M., & Most, R. (1981). Maternal stimulation and infant exploratory competence: Cross-sectional, correlational and experimental analyses. *Child Development, 51,* 1163–1178.

Bennett, A. (1981). Interruption and interpretation of conversation. *Discourse Processes, 4,* 171–188.

Benoit, P. (1981). The use of argument by preschool children: The emergent production of rules for winning arguments. Unpublished manuscript.

Berger, C. (1984). Personal communication, December 12.

Berger, C., & Bradac, J. (1982). *Language and social knowledge: Uncertainty in interpersonal relationships.* London: Edward Arnold.

Berger, P., & Luckmann, T. (1967). *Social construction of reality.* New York: Doubleday.

Bernard, J. (1972). *The future of marriage.* New York: World.

Bernier, N. (1981). Beyond instructional context identificationsome thoughts for extending the analysis of deliberate education. In J. Green & C. Wallat (Eds.), *Ethnography and language in educational settings.* Norwood: Ablex.

Bernstein, B. (1970). Language and socialization with some reference to educability. In F. Williams (Ed.), *Language and poverty.* Chicago: Markham Press.

Bernstein, B. (1971). *Class, codes and control: Volume 1.* London: Routledge Kegan Paul.

Bernstein, B. (1973). *Class, codes and control: Volume 2.* London: Routledge Kegan Paul.

Bernstein, B. (1977). *Class, codes and control: Volume 3.* (Second edition). London: Routledge Kegan Paul.

Berscheid, E., & Peplau, L. (1983). The emerging science of relationships. In H. Kelley, et al. (Eds.), *Close relationships.* New York: Freeman & Company.

Bigelow, B., & LaGaipa, J. (1975). Children's written descriptions of friendship: A multidimensional analysis. *Developmental Psychology, 11,* 857–858.

Bigelow, B. & LaGaipa, J. (1980). The development of friendship values and choice. In H. Foot, A. Chapman, & J. Smith (Eds.), *Friendship and social relations in children.* Chichester: Wiley.

Bigner, J. (1974). A Wernerian developmental analysis of children's descriptions of siblings. *Child Development, 45,* 317–323.

Birdwhistell, R. (1970). *Kinesics and context.* Philadelphia: University of Pennsylvania Press.

Birdwhistell, R. (1972). A kinesic-linguistic exercise: The cigarette scene. In J. Gumperz & D. Hymes (Eds.), *New directions in sociolinguistics* New York: Holt, Rinehart & Winston.

Blau, Z. (1973). *Old age in a changing society.* New York: Franklin Watts.

Block, J., & Block, J. (1981). Studying situational dimensions: A grand perspective and some limited empiricism. In D. Magnusson (Ed.), *Toward a psychology of situations.* Hillsdale, NJ: Lawrence Erlbaum Associates.

Bloom, L., Rocissano, L., & Hood, L. (1976). Adult-child discourse: Developmental interaction between information processing and linguistic interaction. *Cognitive Psychology, 8,* 521–552.

Bochner, A. (1984). Functions of communication in interpersonal bonding. In C. Arnold & J. Bowers (Eds.), *Handbook of rhetoric and communication.* Boston: Allyn & Bacon.

Bochner, A., Krueger, D., & Chmielewski, T. (1982). Interpersonal perceptions and marital adjustment. *Journal of Communication, 32,* 135–147.

Bohannon, N., & Marquis, A. (1977). Children's control of adult speech. *Child Development, 48,* 100–110.

Booth, A. (1972). Sex and social participation. *American Sociological Review, 61,* 189–193.

Botvin, G., & Murray, F. (1975). The efficacy of peer modeling and social conflict in the acquisition of conservation. *Child Development, 46,* 904–912.

Bourdieu, P. (1973). Cultural reproduction and social reproduction. In R. Brown (Ed.), *Knowledge, education and cultural change.* London: Tavistock Press.

Bourdieu, P., & Passeron, J. (1977). *Reproduction in education, society, and culture.* Beverly Hills: Sage Publications.

Bourhis, R., Giles, H., & Rosenthal, D. (1981). Notes on the construction of a "subjective vitality" questionnaire for ethnolinguistic groups. *Journal of Multicultural and Multilingual Development, 2,* 145–155.

Bower, G. (1982). Plans and goals in understanding episodes. *Discourse Processes, 7,* 2–15.

Bowers, K. (1981). Knowing more than we can say leads to saying more than we can know: On being implicitly informed. In D. Magnusson (Ed.), *Toward a psychology of situation.* New York: Academic Press.

Bradley, P. (1981). The folk-linguistics of women's speech: An empirical examination. *Communication Monographs, 48,* 73–90.

Bransford, J., & Franks, J. (1971). The abstraction of linguistic ideas. *Cognitive Psychology, 2,* 331–350.

Bransford, J., & Johnson, M. (1972). Contextual prerequisites for understanding: Some investigations of comprehension and recall. *Journal of Verbal Learning and Verbal Behavior, 11,* 717–726.

Bransford, J., & Johnson, M. (1973). Consideration of some problems in comprehension. In W. Chase (Ed.), *Visual information processing.* New York: Academic Press, 1973.

Bransford, J., & McCarrell, N. (1977). A sketch of a cognitive approach to comprehension: Some thoughts about understanding what it means to comprehend. In P. Johnson-Laird & P. Wason (Eds.), *Thinking: Readings in cognitive science.* Cambridge: Cambridge University Press.

Brazelton, R. (1977). Implications of infant development among the Maya Indians of Mexico. In P. Leiderman, S. Tulkin, & A. Rosenfeld (Eds.), *Culture and infancy: Variations in the human experience.* New York: Academic Press.

Brazil, D. (1983). Kinds of English: Spoken, written, literary. In M. Stubbs & H. Hillier (Eds.), *Readings in language, schools and classrooms.* London: Methuen.

Brenneis, D., & Lein, L. (1976). A sociolinguistic approach to children's dispute settlement. In S. Ervin-Tripp & C. Mitchell-Kernan (Eds.), *Child discourse.* New York: Academic Press.

Brenner, M. (1980). *The structure of action.* Oxford: Blackwell.

Bretherton, I., & Bates, E. (1979). The emergence of intentional communication. *New directions for child development, 4,* 81–100.

Bretherton, I., Bates, E., Benigni, L., Camaioni, L., & Volterra, V. (1979). Relationships between cognition, communication and quality of attachment. In E. Bates et al., (Eds.), *The emergence of symbols.* New York: Academic Press.

Brittan, A. (1973). *Meanings and situations.* London: Routledge & Kegan Paul.

Brophy, J., & Good, T. (1974). *Teacher-student relationships.* New York: Holt, Rhinehart and Winston.

Brown, G. (1983). Understanding spoken language. In M. Stubbs & H. Hillier (Eds.), *Readings on language, schools and classrooms.* London: Methuen.

Brown, G. (1984). Linguistic and situational context in a model of task-oriented dialogue. In L. Vaina & J. Hintikka, (Ed.), *Cognitive constraints on communication.* Berlin: D. Reidel.

Brown, P., & Fraser, C. (1979). Speech as a marker of situation. In K. Scherer & H. Giles (Eds.), *Social markers in speech.* Cambridge: Cambridge University Press.

Brown, P., & Levinson, S. (1978). Universals in language use: Politeness phenomena. In E. Goody (Ed.), *Questions and politeness: Strategies in social interaction.* Cambridge: Cambridge University Press.

Brown, P., & Levinson, S. (1979). Social structure, groups and interaction. In H. Scherer & H. Giles (Eds.), *Social markers in speech.* London: Cambridge University Press.

Brown, R. (1976). New paradigm of reference. *Cognition, 4,* 125–153.

Bruner, J. (1975a). The ontogenesis of speech-acts. *Journal of Child Language, 2,* 1–19.

Bruner, J. (1975b). From communication to language—a psychological perspective. *Cognition, 3,* 255–287.

Bruner, J. (1977). Early social interaction and language acquisition. In H. Schaeffer (Ed.), *Studies in mother-infant interaction.* London: Academic Press.

Bruner, J. (1983). The acquisition of pragmatic commitments. In R. Golinkoff (Ed.), *The transition from prelinguistic to linguistic communication.* Hillsdale, NJ: Lawrence Erlbaum Associates.

Bruner, J. (1984). *Children's talk.* London: Oxford University Press.

Bühler, K. (1934). *Sprachtheories: die darstellungsfunktion der sprache.* Jena: Fischer.

Bull, P. (1983). *Body movement and interpersonal relationships.* New York: Wiley-Interscience.

Burgess, R. (1981). Relationships in marriage and the family. In S. Duck & R. Gilmour (Eds.), *Personal relationships, volume 1.* New York: Academic Press.

Burke, K. (1969). *A grammar of motives.* Berkeley: University of California Press.

Campbell, A. (1975). The American way of mating: Marriage, si; children, only maybe. *Psychology Today,* May, 39–42.

Cantor, N. (1981). Perceptions of situations: Situation Prototypes and person-situation prototypes. In D. Magnusson (Ed.), *Toward a psychology of situations.* Hillsdale: Lawrence Erlbaum Associates.

Cantor, N., Mischel, W., & Schwartz, J. (1982). Social knowledge: Structure, content, use, and abuse. In A. Hastorf & A. Isen (Eds.), *Cognitive social psychology.* North Holland: Elsevier.

Cappella, J., & Planalp, S. (1981). Talk and silence sequences in informal conversations III: Interspeaker influence. *Human Communication Research, 7,* 117–132.

Carlson-Luden, V. (1979). Causal understanding in the 10-month-old. Unpublished doctoral dissertation, University of Colorado.

Carpenter, P., & Just, M. (1977). *Cognitive processes in comprehension.* Hillsdale, NJ: Lawrence Erlbaum Associates.

Carswell, E., & Rommetveit, R. (1971). *Social contexts of messages.* New York: Academic Press.

Carter, A. (1975). The transformation of sensori-motor morphemes into words: A case study of the development of *more* and *mine. Journal of Child Language, 2,* 233–250.

Carter, A. (1978a). The development of systematic vocalizations prior to words: A case study. In N. Waterson & C. Snow (Eds.), *The development of children.* Chicester: Wiley.

Carter, A. (1978b). From sensori-motor vocalizations to words: A case study of attention-directing communication in the second year. In A. Lock (Ed.), *Action, gesture and symbol.* New York: Academic Press.

Chafe, W. (1976). Givenness, contrastiveness, definiteness, subjects, topics, and point of view. In C. Li (Ed.), *Subject and topic.* New York: Academic Press.

Chafe, W. (1977). Creativity in verbalization and its implications for the nature of stored knowledge. In R. Freedle (Ed.), *Discourse production and comprehension.* Norwood, NJ: Ablex.

Chafe, W. (1978). *The pear stories.* Norwood, NJ: Ablex.

Chandler, M. (1977). Social cognition: A selective review of current research. In W. Overton (Ed.), *Knowledge and development.* New York: Plenum Press.

Chandler, M. (1982). Social cognition and social structure. In C. Serafica (Ed.), *Social-cognitive development in context.* New York: Guilford Press.

Charney, R. (1979). The comprehension of 'here' and 'there.' *Journal of Child Language, 6,* 69–80.

Chomsky, N. (1965). *Aspects of a theory of syntax.* Cambridge: MIT Press.

Cicourel, A. (1970). The acquisition of social structure. In J. Douglas (Ed.), *Understanding everyday life.* Chicago: Aldine.

Cicourel, A. (1972). Basic and normative rules in the negotiation of status and role. In D. Sudnow (Ed.), *Studies in social interaction.* New York: Free Press.

Cicourel, A. (1973). *Cognitive sociology: Language and meaning in social interaction.* London: Cox and Wyman.

Cicourel, A. (1980). Three models of discourse analysis: The role of social structure. *Discourse Processes, 3,* 101–132.

Ciolek, T., & Kendon, A. (1980). Environment and the spatial arrangement of conversational encounters. In D. Zimmerman & C. West (Eds.), *Language and social interaction.* Special issue, *Sociological Inquiry, 50,* 237–276.

Clark, H., & Clark, E. (1977). *Psychology and language.* New York: Harcourt Brace Jovanovich.

Clark, R., & Delia, J. (1976). The development of functional persuasive skills in childhood and early adolesence. *Child Development, 47,* 1008–1014.

Clark, R., & Delia, J. (1977). Cognitive complexity, social perspective-taking, and functional persuasive skills in second-to-ninth grade children. *Human Communication Research, 3,* 123–134.

Cochran, M., & Peplau, L. (1983). *Values of attachment and autonomy in heterosexual relationships.* Unpublished manuscript, University of California, Los Angeles.

Cody, M., & McLaughlin, M. (1980). Perceptions of compliance-gaining situations: A dimensional analysis. *Communication Monographs, 47,* 132–148.

Cody, M., & McLaughlin, M. (1985). Models for the sequential structure of accounting episodes: Situational and interactional constraints on message selection and evaluation. In R. Street and J. Capella (Eds.) *Sequence and Pattern in Communicative Behavior,* London: Edward Arnold.

Cody, M., Woelfel, M., & Jordan, W. (1983). Dimensions of compliance-gaining situations. *Human Communication Research, 9,* 99–113.

Cohen, C. (1981). Goals and schemata in person perception: Making sense from the stream of behavior. In N. Cantor & J. F. Kihlstrom (Eds.), *Personality, cognition and social interactionism.* Hillsdale, NJ: Lawrence Erlbaum Associates.

Cole, M., Griffin, P., & Newman, D. (1979). Mid-quarter reports to the National Institute of Education. July, NIE G–78–0159.

Collett, P. (1977). The rules of conduct. In P. Collett (Ed.), *Social rules and social behavior.* Totowa, NJ: Rowman and Littlefield.

Connolly, J., Doyle, A., & Creschin, F. (1983). Forms and functions of social fantasy play in preschoolers. In M. Liss (Ed.), *Social and cognitive skills in children's play.* New York: Academic Press.

Cook-Gumperz, J. (1973). *Social control and socialization.* London: Routledge Kegan Paul.

Cook-Gumperz, J. (1981). Persuasive talk—the social organization of children's talk. In J. Green & C. Wallat (Eds.), *Ethnography and language in educational settings.* Norwood, NJ: Ablex.

Cook-Gumperz, J., & Cosaro, W. (1976). Social-ecological constraints on children's communicative strategies. In J. Cook-Gumperz & J. Gumperz (Eds.), *Papers on language and context.* Berkeley: Language Behavior Research Laboratory.

Cook-Gumperz, J., & Gumperz, J. (1976). Context in children's speech. In J. Cook-Gumperz & J. Gumperz (Eds.), *Papers on language and context*. Berkeley: Language Behavior Research Laboratory.

Cook-Gumperz, J., & Gumperz, J. (1982). Communicative competence in educational perspective. In L.C. Wilkinson (Ed.), *Communicating in the classroom*. New York: Academic Press.

Cooper, C., Ayers-Lopez, S., & Marquis, A. (1981). *Children's discourse in cooperative and didactic interaction: Developmental patterns in effective learning*. Final report, National Institute of Education, NIE G–78–0098.

Cooper, C., Marquis, A., & Ayers-Lopez, S. (1982). Peer learning in the classroom: Tracing developmental patterns and consequences of children's spontaneous interaction. In L. C. Wilkinson (Ed.), *Communicating in classrooms*. New York: Academic Press.

Cosaro, W. (1977). The clarifications request as a feature of adult interactive styles with young children. *Language in Society, 7,* 63–84.

Coulthard, R. (1977). *An introduction to discourse analysis*. Cambridge: Cambridge University Press.

Craik, K. (1981). Environmental assessment and situational analysis. In D. Magnusson (Ed.), *Toward a psychology of situations*. Hillsdale, NJ: Lawrence Erlbaum Associates.

von Cranach, M., & Harre, R. (1982). *The analysis of action*. Cambridge: Cambridge University Press.

Cronen, V., Pearce, B., & Harris, L. (1982). The coordinated management of meaning: A new theory of communication. In F. Dance (Ed.), *Human communication theory*. New York: Harper and Row.

Cushman, D., & Sanders, R. (1981). Rules theories of human communication processes: The structural and functional perspectives. In B. Dervin & M. Voight (Eds.), *Progress in communication research*. Norwood, NJ: Ablex.

Cushman, D., Valentinsen, B., & Dietrich, D. (1981). A rules theory of interpersonal relationships. In F. Dance (Ed.), *Human communication theory*. New York: Harper and Row.

Cushman, D., & Whiting, G. (1972). An approach to communication theory: Towards a consensus on rules. *Journal of Communication, 22,* 217–238.

Damon, W. (1981). Exploring children's social cognition on two fronts. In J. Flavell & L. Ross (Eds.), *Social cognitive development*. Cambridge: Cambridge University Press.

D'Angelo, F. (1982). Rhetoric and cognition: Toward a metatheory of discourse. *Pre/Text, 3,* 105–119.

Dascal, M. (1981). Contextualism. In H. Parret, M. Sbisa, & J. Verschueren (Eds.), *Possibilities and limitations of pragmatics*. Amsterdam: John Benjamins B.V.

Delia, J., & Clark, R. (1977). Cognitive complexity, social perception, and the development of listener-adapted communication in six-, eight-, ten-, and twelve-year-old boys. *Communication Monographs, 44,* 326–345.

Delia, J., Kline, S., & Burleson, B. (1979). The development of persuasive communication strategies in kindergartners through twelfth-graders. *Communication Monographs, 46,* 241–256.

Delia, J., & O'Keefe, B. (1979). Constructivism: The development of communication in children. In E. Wartella (Ed.), *Children communicating*. Beverly Hills: Sage.

Delia, J., O'Keefe, B., & O'Keefe, D. (1982). The constructivist approach to communication. In F. Dance (Ed.), *Human communication theory*. New York: Harper and Row.

DeLong, A. (1974). Kinesic signals at utterance boundaries in preschool children. *Semiotica, 11,* 43–74.

Denny, R. (1985). Marking the interaction order: The social constitution of turn exchange and speaking turns. *Language in Society, 14,* 41–62.

Denzin, N. (1970). Symbolic interactionism and ethnomethodology. In J. Douglas (Ed.), *Understanding everyday life*. Chicago: Aldine.

DeStefano, J., & Pepinsky, H. (1981). *The learning of discourse rules of culturally different children in first grade literacy instruction.* Final report, NIE, NIE G-79-0032.

Detweiler, R., Brislin, R., & McCormack, W. (1983). Situational analysis. In D. Landis and R. Brislin (Eds.), *Handbook of intercultural training, vol. 2.* New York: Pergamon.

deVilliers, P., & deVilliers, J. (1979). *Early language.* Cambridge: Cambridge University Press.

Dickens, W., & Perlman, D. (1981). Friendship over the life-cycle. In S. Duck & R. Gilmour (Eds.), *Personal relationships, volume 2.* New York: Academic Press.

Dickson, W. (1981). *Children's oral communication skills.* New York: Academic Press.

van Dijk, T. (1977a). *Text and context.* London: Longman.

van Dijk, T. (1977b). Context and cognition: Knowledge frames and speech act comprehension. *Journal of Pragmatics, 1,* 211–232.

van Dijk, T. (1980). *Macrostructures.* Hillsdale, NJ: Lawrence Erlbaum Associates.

van Dijk, T. (1981). *Studies in the pragmatics of discourse.* The Hague: Mouton.

van Dijk, T. (1983). *Cognitive situation models in discourse production.* Amsterdam: Working paper no. 5.

van Dijk, T. (1984). *Prejudice in discourse.* Amsterdam: John Benjamins.

van Dijk, T. (Ed.). (1985a). *Handbook of discourse analysis, vol.1–4.* New York: Academic Press.

van Dijk, T. (1985b). Introduction: Dialogue as discourse and interaction. In T. van Dijk (Ed.), *Handbook of discourse analysis: Vol. 3, Discourse and dialogue.* New York: Academic Press.

van Dijk, T., & Kintsch, W. (1983). *Strategies of discourse comprehension.* New York: Academic Press.

DiPietro, R. (1981). Discourse and real-life roles in the ESL classroom. *TESOL Quarterly, 15,* 27–33.

Doise, W., & Mugny, G. (1981). Le developpement social de l'intelligence. As cited in Perret-Clermont & Schubauer-Leoni, in W. Robinson (Ed.), *Communication in development.* New York: Academic Press.

Dore, J. (1974). A pragmatic description of early language development. *Journal of Psycholinguistic Research, 3,* 343–350.

Dore, J. (1977). Children's illocutionary acts. In R. Freedle (Ed.), *Discourse production and comprehension.* Hillsdale, NJ: Lawrence Erlbaum Associates.

Dore, J. (1983). Feeling, form and intention in the baby's transition to language. In R. Golinkoff (Ed.), *The transition from prelinguistic to linguistic communication.* Hillsdale, NJ: Lawrence Erlbaum Associates.

Dore, J. (1985). Cohesion, coherence and context in children's conversations. In T. van Dijk (Ed.), *The handbook of discourse analysis.* New York: Academic Press.

Douglas, J.R. (1970). *Understanding everyday life.* Chicago: Aldine.

Dresher, B., & Hornstein, W. (1977). Reply to Winograd. *Cognition, 5,* 379–392.

Drew, P. (1986). *Po-faced receipt of teases.* Paper, Talk and Social Structure Conference, University of California, Santa Barbara, California, March.

Duck, S. (1973). *Personal relationships and personal constructs: A study of friendship formation.* London: Wiley.

Duck, S. (1976). Interpersonal communication in developing acquaintance. In G. Miller (Ed.), *Explorations in interpersonal communication.* Beverley Hills: Sage.

Duck, S. (1983). *Friends for life.* Brighton, Sussex: The Harvester Press.

Duck, S. (1984a). *Personal relationships, volume 5: Repairing personal relationships.* New York: Academic Press.

Duck, S. (1984b). A perspective on the repair of personal relationships: Repair of what, when? In S. Duck (Ed.), *Personal relationships, volume 5.* New York: Academic Press.

Duck, S., Lock, A., McCall, G., Fitzpatrick, M., & Coyne, J. (1984). Social and personal relationships: A joint editorial. *Journal of Social and Personal Relationships, 1,* 1-11.

Duck, S., Miell, D., & Gaebler, H. (1980). Attraction and communication in children's interactions. In H. Foot, A. Chapman, & J. Smith (Eds.), *Friendship and social relations in children.* New York: Wiley & Sons.

Duncan, H. (1962). *Communication and social order.* New York: Bedminster Press.

Duncan, S. (1973). Toward a grammar for dyadic conversation. *Semiotica, 9,* 29-46.

Duncan, S., & Fiske, D. (1977). *Face-to-face interaction: Research, methods, and theory.* Hillsdale, NJ: Lawrence Erlbaum Associates.

Eakins, B., & Eakins, R. (1978). *Sex differences in human communication.* Boston: Houghton Mifflin Company.

Edelsky, C. (1981). Who's got the floor? *Language in Society, 10,* 383-421.

Eder, D. (1982). Differences in communicative styles across ability groups. In L.C. Wilkinson (Ed.), *Communicating in the classroom.* New York: Academic Press.

Edmondson, W. (1981). *Spoken discourse: A model for analysis.* London: Longman.

Edwards, A. (1981). Analysing classroom talk. In P. French & M. MacLure (Eds.), *Adult-child conversation.* London: Croom Helm.

Eisenberg, A., & Garvey, C. (1981). Children's use of verbal strategies in resolving conflict. *Discourse Processes, 4,* 149-170.

Ekehammar, B. (1974). Interactionism in personality from a historical perspective. *Psychological Bulletin, 81,* 1026-1048.

Ellis, D. (1979). Relational control in two group systems. *Communication Monographs, 46,* 153-166.

Endler, N. (1981). Situational aspects of interactional psychology. In D. Magnusson (Ed.), *Toward a psychology of situations.* Hillsdale: Lawrence Erlbaum Associates.

Endler, N., & Magnusson, D. (1976). *Interactional psychology and personality.* New York: Wiley.

Erickson, F. (1982). Classroom discourse as improvisation: Relationships between academic task structure and social participation structure in lessons. In L. Wilkinson (Ed.), *Communicating in the classroom.* New York: Academic Press.

Erickson, F., & Shultz, J. (1977). When is a context?: Some issues and methods in the analysis of social competence. *The Quarterly Newsletter of the Institute for Comparative Human Development, 1,* 5-10.

Erickson, F., & Shultz, J. (1982). *The counselor as gatekeeper: Social interaction in interviews.* New York: Academic Press.

Ervin-Tripp, S. (1970). Discourse agreement: How children answer questions. In J. Hayes (Ed.), *Cognition and the development of language.* New York: Wiley.

Ervin-Tripp, S. (1976). Is Sybil there? The structure of some American English directives. *Language in Society, 5,* 25-66.

Ervin-Tripp, S. (1977). Wait for me, roller-skate. In S. Ervin-Tripp & C. Mitchell-Kernan (Eds.), *Child discourse.* New York: Academic Press.

Ervin-Tripp, S., & Miller, W. (1977). Early discourse: Some questions about questions. In M. Lewis & L. Rosenblum (Eds.), *Interaction, conversation, and the development of language.* New York: Wiley.

Etaugh, C. (1983). The influences of environmental factors on sex differences in children's play. In M. Less (Ed.), *Social and cognitive skills.* New York: Academic Press.

Faggot, B., & Leinbach, M. (1983). Play styles in early childhood. In M. Liss (Ed.), *Social and cognitive skills.* New York: Academic Press.

Falbo, T. (1977). A multidimensional scaling of power strategies. *Journal of Personality and Social Psychology, 35,* 537-547.

Falbo, T., & Peplau, L. (1980). Power strategies in intimate relationships. *Journal of Personality and Social Psychology, 38,* 618-628.

Fillmore, C. (1971). Towards a theory of deixis. *The PCCLLU Papers, 3 & 4,* 219-241. Department of Linguistics, University of Hawaii.

Fine, G. (1981). Friends, impression management and preadolescent behavior. In S. Asher & J. Gottman (Eds.), *The development of friendship.* Cambridge: Cambridge University Press.

Firth, J. (1957). *Papers in linguistics: 1934-1951.* London: Oxford University Press.

Fitzpatrick, M. (1977). A typological approach to communication in relationships. In B. Ruben (Ed.), *Communication Yearbook, Vol. 1.* New Brunswick, N.J.: Transaction.

Fitzpatrick, M., & Indvik, J. (1982). The instrumental and expressive domains of marital communication. *Human Communication Research, 8,* 195-213.

Fitzpatrick, M., & Winke, J. (1979). You always hurt the one you love: Strategies and tactics in interpersonal conflict. *Communication Quarterly, 27,* 3-11.

Flanders, N. (1963). Intent, action and feedback: A preparation for teaching. In E.J. Amidon & J. Hough (Eds.), *Interaction analysis: Theory research and application.* New York: Holt Rinehart and Winston.

Flanders, N. (1970). *Analyzing teaching behavior.* New York: Addison Wesley.

Flavell, J. (1979). Metacognition and cognitive monitoring: A new area of psychological inquiry. *American Psychologist, 34,* 906-911.

Flavell, J. (1981a). Cognitive monitoring. In W. Dickson (Ed.), *Children's oral communication skills.* New York: Academic Press.

Flavell, J. (1981b). Monitoring social cognitive enterprises: Something else that may develop in the area of social cognition. In J. Flavell & L. Ross (Eds.), *Social cognitive development.* Cambridge: Cambridge University Press.

Flavell, J., Speer, J., Green, F., & August, D. (1981). *The development of comprehension monitoring and knowledge about communication.* Society for Research on Child Development Monograph.

Florio, S., & Clark, C. (1982). What is writing for? Writing in the first weeks of school in a second-third grade class room. In L. C. Wilkinson (Ed.), *Communicating in the classroom.* New York: Academic Press.

Florio, S., & Shultz, J. (1979). Social competence at home and at school. *Theory into practice, 18,* 234-243.

Forbes, D,, & Lubin, D. (1981). *The development of applied strategies in children's social behavior.* Paper, SRCD, April.

Forgas, J. (1978). Social episodes and social structure in an academic setting: The social environment of an intact group. *Journal of Experimental Social Psychology, 14,* 434-448.

Forgas, J. (1983). Language, goals and situations. *Journal of Language and Social Psychology, 2,* 267-293.

Foucault, M. (1972). *The archaeology of knowledge* (Trans. by Alan Sheridan). New York: Pantheon.

Franck, D. (1981). Seven sins of pragmatics: Theses about speech act theory, conversational analysis, linguistics and rhetoric. In H. Parret, M. Sbisa, & J. Verschuren (Eds.), *Possibilities and limitations of pragmatics.* Amsterdam: John Benjamins B.V.

Frederiksen, C. (1977a). Semantic processing units in understanding text. In R. Freedle (Ed.), *Discourse production and comprehension, vol. 1.* Norwood, NJ: Ablex.

Frederiksen, C. (1977b). Structure and process in discourse production and comprehension. In P. Carpenter & M. Just (Eds.), *Cognitive processes in comprehension.* Hillsdale, NJ: Lawrence Erlbaum Associates.

Frederiksen, C. (1981). Inference in preschool children's conversations: A cognitive perspective.

In J. Green & C. Wallat (Eds.), *Ethnography and language in educational settings.* Norwood, NJ: Ablex.

Fredriksen, C., Harris, E., & Duran, R. (1975). Discourse structure and discourse processing. In B. Wolman (Ed.), *International encyclopedia of neurology, psychiatry, psycholanalysis, and psychology.* New York: Macmillan.

French, P., & MacLure, M. (1983). Teachers' questions and pupils' answers. In M. Stubbs & H. Hillier (Eds.), *Readings on language, schools, and classrooms.* London: Methuen.

French, P., & Woll, B. (1981). Context, meaning and strategy in parent-child conversation. In G. Wells (Ed.), *Learning through interaction.* Cambridge: Cambridge University Press.

French, R., & Raven, B. (1960). The bases of social power. In D. Cartwright & A. Zander (Eds.), *Group dynamics.* New York: Harper & Row.

Furnham, A. (1982). The message, the context and the medium. *Language and Communication, 2,* 33–47.

Furnham, A. (1986). Social situations. In W. Gudykunst (Ed.), *Intergroup communication.* London: Edward Arnold.

Ganz, J. (1971). *Rules: A systematic study.* The Hague: Mouton.

Garfinkel, H. (1962). Commonsense knowledge of social structures: the documentary method of interpretation in lay and professional fact finding. In J. Sher (Ed.), *Theories of the mind.* New York: Free Press.

Garfinkel, H. (1967a). *Studies in ethnomethodology.* Englewood Cliffs: Prentice-Hall.

Garfinkel, H. (1967b). Studies of the routine grounds of everyday activities. In H. Garfinkel, *Studies in ethnomethodology.* Englewood Cliffs: Prentice-Hall.

Garfinkel, H., & Sacks, H. (1970). On formal structures of practical actions. In J. McKinney & E. Tiryankian (Eds.), *Theoretical sociology.* New York: Appleton Century Crofts.

Garvey, C. (1974). Some properties of social play. *Merrill-Palmer Quarterly, 20,* 163–180.

Garvey, C. (1975). Requests and responses in children's speech. *Journal of Child Language, 2,* 41–60.

Garvey, C. (1977). Play with language and speech. In S. Ervin-Tripp & E. Mitchell-Kernan (Eds.), *Child discourse.* New York: Academic Press.

Garvey, C., & Berninger, G. (1981). Timing and turn taking in children's conversation. *Discourse Processes, 4,* 27–57.

Garvey, C., & Hogan, R. (1973). Social speech and social interaction: Egocentrism revisited. *Child Development, 44,* 562–568.

Garnica, O. (1981). Social dominance and conversational interaction—the Omega child in the classroom. In J. Green & C. Wallat (Eds.), *Ethnography and language in educational settings.* Norwood, NJ: Ablex.

Gazdar, G. (1979a). *Pragmatics: Implicature, presupposition and logical form.* New York: Academic Press.

Gazdar, G. (1979b). A solution to the projection problem. In Oh & Dineen (Eds.), *Syntax and semantics II: Presupposition.* New York: Academic Press.

Gazdar, G. (1981). Speech act assignment. In A. Joshi, B. Webber, & I. Sag (Eds.), *Elements of discourse understanding.* Cambridge: Cambridge University Press.

Gelman, R., & Shatz, M. (1977). Appropriate speech adjustments: The operation of conversational constraints on talk to two year olds. In M. Lewis & L. Rosenblum (Eds.), *Interaction, conversation and the development of language.* New York: Wiley.

Gelman, R., & Spelke, E. (1981). The development of thoughts about animate and inanimate objects: Implications for research on social cognition. In J. Flavell & L. Ross (Eds.), *Social cognitive development.* Cambridge: Cambridge University Press.

Genishi, C. (1979). Young children communicating in the classroom. *Theory into Practice, 18,* 244–250.

Germain, C. (1979). *Concept of situation in linguistics.* Ottowa: University of Ottowa Press.

Giddens, A. (1976). *New rules of sociological method.* London: Hutchinson.

Giddens, A. (1979). *Central problems in social theory.* London: Macmillan.

Giddens, A. (1982). *Profiles and critiques in social theory.* Los Angeles: University of California Press.

Giles, H. (1977). *Language, ethnicity and intergroup relations.* London: Academic Press, 1977.

Giles, H. (1979). Sociolinguistics and social psychology: An introductory essay. In H. Giles & R. St. Clair, *Language and social psychology.* Baltimore: University Park Press.

Giles, H., & Hewstone, M. (1982). Cognitive structures, speech and social situations: Two integrative models. *Language Sciences, 4,* 188-219.

Giles, H., & Johnson, P. (1981). The role of language in inter-ethnic behavior. In J. Turner & H. Giles (Eds.), *Intergroup behavior.* Oxford: Blackwell.

Giles, H., & Powesland, P. (1975). *Speech style and social evaluation.* London: Academic Press.

Giles, H., & Saint-Jacques, B. (1979). *Language and ethnic relations.* Oxford: Pergamon.

Giles, H., Scherer, K., & Taylor, D. (1979). Speech markers in social interaction. In K. Scherer & H. Giles (Eds.), *Social markers in speech.* Cambridge: Cambridge University Press.

Gilmore, P., & Glatthorn, A. (1982). *Children in and out of school: Ethnography and education.* Washington, D.C.: Center for Applied Linguistics.

Gleitman, L, Gleitman, H., & Shipley, E. (1972). The emergence of the child as grammarian. *Cognition, 1,* 137-164.

Glick, J. (1978). Cognition and social cognition: An introduction. In J. Glick & K. Clarke-Stewart (Eds.), *The development of social understanding.* New York: Gardner Press.

Glucksberg, S., Krauss, R., & Higgins, E. (1975). The development of referential communication skills. In F. Horowitz, E. Hetherington, S. Scarr-Salapatek, & G. Siegel (Eds.), *Review of child development research, vol. 4.* Chicago: University of Chicago Press.

Goffman, E. (1970). *Strategic interaction.* Oxford: Blackwell.

Goffman, E. (1971). *Relations in public.* New York: Harper & Row.

Goffman, E. (1974). *Frame analysis.* New York: Harper & Row.

Goffman, E. (1976). Replies and responses. *Language in society, 5,* 257-313.

Goffman, E. (1981). *Forms of talk.* Philadelphia: University of Pennsylvania Press.

Goldberg, S., & Lewis, M. (1969). Play behavior in the year-old infant: Early sex differences. *Child Development, 40,* 21-31.

Gollin, E. (1958). Organizational characteristics of social judgment: A developmental investigation. *Journal of Personality, 26,* 139-154.

Golinkoff, R. (1983). *The transition from prelinguistic to linguistic communication.* Hillsdale, NJ: Lawrence Erlbaum Associates.

Gottman, J. (1979). *Marital interaction.* New York: Academic Press.

Good, C. (1979). Language as social activity: Negotiating conversation. *Journal of Pragmatics, 3,* 151-167.

Goodwin, C. (1979). Language as social activity: Negotiating conversation. *Journal of Pragmatics, 3,* 151-167.

Goodwin, C. (1981). *Conversational organization: Interaction between speakers and hearers.* New York: Academic Press.

Gouldner, A. (1960). The norm of receiprocity. *American Sociological Review, 25,* 160-179.

Gouldner, H. (1984). *Adult friendships among women.* Lecture, University of Delaware, April.

Graham, J., Argyle, M., & Furnham, A. (1980). The goal structure of situations. *European Journal of Social Psychology, 10,* 345-366.

Green, J. (1983). Research on teaching as a linguistic process: A state of the art. *Review of Research in Education, 10,* 151-252.

Green, J., & Harker, J. (1982). Gaining access to learning: Conversational, social and cognitive demands of group participation. In L. Wilkinson (Ed.), *Communicating in classrooms.* New York: Academic Press.

Green, J., & Wallat, C. (1981a). *Ethnography and language in educational settings.* Norwood, NJ: Ablex.

Green, J., & Wallat, C. (1981b). Mapping instructional conversations. In J. Green & C. Wallat (Eds.), *Ethnography and language in educational settings.* Norwood, NJ: Ablex.

Greenspan, S., Barenboim, C., & Chandler, M. (1974). *Children's affective judgments in response to videotaped stories.* Paper, SRCD.

Grice, H. (1975). Logic and conversation. In P. Cole & J. Morgan (Eds.), *Syntax and semantics, vol. 3: Speech acts.* New York: Academic Press.

Grice, H. (1978). Further notes on logic and conversation. In P. Cole (Ed.), *Syntax and semantics, vol. 9: Pragmatics.* New York: Academic Press.

Griffin, M., & Mehan, H. (1981). Sense and ritual in classroom discourse. In F. Coulmas (Ed.), *Conversational routine.* The Hague: Mouton.

Grimes, J. (1975). *The thread of discourse.* The Hague: Mouton.

Gumperz, J. (1977). Sociocultural knowledge in conversational inference. In M. Saville-Troike (Ed.), *Georgetown 28th Round Table on language and linguistics monograph series.* Washington, D.C.: Georgetown University Press.

Gumperz, J. (1981a). Sociocultural knowing in conversational inference. In M. Saville-Troike (Ed.), *Georgetown 28th. round table on language and linguistics monograph series.* Washington, D.C.: Georgetown University Press.

Gumperz, J. (1981b). *Language and social identity.* Cambridge: Cambridge University Press.

Gumperz, John J. (1982). *Discourse strategies.* Cambridge: Cambridge University Press.

Gumperz, J., & Herasimchuk, E. (1973). Conversational analysis of social meaning. In R. Shuy (Ed.), *Sociolinguistics: Current trends and prospects.* Georgetown: GURT.

Gumperz, J., & Hymes, D. (1972). *Directions in sociolinguistics.* New York: Holt, Rinehart & Winston.

Haas, A. (1979). Male and female spoken language differences: Stereotypes and evidence. *Psychological Bulletin, 86,* 616–626.

Hall, E. (1959). *Silent language.* Garden City, NJ: Doubleday.

Hall, E. (1969). *The hidden dimension.* Garden City, NY: Doubleday.

Hall, J., & Braunwald, K. (1981). Gender cues in conversations. *Journal of Personality and Social Psychology, 40,* 99–110.

Hall, W.S., & Guthrie, L. (1980). On the dialect question and reading. *Psychology of reading, 80,* 439–450.

Halliday, M.A.K. (1970). *A course in spoken English: Intonation.* London: Oxford University Press.

Halliday, M.A.K. (1973). *Explorations in the functions of language.* London: Edward Arnold.

Halliday, M.A.K. (1975). *Learning how to mean: Explorations in the functions of language.* London: Edward Arnold.

Halliday, M.A.K. (1978). *Language as a social semiotic.* London: Edward Arnold.

Halliday, M.A.K. (1979). Development of texture in child language. In T. Myers (Ed.), *The development of conversation and discourse.* Edinburgh: Edinburgh University Press.

Halliday, M.A.K., & Hasan, R. *Cohesion in English.* London: Longman.

Halliday, M.A.K., & Martin, J.R. (1981). *Readings in systematic linguistics.* London: Batford.

Hancher, M. (1979). The classification of co-operative illocutionary acts. *Language in Society, 8,* 1–14.

Harding, C. (1983). Setting the stage for language acquisition: Communication development in the first year. In R. Golinkoff (Ed.), *The transition from prelinguistic to linguistic communication.* Hillsdale, NJ: Lawrence Erlbaum Associates.

Harre, R. (1979). *Social being: A theory for social psychology.* Totowa, NJ: Rowman & Littlefield.

Harre, R., & Secord, P. (1972). *The explanation of social behavior.* Oxford: Basil Blackwell.

Hartmann, E., & Haavind, H. (1981). Mothers as teachers. In W.P. Robinson (Ed.), *Communication in development.* New York: Academic Press.

Hart, R., & Burks, S. (1972). Rhetorical sensitivity and social interaction. *Speech Monographs, 39,* 75-91.

Hartup, W. (1978). Perspectives on child and family interaction: Past, present, and future. In R. Lerner & G. Spanier (Eds.), *Child influences on marital and family interaction: A life-span perspective.* New York: Academic Press.

Hasan, R. (n.d.). *What's going on: A dynamic view of context in language.* Australia: Macquarie University.

Haslett, B. (1979). Patterns of teacher/child interaction in preschool settings. In R. DiPietro, W. Frawley & A. Wedel (Eds.), *The Delaware symposium on language studies.* Newark: University of Delaware Press.

Haslett, B. (1982). *A critique of Searle's speech acts.* Remarks presented at the Temple University Discourse Conference, Philadelphia.

Haslett, B. (1983a). Children's strategies for maintaining cohesion in their written and oral stories. *Communication Education, 32,* 91-106.

Haslett, B. (1983b). Communicative functions and strategies in children's conversations. *Human Communication Research, 9,* 115-124.

Haslett, B. (1983c). Preschoolers' communicative strategies in gaining compliance from peers: A developmental study. *Quarterly Journal of Speech, 69,* 84-99.

Haslett, B. (1984a). Acquiring conversational competence. *Western States Journal of Communication, 48,* 107-124.

Haslett, B. (1984b). Communicative development: The state of the art. In R. Bostrom (Ed.), *Communication Yearbook, Vol. 8,* 198-267.

Haslett, B. (1986a). A critique of van Dijk's theory of discourse. In B. Dervin & M. Voight (Eds.), *Progress in the communication sciences, vol. 7.* Norwood, NJ: Ablex.

Haslett, B. (1986b). *Talk and social structure: Expanding conversational analysis.* Paper, Talk and Social Structure Conference, University of California at Santa Barbara, March.

Haslett, B. (1986c). A developmental analysis of narratives. In D. Ellis & W. Donohue (Eds.), *Discourse and language processes.* Hillsdale, NJ: Lawrence Erlbaum Associates.

Haslett, B. (1986d). Intergroup relations: The influence of age, sex and social class. In W. Gudykunst (Ed.), *Intergroup relations.* London: Edward Arnold.

Haslett, B., & Bowen, S. (1986). *On becoming a competent communicator: Initiating and sustaining interaction.* Unpublished manuscript, Department of Communication, University of Delaware.

Hauser, G. (1968). The example in Aristotle's Rhetoric: Bifurcation or contradiction? *Philosophy and Rhetoric, 1,* 78-90.

Haviland, S., & Clark, H. (1974). What's new? Acquiring new information as a process in comprehension. *Journal of Verbal Learning and Verbal Behavior, 18,* 91-108.

Heath, S. (1981). Protean shapes in literacy events: Evershifting oral and literate traditions. In D. Tannen (Ed.), *Spoken and written language.* Norwood, NJ: Ablex.

Heath, S. (1982a). Ethnography in education: Defining the essentials. In P. Gilmore & A. Glatthorn (Eds.), *Children in and out of school.* Washington, D.C.: Center for Applied Linguistics.

Heath, S. (1982b). Questioning at home and at school: A comparative study. In G. Spindler (Ed.), *Doing ethnography: Educational anthropology in action.* New York: Holt, Rinehart & Winston.

Heath, S. (1982c). What no bedtime story means: Narrative skills at home and at school. *Language in Society, vol. 11,* 49-76.

Heath, S. (1983). *Ways with words: Language, life and work in communities and classrooms.* Cambridge: Cambridge University Press.

Hecht, M. (1984a). Satisfying communication and relationship labels: Intimacy and length of relationship as perceptual frames of naturalistic conversations. *Western Journal of Speech Communication, 48,* 201-217.

Hecht, M. (1984b). Persuasive efficacy: A study of the relationships among type and degree of change, message strategies, and satisfying communication. *Western Journal of Speech Communication, 48,* 373-389.

Heritage, J. (1980). *Context.* Unpublished manuscript.

Heritage, J. (1984). *Garfinkel and ethnomethodology.* Cambridge: Polity Press.

Heritage, J., & Watson, D.R. (1979). Formulations as conversational objectives. In G. Psathas (Ed.), *Everyday language: Studies in ethnomethodology.* New York: Irvington.

Hess, R., & Shipman, V. (1965). Early experience and the socialization of cognitive modes in children. *Child Development, 36,* 869-896.

Hess, R., & Shipman, V. (1967). Cognitive elements in maternal behavior. In J. Hill (Ed.), *Minnesota Symposium on Child Development,* vol. 1. Minneapolis: University of Minnesota Press.

Hess, R., & Shipman, V. (1968). Maternal influences upon early learning. In R. Hess & R. Bear (Eds.), *Early education.* Chicago: University of Chicago Press.

Hess, R., Shipman, V., Bear, R., & Brophy, J. (1968). *The cognitive environments of urban pre-school children.* Chicago: University of Chicago Press.

Hewitt, J., & Stokes, R. (1975). Disclaimers. *American Sociological Review, 40,* 1-11.

Hicks, M., & Platt, M. (1970). Marital happiness and stability: A review of the research in the sixties. *Journal of Marriage and the Family, 32,* 553-574.

Higgins, E. (1981). Role taking and social judgment: Alternative developmental perspectives and processes. In J. Flavell & L. Ross (Eds.), *Social cognitive development.* Cambridge: Cambridge University Press.

Hinde, R. (1979). *Towards understanding relationships.* New York: Academic Press.

Hinde, R. (1981). The bases of a science of interpersonal relationships. In S. Duck & R. Gilmour (Eds.), *Personal relationships, volume 1.* London: Academic Press.

Hoffman, L. (1981). *Foundations of family therapy.* New York: Basic Books.

Hopper, R. (1981). The taken-for-granted. *Human Communication Research, 7,* 195-211.

Howe, C. (1980). Mother-child conversation and semantic development. In H. Giles, W. Robinson, & P. Smith (Eds.), *Language: Social psychological perspectives.* London: Pergamon Press.

Hymes, D. (1972). Model of interaction of language and social settings. In J. Gumperz & D. Hymes (Eds.), *Directions in sociolinguistics: The ethnography of communication.* New York: Holt, Rinehart & Winston.

Hymes, D. (1974). *Foundations in sociolinguistics: An ethnographic approach.* Philadelphia: University of Pennsylvania Press.

Hymes, D. (1977). Critique. *Anthropology and Educational Quarterly, 8,* 91-93.

Hymes, D. (1980). Foreword. In S. Shimanoff, *Communication rules.* Beverly Hills, CA: Sage.

Hyrbyk, M., & Farnham-Diggory, S. (1981). *Children's groups in a school: A developmental case study* (NIE G-79-0124). National Institute of Education final report.

Isbell, B., & McKee, L. (1980). Society's cradle: An anthropological perspective on the socialisation of cognition. In J. Sant (Ed.), *Developmental psychology and society.* London: MacMillan.

Jacobs, S., & Jackson, S. (1982). Conversational argument: A discourse analytic approach. In J. Cox & C. Willard (Eds.), *Recent advances in argumentation theory and research.* Carbondale: Southern Illinois University Press.

Jaffe, J., & Feldstein, S. (1970). *Rhythms of dialogue.* New York: Academic Press.

Jakobson, R. (1960). Concluding statement: Linguistics and poetics. In T. Sebeok (Ed.), *Style in language.* New York: Wiley.

Jefferson, G. (1972). Side sequences. In D. Sudnow (Ed.), *Studies in social interaction.* New York: Free Press.

Jefferson, G. (1973). A case of precision timing in ordinary conversation. *Semiotica, 9,* 47-93.

Jefferson, G. (1978). Sequential aspects of storytelling in conversation. In J. Schenkein (Ed.), *Studies in the organization of conversational interaction.* New York: Academic Press.

Jefferson, G. (1984b). On stepwise transition from talk about a trouble to inappropriately next-positioned matters. In M. Atkinson & J. Heritage (Eds.), *Structures of social action.* Cambridge: Cambridge University Press.

Jefferson, G., & Schenkein, J. (1978). Some sequential negotiations in conversation: Unexpanded and expanded versions of projected action sequences. In J. Schenkein (Ed.), *Studies in the organization of conversational interaction.* New York: Academic Press.

Johnson, F. (1983). Political and pedagogical implications of attitudes towards women's language. *Communication Quarterly, 31,* 133-138.

Jones, J., Delia, J., & Clark, R. (1979). *Person-centered parental communication and the development of communication in children.* Unpublished manuscript, Department of Speech Communication, University of Illinois.

Jourard, S. (1971). *Self disclosure.* New York: Wiley.

Josephson, J., & DeStefano, J. (1979). An analysis of productive control over an educational register in school age children's language. *International Journal of Psycholinguistics, 16,* 41-55.

Juhasz, A. (1979). A concept of divorce: Not busted bond but severed strand. *Alternative Lifestyles, 2,* 471-482.

Karttunen, L., & Peters, S. (1979). Conversational implicature. In C.K. Oh & D.A. Dineen (Eds.), *Syntax and semantics, 3: Presupposition.* New York: Academic Press.

Kaye, K., & Charney, R. (1981). Conversational asymmetry between mothers and children. *Journal of Child Language, 8,* 35-49.

Keenan, E. (1974). Conversational competence in children. *Journal of Child Language, 1,* 163-183.

Keenan, E., & Schieffelin, B. (1976). Topic as a discourse notion: A study of topic in the conversation of children and adults. In C. Li (Ed.), *Subject and topic.* New York: Academic Press.

Kelley, H., Berscheid, E., Christensen, A., Harvey, J., Huston, T., Levinger, G., McClintock, E., Peplau, L., & Peterson, D. (1983) *Close relationships.* New York: Freeman & Company.

Kelly, G. (1955). *The psychology of personal constructs.* New York: Norton.

Kelly, G. (1970). A brief introduction to personal construct theory. In D. Bannister (Ed.), *Perspectives in personal construct theory.* New York: Academic Press.

Kemper, S. (1982). Filling in the missing links. *Journal of Verbal Learning and Verbal Behavior, 21,* 99-107.

Key, M. (1975). *Male/female language.* Metuchen, N.J.: Scarecrow Press.

Kintsch, W., & Kintsch, E.H. (1978). The role of schemata in text comprehension. *International Journal of Psycholinguistics, 10,* 17-29.

Knapp, M. (1978). *Social intercourse: From greeting to goodbye.* Boston: Allyn & Bacon.

Kon, I., & Losenkov, V. (1978). Friendship in adolescence: Values and behavior. *Journal of Marriage and the Family, 40,* 143-155.

Kramarae, C. (1981). *Women and men speaking.* Rowley, Mass.: Newbury House.

Kramarae, C., Schulz, M., & O'Barr, W. (1984). *Language and power.* Beverly Hills: Sage.

Kreckel, M. (1981). *Communicative acts and shared knowledge in natural discourse.* New York: Academic Press.

Kress, G. (1976). *Halliday: System and function in language.* London: Oxford University Press.

Kuhn, T. (1970). *The structure of scientific revolutions.* Chicago: University of Chicago Press.

Labov, W., & Fanschel, D. (1977). *Therapeutic discourse.* Philadelphia: University of Pennsylvania Press.

LaGaipa, J. (1981a). A systems approach to personal relationships. In S. Duck & R. Gilmour (Eds.), *Personal relationships, vol. 1.* New York: Academic Press.

LaGaipa, J. (1981b). Children's friendships. In S. Duck & R. Gilmour (Eds.), *Personal relationships, vol. 2.* New York: Academic Press.

Lakoff, R. (1975). *Language and woman's place.* New York: Harper & Row.

Langer, E. (1978). Rethinking the role of thought in social interaction. In J. Harvey, W. Ickes, & R. Kidd (Eds.), *New directions in attribution research, vol. 2.* Hillsdale, NJ: Lawrence Erlbaum Associates.

Langer, E. (1983). *The psychology of control.* Beverly Hills: Sage.

Leech, G. (1983). *Principles of pragmatics.* London: Longman.

Lehnert, W.G. (1979). The role of scripts in understanding. In D. Metzing (Ed.), *Frame conceptions and text understanding.* Berlin: de Gruyter.

LeVine, R. (1977). Child rearing as cultural adaptation. In P. Leiderman, S. Tulkin, & A. Rosenfeld (Eds.), *Culture and infancy: Variations in the human experience.* New York: Academic Press.

Levinson, S. (1979). Activity types and language. *Linguistics, 17,* 356–399.

Levinson, S. (1983). *Pragmatics.* Cambridge: Cambridge University Press.

Lieven, E. (1978). Conversation between mothers and young children: Individual differences and their possible implication for the study of language learning. In N. Waterson & C. Snow (Eds.), *The development of communication.* New York: Wiley.

Lindley, P. (1983). *Analytic and constructive processes in the comprehension of texts.* Unpublished doctoral dissertation, University of Hull, Department of Psychology, England.

Liss, M. (1983). *Social and cognitive skills, sex roles and children's play.* New York: Academic Press.

Lloyd, P., & Beveridge, M. (1981). *Information and meaning in child communication.* London: Academic Press.

Lubin, D., & Forbes, D. (1981). *Understanding sequential aspects of children's social behavior: Conceptual issues in the development of coding schemes.* Paper, SRCD.

Lyons, J. (1977a). *Semantics, vols. 1 & 2.* Cambridge: Cambridge University Press.

MacWhinney, B., & Bates, E. (1978). Sentential devices for conveying givenness and newnew: A cross-cultural developmental study. *Journal of Verbal Learning and Verbal Behavior, 17,* 539–558.

Magnusson, D. (1981a). Problems in environmental analyses—an introduction. In D. Magnusson (Ed.), *Toward a psychology of situation.* Hillsdale, NJ: Lawrence Erlbaum Associates.

Magnusson, D. (1981b). An analysis of situational dimensions. In D. Magnusson (Ed.), *Toward a psychology of situations.* Hillsdale, NJ: Lawrence Erlbaum Associates.

Magnusson, D. (1981c). *Toward a psychology of situation.* Hillsdale, NJ: Lawrence Erlbaum Associates.

Malinowski, B. (1923). The problem of meaning in primitive languages. In C. Ogden & I. Richards (Eds.), *The meaning of meaning.* London: Routledge & Kegan Paul.

Maltz, D., & Borker, R. (1982). A cultural approach to male-female miscommunication. In J. Gumperz (Ed.), *Language and social identity.* Cambridge: Cambridge University Press.

Mandler, J. (1984). *Stories, scripts, and scenes: Aspects of schema theory.* Hillsdale, NJ: Lawrence Erlbaum Associates.

Mannarino, A. (1980). The development of children's friendships. In H. Foot, A. Chapman & J. Smith (Eds.), *Friendship and social relations in children.* New York: Wiley & Sons.

Marwell, C., & Schmitt, D. (1967). Dimensions of compliance-gaining behavior: An empirical analysis. *Sociometry, 30,* 350–364.

Maynard, D. (1985). How children start arguments. *Language in Society, 14,* 1–30.

McLaughlin, M. (1984). *How talk is organized.* Beverley Hills: Sage.

McLaughlin, M., & Cody, M. (1982). *Situation perception factors and the selection of message strategies.* Paper, Speech Communication Association Convention.

McLaughlin, M., Cody, M., & O'Hair, H. (1983). The management of failure accounts: Some contextual determinants of accounting behavior. *Human Communication Research, 7,* 14–36.

McLaughlin, M., Cody, M., & Robey, C. (1980). Situational influences on the selection of strategies to resist compliance-gaining attempts. *Human Communication Research, 7,* 14–36.

McMillan, M., Clifton, A., McGrath, C., & Gale, S. (1977). Women's language: Uncertainty of interpersonal sensitivity and emotionality. *Sex Roles, 3,* 545–559.

McNew, S. (1981). *Maternal gestures: An exploration of contingency.* Unpublished paper.

Mead, G.H. (1934). *Mind, self and society.* Chicago: University of Chicago Press.

Mehan, H. (1974). Accomplishing classroom lessons. In A. Cicourel et al. (Eds.), *Language use and school performance.* New York: Academic Press.

Mehan, H. (1979). *Learning lessons.* Cambridge: Harvard University Press.

Mehan, H. (1986). *Power in the language of organizational process.* Paper, Talk and Social Structure Conference, Santa Barbara, California, March.

Mehan, H., Cazden, C., Coles, L., Fisher, S., & Maroules, N. (1976). *The social organization of classroom lessons.* LaJolla, CA: University of San Diego, Center for Human Information Processing.

Mettetal, G., & Gottman, J. (n.d.). *Affective responsiveness in spouses: Investigating the relationship between communication behavior and marital satisfaction.* University of Illinois at Urbana-Champaign., unpublished paper.

Merrit, M. (1982). Repeats and reformulations in primary classrooms as windows of the nature of talk engagement. *Discourse Processes, 5,* 127–145.

Merritt, M., & Humphrey, F. (1979). Teacher, talk, and task: Communicative demands during individualized instruction time. *Theory into Practice, 18,* 298–303.

Merritt, M., & Humphrey, F. (1981). *Service-like events during individual work time and their contribution to the nature of communication in primary classrooms.* (NIE G-78-0159). Washington, D.C.: National Institute of Education.

Meyer, B. (1975). *The organization of prose and its effects on memory.* Amsterdam: North-Holland.

Millar, F., Rogers, L.E., & Bavelas, J. (1984). Identifying patterns of verbal conflict in interpersonal dynamics. *Western Journal of Speech Communication, 48,* 231–246.

Miller, G. (1976). Foreword. In G. Miller (Ed.), *Explorations in interpersonal communication.* Beverley Hills: Sage.

Miller, G. (1978). The current status of theory and research in interpersonal communication. *Human Communication Research, 4,* 164–191.

Miller, G., Boster, R., Roloff, M., & Seibold, D. (1977). Compliance-gaining message strategies: A typology and some findings concerning effects of situational differences. *Communication Monographs, 44,* 37–51.

Miller, G., & Steinberg, M. (1975). *Between people: A new analysis of interpersonal communication.* Chicago: Science Research Associates.

Mills, C. (1940). Situated actions and vocabularies of motive. *American Sociological Review, 5,* 912–913.

Minsky, M. (1975). A framework for the representation of knowledge. In P. Winston (Ed.), *The psychology of computer vision.* New York: McGraw-Hill.

Minsky, M. (1977). Frame-system theory. In P. Johnson-Laird & P. Wason (Eds.), *Thinking*. Cambridge: Cambridge University Press.

Minsky, M. (1979). A framework for representing knowledge. In D. Metzing (Ed.), *Frame conceptions and text understanding*. Berlin: de Gruyter.

Minuchin, S. (1974). *Families and family therapy*. Cambridge: Harvard University Press.

Mishler, E. (1975). Studies in dialogue and discourse: II. Types of discourse initiated by and sustained through questioning. *Journal of Psycholinguistic Research, 4*, 99–121.

Mishler, E. (1976). Studies in dialogue and discourse: III. Utterance structure and utterance function in interrogative sequences. *Journal of Psycholinguistic Research, 5*, 279–305.

Mishler, E. (1979). Would you trade cookies for popcorn: Talk of trade among six-year-old-children. In O. Garnica & M. King (Eds.), *Language, children and society*. New York: Pergamon Press.

Mishler, E., & Waxler, N. (1968). *Interaction in families: An experimental study of family process and schizophrenia*. New York: Wiley.

Mitchell-Kernan, C., & Kernan, K. (1977). Pragmatics of directive choice among children. In S. Ervin-Tripp & C. Mitchell-Kernan (Eds.), *Child discourse*. New York: Academic Press.

Moerk, E. (1974). Changes in verbal child-mother interactions with increasing language skills of the child. *Journal of Psycholinguistic Research, 3*, 101–115.

Monson, T. (1981). Implications of the traits v. situations controversy for differences in the attributions of actors and observers. In M. Hewstone, F. Fincham & J. Jaspars, (Eds.), *Attribution theory and research*. New York: Academic Press.

Montgomery, B. (1984). Communication in intimate relationships: A research challenge. *Communication Quarterly, 32*, 318–327.

Morris, G. (1985). The remedial episode as a negotiation of rules. In R. Street & J. Cappella (Eds.), *Sequence and pattern in communicative behavior*. London: Edward Arnold.

Morton, T., & Douglas, M. (1981). Growth relationships. In S. Duck & R. Gilmour (Eds.), *Personal relationships, vol. 2*. New York: Academic Press.

Morine-Dershimer, G., & Tenenberg, M. (1981). *Participant perspectives of classroom discourse*. NIE-G-78-0161, awarded to California State University, Hayward.

Mosenthal, P., & Na, T. (1981). Classroom competence and children's individual differences in writing. *Journal of Educational Psychology, 73*, 106–121.

Mueller, E., & Lucas, T. (1975). A developmental analysis of peer interaction among toddlers. In M. Lewis & L. Rosenblum (Eds.), *Friendship and peer relations*. New York: Wiley.

Mugny, G., Perret-Clermont, A., & Doise, W. (1981). Interpersonal coordination and sociological differences in intellectual growth. In G. Stephenson & J. Davis (Eds.), *Progress in applied social psychology*. Chichester: Wiley.

Mulkay, M. (1981). Action and belief or scientific discourse? A possible way of ending intellectual vassalage in social studies of science. *Philosophy of the Social Sciences, 11*, 163–171.

Mulkay, M., & Gilbert, G. (1982). Joking apart: some recommendations concerning the analysis of scientific culture. *Social Studies of Science, 12*, 585–613.

Murray, F., Ames, G., & Botvin, F. (1977). Acquisition of conservation through cognitive dissonance. *Journal of Educational Psychology, 69*, 519–527.

Murray, L. (1980). *The sensitivities and expressive capacities of young infants in communication with their mothers*. Doctoral dissertation, Edinburgh University.

Narvan, I. (1967). Communication and adjustment. *Family Process, 6*, 173–184.

Nash, R. (1973). *Classrooms observed: Teachers' perceptions and pupils' response*. London: Routledge.

Nelson, K. (1973). Structure and strategy in learning how to talk. *Monographs of the Society for Research on Child Development, 38*, (149), 1–2.

Nelson, K. (1976). Some attributes of adjectives used by young children. *Cognition, 4*, 13–80.

Nelson, K. (1977). Facilitating syntax acquisition. *Developmental Psychology, 13*, 101–107.

Nelson, K. (1978). Early speech in its communicative context. In F. Minifie & L. Lloyd (Eds.), *Communicative and cognitive abilities: Early behavioral assessment.* Baltimore: University Park Press.

Nelson, K. (1981). Social cognition in a script framework. In J. Flavell & L. Ross (Eds.), *Social cognitive development.* Cambridge: Cambridge University Press.

Nelson, K., Carskaddon, G., & Bonvillian, J. (1973). Syntax acquisition: Impact of experimental variation in adult verbal interaction with the child. *Child Development, 44,* 497–504.

Newcomb, T., & Bentler, P. (1981). Marital breakdown. In S. Duck & R. Gilmour (Eds.), *Personal relationships, vol. 3.* New York: Academic Press.

Newport, L., Gleitman, H., & Gleitman, L. (1977). Mother, I'd rather do it myself: Some effects and non-effects of maternal speech styles. In C. Snow & C. Ferguson (Eds.), *Talking to children.* London: Cambridge University Press.

Nicolich, L. (1975). *A longitudinal study of representational play in relation to spontaneous imitation and development of multiword utterances: Final report.* ERIC Document PS007 854.

Nisbett, R., & Ross, L. (1980). *Human inference: Strategies and shortcomings of social judgment.* Englewood Cliffs, NJ: Prentice-Hall.

Nisbett, R., & Wilson, T. (1977). Telling more than we can know: Verbal reports on mental processes. Psychological Review, 84, 231–259.

Norton, R. (1983). *Communicator style.* Beverly Hills: Sage.

Nofsinger, R. (1976). Answering questions indirectly. *Human Communication Research, 2,* 172–181.

Nowakowska, M. (1981). Structure of situation and action: Some remarks on formal theory of actions. In D. Magnusson (Ed.), *Toward a psychology of situations.* Hillsdale, NJ: Lawrence Erlbaum Associates.

Nystedt, L. (1981). A model for studying the interaction between the objective situation and a person's construction of the situation. In D. Magnusson (Ed.), *Toward a psychology of situations.* Hillsdale, NJ: Lawrence Erlbaum Associates.

Ochs, E., & Schieffelin, B. (1979). *Developmental pragmatics.* New York: Academic Press.

Ogbu, J. (1974). *The next generation: An ethnography of education in an urban neighborhood.* New York: Academic Press.

Ogbu, J. (1978). *Minority education and caste.* New York: Academic Press.

Ogilvie, J., & Haslett, B. (1985). Communicating peer feedback in a task group. *Human Communication Research, 12,* 79–98.

O'Keefe, B., & Benoit, P. (1982). Children's argument. In R. Cox & C. Willard (Eds.), *Advances in argumentation theory.* Carbondale: Southern Illinois University Press.

O'Keefe, B., & Delia, J. (1979). Construct comprehensiveness and cognitive complexity as predictors of the number and strategic adaptation of arguments and appeals in a persuasive message. *Communication Monographs, 46,* 221–240.

O'Keefe, B., & Delia, J. (1982). Impression formation processes and message production. In M. Roloff & C. Berger (Eds.), *Social cognition and communication.* Beverly Hills: Sage.

Olson, D., & Hildyard, A. (1981). Assent and compliance in children's language. In W. Dickson (Ed.), *Children's oral communication skills.* New York: Academic Press.

Orford, J., & O'Reilly, P. (1981). Disorders in the family. In S. Duck & R. Gilmour (Eds.), *Personal relationships, vol. 3.* New York: Academic Press.

Parisi, D. & Castelfranchi, P. (1981). A goal analysis of some pragmatic aspects of language. In H. Parret, M. Sbisa, & J. Vershueren (Eds.), *Possibilities and limitations of pragmatics.* Amsterdam: John Benjamins B.V.

Parret, H., Sbisa, M., & Verschueren, J. (1981). Introduction. In H. Parret, M. Sbisa, & J. Verschueren (Eds.), *Possibilities and limitations of pragmatics.* Amsterdam: John Benjamins B.V.

Pearce, W., & Cronen, V. (1981). *Communication, action and meaning.* New York: Praeger.

Pearson, J. (1985). *Gender and communication.* Dubuque, Iowa: W.C. Brown & Company.

Peplau, L. (1983). Roles and gender. In H. Kelley et al. (Eds.), *Close relationships.* New York: W.H. Freeman & Company.

Perret-Clermont, A. (1980). *Social interaction and cognitive development in children.* London: Academic Press.

Perinbanayagam, R.S. (1974). The definition of the situation: An analysis of the ethnomethodological and dramaturgical view. *The Sociological Quarterly, 15,* 521–541.

Philips, S. (1972). Participant structures and communicative competence: Warm Springs children in community and classroom. In C. Cazden, J. Gumperz, & D. Hymes (Eds.), *Functions of language in the classroom.* New York: Teachers College Press.

Philips, S. (1974). Warm Springs Indian time: How the regulation of participation affects the progression of events. In R. Bauman & J. Sherzer (Eds.), *Explorations in the ethnography of speaking.* Cambridge: Cambridge University Press.

Philips, S. (1976). Some sources of cultural variability in the regulation of talk. *Language in Society, 5,* 81–95.

Pinker, S. (1978). Formal models of language learning. *Cognition, 1,* 217–283.

Planalp, S., & Tracy, K. (1980). Not to change the topic but . . . : A cognitive approach to the study of conversation. In D. Nimmo (Ed.), *Communication Yearbook, 4.* New Brunswick, NJ: Transaction.

Polanyi, L. (1979). So what's the point? *Semiotica, 25,* 207–236.

Polanyi, L. (1985). Conversational storytelling. In T. van Dijk (Ed.), *Handbook of discourse analysis: vol. 3 discourse and dialogue.* New York: Academic Press.

Pomerantz, A. (1978a). Compliment responses: Notes on the co-operations of multiple constraints. In J. Schenkein (Ed.), *Studies in the organization of conversational interaction.* New York: Academic Press.

Pomerantz, A. (1978b). Attributions of responsibility: blamings. *Sociology, 12,* 115–121.

Pondy, L. (1967). Organizational conflict—concepts and models. *Administrative Science Quarterly, 12,* 296–320.

Poyatos, F. (1983). *New perspectives in nonverbal communication.* Oxford: Pergamon Press.

Raffler-Engel, W. von. (1977). *The unconscious element in inter-cultural communication.* Unpublished manuscript, Linguistics Department, University of Vanderbilt, Nashville, TN.

Rappoport, R., & Rappoport, R. (1971). *Dual-career families.* Baltimore: Penguin.

Read, B., & Cherry, L. (1978). Preschool children's production of directive forms. *Discourse Processes, 1,* 233–245.

Rees, N. (1978). Pragmatics of language. In R. Schieffelbush et al., (Eds.), *The bases of language.* College Park: University Park Press.

Reichman, R. (1978). Conversational coherency. *Cognitive Science, 2,* 283–327.

Reinhart, T. (1981). Pragmatics and linguistics: An analysis of sentence topics. *Philosophica, 27,* 53–94.

Remler, J. (1978). Some repairs on the notion of repairs in the interests of relevance. *Papers from the Regional Meetings of the Chicago Linguistic Society, 14,* 391–402.

Ricoeur, P. (1981). The model of the text: Meaningful action considered as a text. *Social Research, 38,* 529–555.

Riesser, H. (1977). On the development of text grammar. In H. Dressler (Ed.), *Current trends in text linguistics.* Berlin: de Gruyter.

Robinson, E. J., & Robinson, W. P. (1976a). Development changes in the child's explanation of communication failure. *Australian Journal of Psychology, 28,* 155–65.

Robinson, E., & Robinson, W. (1976b). The young child's understanding of communication. *Developmental Psychology, 12,* 328–333.

Robinson, E.J., & Robinson, W. P. (1977a). The young child's understanding of communication. *Developmental Psychology, 12,* 328–333.

Robinson, E.J., & Robinson, W.P. (1977b). Development in the understanding of causes of success and failure in verbal communication. *Cognition, 5,* 363–378.

Robinson, E.J., & Robinson, W.P. (1978a). Explanations of communication failure and ability to give bad messages. *British Journal of Social and Clinical Psychology, 17,* 219–225.

Robinson, E.J., & Robinson, W.P. (1978b). Development of understanding about communication: Message inadequacy and its role in causing communication failure. *Genetic Psychological Monographs, 98,* 233–279.

Robinson, E.J., & Robinson, W.P. (1978c). The roles of egocentrism and of weakness in comparing children's explanations of communication failures. *Journal of Experimental Psychology, 26,* 147–160.

Robinson, W.P. (1981a). Mother's answers to children's questions. In W. Robinson (Ed.), *Communication in development.* New York: Academic Press.

Robinson, W. P. (1981b). Some problems for theory, methodology, and methods for the 1980's. In W. Robinson (Ed.), *Communication in development.* New York: Academic Press.

Robinson, W., & Rackstraw, S. (1967). Variations in mothers' answers to children's questions. *Sociology, 1,* 259–279.

Robinson, W., & Rackstraw, S. (1972). *A question of answers, vol 1 and 2.* London: Routledge.

Rogers, L. (1983). *Analyzing relational communication: Implications of a pragmatic approach.* Paper, Speech Communication Association, Louisville, Kentucky.

Rogers-Millar, L.E., & Millar, F. (1979). Domineeringness and dominance: A transactional view. *Human Communication Research, 5,* 238–246.

Romaine, S. (1984). *The language of children and adolescents.* Oxford: Basil Blackwell.

Rosenthal, R., & Jacobsen, L. (1968). *Pygmalion in the classroom: Teacher expectation and pupils intellectual development.* New York: Holt, Rinehart & Winston.

Rosenstein, N., & McLaughlin, M. (1983). *Characterization of interruption as a function of temporal placement.* Paper, Speech Communication Association, Louisville, Kentucky.

Ross, L. (1981). The "intuitive scientist" formulation and its developmental implications. In J. Flavell & L. Ross (Eds.), *Social cognitive development.* Cambridge: Cambridge University Press.

Rubin, D. (1982). *"Nobody play by the rules he know:" Cultural interference in classroom questioning events.* Paper, Speech Communication Association, San Francisco.

Rubin, Z. (1980). *Children's friendships.* Cambridge: Harvard University Press.

Ryan, J. (1974). Early language development. In M. Richards (Ed.), *The integration of the child into a social world.* Cambridge: Cambridge University Press.

Sachs, J. (1977). The adaptive significance of linguistic input to prelinguistic infants. In C. Snow & G. Ferguson (Eds.), *Talking to children.* London: Cambridge University Press.

Sacks, H. (1974). An analysis of the course of a joke's telling in conversation. In R. Bauman & J. Sherzer (Eds.), *Explorations in the ethnography of speaking.* Cambridge: Cambridge University Press.

Sacks, H., Schegloff, E., & Jefferson, G. (1974). A simplest systematics for the organization of turn taking for conversation. *Language, 50,* 696–735.

St. Clair, R., & Giles, H. (1980). The social and psychological contexts of language. Hillsdale, NJ: Lawrence Erlbaum Associates.

Sanford, A., & Garrod, S. (1981). *Understanding written languages: Explorations of comprehension beyond the sentence.* Chichester: Wiley and Sons.

Scarlett, H., Press, A., & Crockett, W. (1971). Children's descriptions of peers: A Wernerian developmental analysis. *Child Development, 42,* 439–453.

Schaffer, H. (1979). Acquiring the concept of dialogue. In M. Bornstein & W. Kessen (Eds.),

Psychological development from infancy: Image to intention. Hillsdale, NJ: Lawrence Erlbaum Associates.

Schaffer, H., Collis, G., & Parsons, G. (1977). Vocal exchange and visual regard in verbal and preverbal children. In H. Schaffer (Ed.), *Studies in mother-infant interaction.* London: Academic Press.

Schank, R. (1977). Rules and topics in conversation. *Cognitive Science, 1,* 421–444.

Schank, R. (1979). Interestingness: Controlling inferences. *Artificial Intelligence, 12,* 273–297.

Schank, R., & Abelson, R. (1977). *Scripts, plans, goals and understanding.* Hillsdale, NJ: Lawrence Erlbaum Associates.

Scheflen, A. (1963). Communication and regulation in psychotherapy. *Psychiatry, 26,* 126–136.

Scheflen, A. (1972). *Body language and the social order.* Englewood Cliffs, NJ: Prentice-Hall.

Scheflen, A. (1974). *How behavior means.* New York: Doubleday.

Schegloff, E., Jefferson, G., & Sacks, H. (1977). The preference for self-correction in the organization of repair in conversation. *Language, 53,* 361–382.

Schenkein, J. (1978). *Studies in the organization of conversational interaction.* New York: Academic Press.

Scherer, K., & Giles, H. (1979). *Social markers in speech.* Cambridge: Cambridge University Press.

Schieffelin, B. (1981). A sociolinguistic analysis of relationship. *Discourse Processes, 4,* 189–196.

Schieffelin, B., & Ochs, E. (1983). A cultural perspective on the transition from prelinguistic to linguistic communication. In R. Golinkoff (Ed.), *The transition from prelinguistic to linguistic communication.* Hillsdale, NJ: Lawrence Erlbaum Associates.

Schiffrin, D. (1977). Opening encounters. *American Sociological Review, 42,* 679–691.

Schiffrin, D. (1980). Meta-talk: Organizational and evaluative brackets in discourse. *Sociological Inquiry, 50,* 199–236.

Schonbach, P. (1980). A category system for account phases. *European Journal of Social Psychology, 10,* 195–200.

Schutz, A. (1962a). Commonsense and scientific interpretations of human action. In A. Schutz, *Collected papers, vol. 1.* The Hague: Martinus Nijhoff.

Schutz, A. (1962b). Concept and theory formation in the social sciences. In A. Schutz, *Collected papers, vol. 1.* The Hague: Martinus Nijhoff.

Schutz, A. (1964). *Collected papers, vol. 2.* The Hague: Martinus Nijhoff.

Schutz, A. (1967). *The phenomenology of the social world.* Trans. G. Walsh & F. Lehnert. Evanston, Ill.: Northwestern University Press.

Scollon, R., & Scollon, S. (1981). *Narrative literacy and face in interethnic communication.* Norwood, NJ: Ablex.

Scott, M., & Lyman, S. (1968). Accounts. *American Sociological Review, 33,* 46–62.

Searle, J. (1969). *Speech acts.* Cambridge: Cambridge University Press.

Searle, J. (1976). The classification of illocutionary acts. *Language in Society, 5,* 1–24.

Searle, J. (1982). The myth of the computer. *New York Review of Books, Vol. 29,* No. 7.

Searle, J. (1983). *Intentionality.* Cambridge: Cambridge University Press.

Selman, R., & Byrne, D. (1975). A structural analysis of role-taking levels in middle childhood. *Child Development, 45,* 803–806.

Selman, R., & Selman, A. (1979). Children's ideas about friendship: A new theory. *Psychology Today, 114,* 71–80.

Shantz, C. (1981). The role of role taking in children's referential communication. In W. Dickson (Ed.), *Children's oral communication skills.* New York: Academic Press.

Shantz, C. (1982). Children's understanding of social rules and the social context. In C. Serafica (Ed.), *Social-cognitive development in context.* New York: Guilford.

Shatz, M. (1974). *The comprehension of indirect directives: Can two-year-olds shut the door?* Paper, Linguistic Society of America, Amherst.

Shatz, M. (1978). The relationship between cognitive processes and the development of communication skills. *Proceedings of the Nebraska Symposium on Motivation.* Lincoln: University of Nebraska Press.

Shatz, M. (1982). On mechanisms of language acquisition: Can features of the communicative environments account for development? In L. Gleitman & E. Warren (Eds.), *Language acquisition: The state of the art.* New York: Cambridge University Press.

Shatz, M., & Gelman, R. (1973). The development of communication skills: Modifications in the speech of young children as a function of listener. *Monographs of the Society for Research on Child Development, 38,* 5.

Shaw, M., & Sadler, O. (1965). Interaction patterns in heterosexual dyads varying in degree of intimacy. *Journal of Social Psychology, 66,* 345–351.

Shimanoff, S. (1980). *Communication rules: Theory and research.* Beverly Hills: Sage.

Shimanoff, S. (1983). The role of gender in linguistic references to emotive states. *Communication Quarterly, 30,* 174–179.

Shotter, J. (1984). *Social accountability and self-hood.* Oxford: Blackwell.

Sillars, A. (1980). The stranger and the spouse as target persons for compliance-gaining strategies: A subjective expected utility model. *Human Communication Research, 6,* 265–279.

Sinclair, J., & Coulthard, M. (1975). *Towards an analysis of discourse.* London: Oxford University Press.

Sjoberg, L. (1981). Life situations and episodes as a basis for situational influence on action. In D. Magnusson (Ed.), *Toward a psychology of situations.* Hillsdale, NJ: Lawrence Erlbaum Associates.

Slater, P. (1968). Some social consequences of temporary systems. In W. Benneis & P. Slater (Eds.), *The temporary society.* New York: Harper & Row.

Smith, M.J. (1984). Contingency rules theory, context and compliance behaviors. *Human Communication Research, 10,* 489–512.

Smith, N.V. (1982). *Mutual knowledge.* London: Academic Press.

Snow, C. (1972). Mothers' speech to children learning language. *Child Development, 43,* 543–565.

Snow, C. (1977a). The development of conversation between mothers and babies. *Journal of Child Language, 4,* 1–22.

Snow, C. (1977b). Mother's speech research: From input to interaction. In C. Snow & C. Ferguson (Eds.), *Talking to children.* Cambridge: Cambridge University Press.

Snow, C. (1979). The role of social interaction in language acquisition. In W.A. Collins (Ed.), *Children's language and communication, vol. 12, the Minnesota Symposium on Child Psychology.* Hillsdale, NJ: Lawrence Erlbaum Associates.

Snow, C., & Gilbreath, B. (1983). Explaining transitions. In R. Golinkoff (Ed.), *The transition from prelinguistic to linguistic communication.* Hillsdale, NJ: Lawrence Erlbaum Associates.

Snyder-McLean, L., & McLean, J. (1978). Verbal information gathering strategies: The child's use of language to acquire language. *Journal of Speech and Hearing Disorders, 43,* 305–313.

Solomon, D., Bezdek, W., & Rosenberg, L. (1963). *Teaching styles and learning.* Chicago: Center for the Study of Liberal Education for Adults.

Sperber, D., & Wilson, D. (1986). *Relevance: Communication and cognition.* Oxford: Basil Blackwell.

Spitzberg, B., & Cupach, W. (1984). *Communicative competence.* Beverly Hills: Sage.

Stein, N., & Glenn, C. (1979). An analysis of story comprehension in elementary school children. In R. Freedle (Ed.), *New directions in discourse processing, vol. 2.* Norwood, NJ: Ablex.

Steinberg, Z., & Cazden, C. (1979). Children as teachers—of peers and ourselves. *Theory into Practice, 18,* 284–291.

Steiner, G. (1969). The language animal. *Encounter, 33,* 7–24.

Stern, D. (1977). *The first relationship.* Cambridge: Cambridge University Press.

Stokes, R., & Hewitt, J. (1976). Aligning actions. *American Sociological Review, 41,* 838–849.

Strawson, P. (1979). Identifying reference and truth values. In D. Steinberg & L. Jakobovits (Eds.), *Semantics.* London: Cambridge University Press.

Stubbs, M. (1975). Teaching and talking: A sociolinguistic approach to classroom interaction. In G. Channan & S. Delamont (Eds.), *Frontiers of classroom research.* Slough, England: National Federation for Educational Research.

Stubbs, M., & Hillier, H. (1983). *Readings on language, schools and classrooms.* London: Metheun.

Sugarman, S. (1973). *Description of communicative development in the prelanguage child.* Unpublished manuscript, Hampshire College, Amherst.

Sugarman, S. (1977). A description of communicative development in the prelanguage child. In I. Markova (Ed.), *The social context of language.* London: Wiley.

Sugarman, S. (1983). Empirical versus logical issues in the transition from prelinguistic to linguistic communication. In R. Golinkoff (Ed.), *The transition from prelinguistic to linguistic communication.* Hillsdale, NJ: Lawrence Erlbaum Associates.

Sylvester-Bradley, B. (1980). *A study of young infants as social beings.* Doctoral dissertation, Edinburgh University.

Tajfel, H. (1978). *Differentiation between social groups.* London: Academic Press.

Tajfel, H., & Turner, J. (1979). An integrative theory of intergroup conflict. In W. Austin & S. Worchel (Eds.), *The social psychology of intergroup relations.* Monterey, Calif.: Brooks/Cole, 1979.

Tannen, D. (1979). What's in a frame? Surface evidence for underlying expectations. In R. Freedle (Ed.), *New directions in discourse processing.* Norwood, NJ: Ablex.

Tannen, D. (1981). *Analyzing discourse: Text and talk.* Georgetown: Georgetown University Round Table.

Tannen, D. (1982). *Spoken and written language, vol. ix.* Norwood, NJ: Ablex.

Tannen, D. (1985). Cross-cultural communication. In T. van Dijk (Ed.), *Handbook of discourse processes.* New York: Academic Press.

Ten Have, P. (1986). *On the achievement of asymmetry in doctor-patient interaction.* Paper, Talk and Social Structure Conference, University of California at Santa Barbara, March.

Tough, J. (1973). *Focus on meaning.* London: Allen & Unwin.

Tough, J. (1977). *The development of meaning.* New York: Wiley.

Tough, J. (1983). Learning to represent meaning. In B. Hutson (Ed.), *Advances in reading/language research, 2,* 55–82.

Toulmin, S. (1974). Rules and their relevance for understanding human behavior. In T. Mischel (Ed.), *Understanding other persons.* Totowa, NJ: Rowman & Littlefield.

Tracy, K. (1982). On getting the point: Distinguishing "issues" from "events," an aspect of conversational coherence. In M. Burgoon (Ed.), *Communication yearbook, vol. 5.* New Brunswick, NJ: Transaction.

Tracy, K., & Craig, R. (1983). *Conversational coherence.* Beverly Hills: Sage.

Tracy, K., & Moran, J. (1983). Conversational relevance in multiple-goal settings. In K. Tracy & R. Craig (Eds.), *Conversational coherence.* Beverly Hills: Sage.

Trevarthen, C. (1977). Descriptive analyses of infant communication behavior. In H. Schaffer (Ed.), *Studies in mother-infant interaction.* London: Academic Press.

Trevarthen, C. (1979a). Communication and co-operation in early infancy. A description of primary intersubjectivity. In M. Bullowa (Ed.), *Before speech: The beginnings of human communication.* London: Cambridge University Press.

Trevarthen, C. (1979b). Instincts for human understanding and for cultural co-operation: Their development in infancy. In M. von Cranach, K. Foppa, W. Lepenies, & D. Ploog (Eds.), *Human ethology.* Cambridge: Cambridge University Press.

Trevarthen, C. (1980a). Brain development and the growth of psychological functions. In J. Sants (Ed.), *Development of psychology and society.* London: Macmillan.

Trevarthen, C. (1980b). The foundations of intersubjectivity: Development of interpersonal and co-operative understanding in infants. In D. Olsen (Ed.), *The social foundations of language and thought: Essays in honor of J.S. Bruner.* New York: W.W. Norton.

Trevarthen, C. (1982). The primary motives for cooperative understanding. In G. Butterworth & P. Light (Eds.), *Social cognition.* Chicago: University of Chicago Press.

Trevarthen, C., & Hubley, P. (1978). Secondary intersubjectivity: Confidence, confiding and acts of meaning in the first year. In A. Lock (Ed.), *Action, gesture and symbol: The emergence of language.* London: Academic Press.

Triandis, H. (1972). *The analysis of subjective culture.* New York: Wiley-Interscience.

Turner, G. (1973). Social class and children's language of control at ages five and seven. In B. Bernstein (Ed.), *Class, codes and control, vol. 2.* London: Routledge.

Turner, J., & Giles, H. (1981). *Intergroup behavior.* Oxford: Blackwell.

Tyack, D., & Ingram, D. (1977). Children's production and comprehension of questions. *Journal of Child Language, 4,* 211–225.

Ventola, E. (1979). The structure of casual conversation in English. *Journal of Pragmatics, 3,* 267–298.

Wallat, C., & Green, J. (1979). Social rules and communicative contexts in kindergarten. *Theory into practice, 18,* 275–284.

Waldrop, M., & Halverson, C. (1975). Intensive and extensive peer behavior: Longitudinal and cross-sectional analysis. *Child Development, 46,* 19–26.

Watson, D.R. (1981). Conversational and organisational uses of proper names; an aspect of counsellor-client interaction. In P. Atkinson & C. Heath (Eds.), *Medical work: Realities and routines.* Farnborough: Gower.

Watzlawick, P., Beavin, J., & Jackson, D. (1967). *Pragmatics of human communication: A study of interactional patterns, pathologies, and paradoxes.* New York: Norton.

Weick, K. (1979). *The social psychology of organizing.* Second edition. Reading, Mass.: Addison-Wesley.

Weiner, S., & Goodenough, D. (1977). A move toward a psychology of conversation. In R. Freedle (Ed.), *Discourse production and comprehension.* Norwood, NJ: Ablex.

Wells, G. (1981). *Learning through interaction.* Cambridge: Cambridge University Press.

Wells, G. (1985). *Language development in the pre-school years.* Cambridge: Cambridge University Press.

Wells, G., MacLure, M., & Montgomery, M. (1981). Some strategies for sustaining conversation. In P. Werth (Ed.), *Conversation and discourse.* New York: St. Martins.

Wells, G., & Montgomery, M. (1981). Adult-child interaction at home and at school. In P. French & M. MacLure (Eds.), *Adult child conversation.* London: Croom Helm.

Wells, G., Montgomery, M., & MacLure, M. (1979). Adult-child discourse: Outline of a model of analysis. *Journal of Pragmatics, 3,* 337–380.

Wentworth, W. (1980). *Context and understanding.* New York: Elsevier North Holland, Inc.

Werth, P. (1981). The concept of 'relevance' in conversational analysis. In P. Werth (Ed.), *Conversation and discourse.* New York: St. Martins.

West, C., & Zimmerman, D. (1985). Gender, language and discourse. In T. van Dijk (Ed.), *Handbook of discourse analysis: vol. 4, discourse analysis in society.* New York: Academic Press.

Whitehurst, G., & Sonnenschein, S. (1981). The development of informative messages in referential communication: Knowing when versus knowing how. In W. Dickson (ed.), *Children's oral communication skills.* New York: Academic Press.

Wilensky, R. (1978). Why John married Mary—understanding stories involving recurring goals. *Cognitive Science, 2,* 235–266.

Wilkinson, L. (1982a). *Communicating in the classroom.* New York: Academic Press.

Wilkinson, L. (1982b). Introduction: A sociolinguistic approach to communicating in the classroom. In L. Wilkinson (Ed.), *Communicating in the classroom.* New York: Academic Press.

Wilkinson, L., & Calculator, S. (1982). Effective speakers: Students' use of language to request and obtain information and action in the classroom. In L. Wilkinson (Ed.), *Communicating in the classroom.* New York: Academic Press.

Wilkinson, L., Calculator, S., & Dollaghan, C. (1982). Ya wanna trade—just for awhile: Children's requests and responses to peers. *Discourse Processes, 5,* 161–176.

Wilson, D. (1975). *Presuppositions and non-truth conditional semantics.* New York: Academic Press.

Wilson, D., & Sperber, D. (1979). Ordered entailments: An alternative to presuppositional theories. In Oh & D. Dineen (Eds.), *Syntax and semantics II: Presupposition.* New York: Academic Press.

Wilson, D., & Sperber, D. (1981). On Grice's theory of conversation. In P. Werth (Ed.), *Conversation and discourse.* London: Croom Helm.

Wilson, T. (1970). Normative and interpretive paradigms in sociology. In J. Douglas (Ed.), *Understanding everyday life.* Chicago: Aldine.

Winograd, T. (1977). A framework for understanding discourse. In M. Just & P. Carpenter (Eds.), *Cognitive processes in comprehension.* Hillsdale, NJ: Lawrence Erlbaum Associates.

Winograd, T. (1980). What does it mean to understand language? *Cognitive Science, 4,* 209–241.

Wish, M., Deutsch, M., & Kaplan, S. (1976). Perceived dimensions of interpersonal relations. *Journal of Personality and Social Psychology, 33,* 409–420.

Wittgenstein, L. (1958). *Philosophical investigations.* Oxford: Blackwell.

Wolf, D. (1981). Understanding others: A longitudinal case study of the concept of independent agency. In G. Forman (Ed.), *Action and thought.* New York: Academic Press.

Wood, J. (1982). Communication and relational cultures: Bases for the study of human relationships. *Communication Quarterly, 30,* 75–84.

Wootton, A. (1981). Conversation analysis. In P. French & M. MacLure (Eds.), *Adult-child conversation.* London: Croom Helm.

Wright, G. H. von. (1968). The logic of practical discourse. In R. Klikansky (Ed.), *Contemporary philosophy.* Italy: La Nuava Italia Editrice.

Zimmerman, D., & West, C. (1975). Sex roles, interruptions and silence in conversations. In B. Thorne & N. Henley (Eds.), *Language and sex: Difference and dominance.* Rowley, Mass.: Newbury.

Zimmerman, D., & Whitehurst, G. (1979). Structure and function: A comparison of two views of the development of language and cognition. In G. Whitehurst & D. Zimmerman, *Functions of language and cognition.* New York: Academic Press.

Author Index

277

Subject Index

DATE DUE